Library of
Davidson College

This pathbreaking study of the Indian cinema is concerned particularly with cinema-goers in Madurai, a city in Tamil Nadu, South India. Sara Dickey reviews the history of Tamil film, explains the structure of the industry, and presents the perspective of the filmmakers. But the core of the book is an analysis of the films themselves and the place they have in the lives of poor people, who organize fan clubs, discuss the films and the actors, and in various ways relate these fantasy worlds to their own lives. Dickey argues that the effect of these films is ultimately conservative, for they glorify poverty while holding out the hope of a better future. Her rich ethnography makes an original contribution to the study of film in India and, more generally, to the understanding of popular culture in an Indian city.

Cambridge Studies in Social and Cultural Anthropology

Editors: Ernest Gellner, Jack Goody, Stephen Gudeman, Michael Herzfeld, Jonathan Parry

92

Cinema and the urban poor in South India

A list of books in the series will be found at the end of the volume

CINEMA AND THE URBAN POOR IN SOUTH INDIA

SARA DICKEY
Bowdoin College, Maine

Published by the Press Syndicate of the University of Cambridge
The Pitt Building, Trumpington Street, Cambridge CB2 1RP
40 West 20th Street, New York, NY 1011–4211, USA
10 Stamford Road, Oakleigh, Melbourne 3166, Australia

© Cambridge University Press 1993

First published 1993

Printed in Great Britain at the University Press, Cambridge

A catalogue record for this book is available from the British Library

Library of Congress cataloguing in publication data

Cinema and the urban poor in South India / Sara Dickey.
    p.   cm. – (Cambridge studies in social and cultural anthropology: 92)
Includes bibliographical references
ISBN 0 521 44084–X
1. Motion pictures – Social aspects – India – Tamil Nadu. 2. Urban poor – India – Tamil Nadu. 3. Motion picture audiences – India – Madurai. 4. Madurai (India) – Popular culture.
I. Title.
II. Series.
PN1993.5.I8D5   1993
302.23′43′095482 – dc20   92–32196   CIP

ISBN 0 521 44084 X hardback

CE

Contents

List of illustrations	*page*	viii
Acknowledgements		ix
Note on transliteration		xiii

PART I

1	Introduction	3
2	Lives in Madurai	15
3	Activities and attitudes	36

PART II

4	History of Tamil cinema	47
5	Films	57
6	Film themes	89

PART III

7	Filmmakers	119
8	Audiences	134
9	Fan clubs and politics	148
10	Conclusions	173
	Appendix	177
	Notes	179
	List of references	195
	Index	203

Illustrations

Map
India and Sri Lanka (map by Cathy E. Brann). *page* 4

Plates
1. Decorated autorickshaw (photo by Raja Enok). 7
2. Movie billboards (photo by Sara Dickey). 16
3. A street in downtown Madurai (photo by Sara Dickey). 30
4. Line outside a Madras film theater (photo by Raja Enok). 38
5. Film paraphernalia vendor (photo by Raja Enok). 41
6. Rajnikanth in an opticals shop signboard (photo by Sara Dickey). 62
7. Bharatiraja in a Madras billboard (photo by Raja Enok). 125
8. Kamalhasan fan club signboard and two club officers (photo by Sara Dickey). 149
9. The stage for an MGR fan club's presentation ceremony (photo by Sara Dickey). 162
10. Jayalalitha cutout in Madras (photo by Raja Enok). 166
11. Jayalalitha in an old film poster (photo by Raja Enok). 167

Acknowledgements

Multiple periods of research, writing, and thinking have gone into this work, and over the years many friends, guides, and critics in India and the US have given generously to help shape it.

One of my fondest debts is to the family of V. Natarajan and N. Gomati, who welcomed me into their home soon after I first arrived in Madurai. They listened with kind restraint to my early Tamil, translating it among themselves and repeating their own responses to me in as many versions as necessary. They and the six other families in their compound were always willing to talk and share, despite their heavy workloads, and their friendliness and humor helped ease me into the city and my work. The words and experiences of these and all the other people in Madurai who talked with and listened to me, shared in movies and rituals and other festive-everyday events, are the life of this book. My desire here is to communicate some sense of that life, partial as it must be.

V. Shyamala, V. Kirushnasamy, N. Prakash, and D. Jemima Chrisanthi worked as research assistants at different times in Madurai. Each helped in many ways, providing contacts and answering innumerable questions in addition to more mundane work such as accompanying me to interviews. Their aid sped the research both by increasing my level of understanding and by making my time more efficient.

In Madras, two men enabled me to enter the "cine world." Without their generous help, the portion of my research focussing on filmmakers would without question have been impossible. N. R. Chendur, writer, editor and publisher of the Telugu monthly *Jagati*, donated many, many hours of his time to introduce me to critics, producers, directors, actresses, and actors. He accompanied me to interviews as well as film screenings and other insider events. Some of my most relaxed moments were spent with Mr. Chendur's family, including his wife Malathi, a noted journalist and author, and her sister Saradamba, a librarian, as they made my trips to the "big city" more comfortable with their wicked wit and delicious food. I was given further assistance in gaining access to film artists by Mr. P. "Filmnews" Anandan, a renowned film historian and public relations officer for a number of Tamil stars, who also accompanied me to several interviews and gave generously of his time despite the many other demands made upon it. All of these people gave without hesitation, and each has my most grateful thanks.

A number of Madras film industry members shared their scarce time with notable graciousness. They include Balaje, Dr. Bhanumathi Ramakrishna, Bharatiraja, Joseph Enok, Kamalhasan, Kommineni, Muktha Srinivasan, A. V. Narayanan, L. V. Prasad, A. Ramesh, D. V. S. Raju, and Sowcar Janaki. I owe a debt to them all; and I hope they will find that my account of the production side of cinema, while perhaps presenting a different picture than they would draw themselves, is a fair representation.

During my travels in India I have from time to time had the great good fortune of being made to feel at home when I was away from my own. Nargis Cama took me into her peaceful house in Kodaikanal when I needed a retreat for writing, and generously gave me all the sustenance I needed at the end of my fieldwork. In Madras, Joseph and Julie Enok and their family have taken me in again and again since 1990. They have given me great cheer and allowed me to be a non-guest as far as hospitality could permit. Their daughter Prema and her husband Lawrence have also cared for me in Madurai and have been supportive friends over the years.

Many individuals have contributed to the writing of this book. Foremost is F. G. Bailey, who was the best of dissertation advisors and has remained just as steady and incisive a critic since my passage from graduate school. He has read the numerous versions of each chapter, often conferring by mail or telephone. His stimulating intellect, unfailing insight and common sense continue to guide me over many hurdles. He and Mary Bailey have opened their home to me several times, providing a restorative place of hospitality and wit at the moments when I was most in need of a haven.

Fitz John Porter Poole and Chandra Mukerji were members of my dissertation committee who provided catalyzing comments that have helped me transform my analysis of this material in the years since. Their marks remain in this material, however, transformed. So do those of three earlier teachers – John Atkins, Stevan Harrell, and E. V. Daniel – who have most significantly affected the form and discipline of my questions/ thoughts, and whose influence I would like to acknowledge here.

A number of people have read some version of this book in its entirety. They are Theodore Baskaran, Carol Breckenridge, Michael H. Fisher, JoEllen Fisherkeller, Celeste Goodridge, Ernestine McHugh, Carol Padden, Pamela Price, and Carol Slingo. Their compassioned and dispassionate responses have challenged me to ask hard and rewarding questions of this material. In many cases their faith and contributions have been enormous. Several of these readers have provided a kind of offering that cannot be repaid, nor is such a language appropriate in this context; I wish simply to acknowledge their gift.

Others have read portions of the manuscript and provided crucial formative comments. The remarks of E. V. Daniel, Guenther Roth, and Arjun Appadurai have been especially valuable, encouraging me to examine rigorously and look past the easy answers. I have not always lived up to the models of these and my other readers, but their contributions have strengthened my work significantly, and I hope that they can detect some of their influence.

Many acquaintances and friends have given support along the way. Kausalya Hart, a *racikai* of Tamil movies, facilitated my work substantially when she located and shared videos of the three main films analyzed in the text. Eunice and Sam Sudanandha helped with early interview translations during the days we all lived in Seattle, and have provided friendship in Madurai since then. David Kertzer, then still my colleague at Bowdoin College, provided invaluable help with the early stages of publishing. Jack Kimball and Janet and Rachel Norstrand went out of their way to assist me with library resources and transportation in Boston at a critical point in the revision process. Alison Kipp did an excellent job of coding and interpreting survey data as we worked to make sense of difficult responses, and Katy Biron and Ken Legins saved me much time by helping with wordprocessing. Guy Saldanha of Bowdoin's interlibrary loan office has been unfailingly patient and accommodating with last-minute requests at deadline times. Others who have helped in ways practical and spiritual include Laura Adams, Charlton Clay, Kay and Mike Fagan, Peg Hoey-Daniel, Paula Levin, Premila Paul, Paula Richman, and Maureen and Maddie Terada. All of these people have lightened my work with their good spirits and friendship.

My family has supported me in all these ways and more, giving intellectual, material, and emotional support. Their faith in my academic aims has been constant and encouraging, and they are the source of my desire to learn. Among them they have read parts or all of this manuscript, challenged me with important questions, and tried not to worry when I did things they would prefer I didn't. My appreciation of them, despite this attempt to express it, is outside the bounds of language.

The person who shared the most in this work is Ted Adams. Ted accompanied me during most of my first stay in Madurai, speeding my awareness and understanding through his widespread knowledge of and sensitivity to South India. He provided patient and constant help in the early stages of writing as well, much of it involving tedious proofreading, library searches, and bibliographic work. Later his assumption of household tasks allowed me to devote whatever time I could wrest from teaching to this work. His love, support, and companionship have sustained me throughout as none else could.

My doctoral fieldwork in 1985–87 was funded by a fellowship from the American Institute of Indian Studies. Of its representatives, I would like especially to thank Dr. P. Venugopala Rao, regional director in Madras, and the late Dr. K. Paramasivam, a willing and gifted teacher of Tamil. The dissertation writing was funded by the final year of a National Science Foundation Graduate Fellowship, and subsequent trips to India and periods of writing have been supported by small grants from Bowdoin College. I am most grateful to all of these organizations for their crucial assistance.

Small portions of this work have appeared in similar form in "Accommodation and Resistance: Expression of Working-Class Values through Tamil Cinema," *Wide Angle* 11, 3 (July 1989); "Consuming Utopia: Filmwatching in Tamil Nadu," in Carol A. Breckenridge and Arjun Appadurai, editors, *Modern Sites: Consumption and Contestation in a Postcolonial World* (University of Minnesota Press, forthcoming); and "The Politics of Adulation: Cinema and the Production of Politicians in South India," *The Journal of Asian Studies* (forthcoming).

Note on transliteration

The following notes are meant as an aid to readers unfamiliar with Tamil transliteration systems. In order to keep the text as readable as possible, diacritics have been restricted to instances where they affect pronunciation.

1 Almost all Tamil vowels have both short and long forms, rendered here by single ("a") and double ("aa") vowels respectively.
2 Stops (written, in correspondence with Tamil orthographic conventions, as "k," "c," "t," "p") are voiceless when they occur at the beginning of a word, doubled within a word, or combined with another stop; otherwise they are usually voiced. Thus *koncam* is pronounced "konjam," and *makaacakti* as "magaasakti" or "mahaasakti."
3 In Tamil, "t," "n," and "l" have both retroflex and dental forms. The dental forms are unmarked; the retroflex forms are represented here as "ṭ," "ṇ," and "ḷ."

These three rules cover most of the Tamil words in this text. The following are necessary for the remainder:

4 The constant transliterated as "zh" is unique to Tamil and pronounced similarly to Standard American English "r" (though formed further back in the mouth) in literary or "high" Tamil but pronounced as a retroflex "l" in spoken or colloquial Tamil. "Tamil" itself would be transliterated *tamizh*.
5 When "n" precedes "k" it is pronounced "ng."
6 In this text, any time the combination "nr" appears it is pronounced "ndr"; thus *manram* is "mandram."
7 The "sh" sound, which is not indigenous to Tamil, is written as in English.

Film names are transliterated according to this system except for several famous films with established romanized spellings, and those based on proper names. Examples include *Parasakthi* (which I would otherwise transliterate *Paraacakti*), *Nadodi Mannan* (*Naaṭoṭi Mannan*), and *Sindhu Bairavi* (*Cintu Pairavi*). Other words with common English spellings, such as *jati, bhakti, guru,* and *puja,* retain these spellings.

PART I

1

Introduction

In the city of Madurai, cinema is everywhere. Glittering billboards advertise the latest films, and smaller posters are slapped on to spare inches of wall space. Movie songs blare from horn speakers and cassette players at weddings, puberty rites, and temple and shrine festivals. Tapes of movie dialogues play at coffee stalls, while patrons join in reciting them. Rickshaws and shop boards are painted with movie stars' pictures. Young men and women follow dress and hairstyle fashions dictated by the latest films. Younger children trade movie star cards, learn to disco dance like the film actors, and recreate heroic battles in imitation of their favorite stars. Fan club members meet in the streets to boast about their star and make fun of his rivals.

The visual and aural presence of cinema in this part of South India (see map for location of Madurai) is matched by one of the highest production and filmwatching rates in the world. India regularly produces more films than any other country (see Dharap 1985: 626; Thomas 1985: 116), and of the three major centers for film production within India, the southern industry in Madras is the largest in terms of number of studios, capital investment, gross income, and number of people engaged in production. It was reported in 1975 that one fourth of all India's cinema houses are in the state of Tamil Nadu (Hardgrave and Neidhart 1975: 27); by 1990, when Tamil Nadu had 2,431 cinema theaters, this proportion still held.[1] More than 85 percent of the adults I questioned went to the movies at least three or four times a month. The state's last five Chief Ministers have been movie actors or filmmakers, some of them swept to power by their fan clubs.[2] The sheer quantity of all this cinematic activity suggests that film has something significant to do with the lives in Tamils in South India.

What is the appeal of Tamil cinema? Why is it important to its urban

4   *Cinema and the urban poor in South India*

Map of India and Sri Lanka.

viewers?³ What do they gain from frequent attendance? And how do viewers and filmmakers together negotiate the content and meaning of cinema? The answers to these questions will reveal the significance that cinema holds for its viewers and the meanings these viewers make of what they see.

To look at meaning-making in cinema as a process of negotiation requires attention to the different participants, activities, and texts of cinema. Because my interest lies particularly in what the audiences make of the medium, the focus of this study falls primarily on viewers. This audience-centered analysis contrasts with most previous critiques of Tamil and other Indian film, which tend to dismiss popular cinema as mindless, immoral, and divorced from reality.⁴ Rosie Thomas, one of the few English-language writers to analyze mainstream Indian cinema in terms of its own canons, has noted that typical western reactions vary from "impertinent criticism" based on western filmmaking conventions to patronizing congratulations for quaint achievements (1985: 117–18). Indian critics often reveal a similar lack of understanding; Thomas quotes a common complaint by journalists that "all that the films stand for is exotica, vulgarity and absurdity" (1985: 119). Indian as well as foreign critics frequently make unfavorable comparisons between Indian popular films and "art" or "parallel" cinema, which generally follows the canons of European art cinema. Chidananda Das Gupta, one of the most thoughtful critics of Indian film, denies that popular filmmakers take a "serious approach to cinema" (1981: 102).⁵

If most critics pass judgment on popular movies from high-culture perspectives and refuse to examine the films on their own terms, they betray a similar resistance to viewing the audience's interest in films as anything more than titillation or mindless fantasy. The notion that popular cinema could hold meaning for its audiences or provide insight into their lives is, as Pradip Krishen (1981: 4) points out, greeted with disdain. Even as thoughtful an analyst as the anthropologist Beatrix Pfleiderer has claimed that the world presented on screen is "incomprehensible ... not related to the spectators' desires and needs," a "remote reality" at best (1985: 108). What is missing from these perspectives is not only serious engagement with popular cinema, but also attention to the opinions of those others who take these films seriously – the everyday audiences. In fact cinema is deeply connected to some of the most poignant concerns of viewers' lives and, far from being divorced from those lives, influences their everyday conduct.

This is not to say that moral or aesthetic criticism of a negative kind is limited to formal critics; popular opinion in Tamil Nadu can be equally pejorative. When I first went to Madurai, I believed that cinema's popularity would make it easy to get people to talk about films and filmgoing. It quickly became apparent, however, that for all its popularity cinema does not enjoy unequivocal support, even among its most frequent viewers. Many say it undermines traditional values, and even those who go most often and praise favorite stars most vociferously among friends may not admit their passion to others for fear of social censure. Viewers praise actors and actresses one moment and malign their morals the next. Filmmakers who have made fortunes from audiences disparage viewers' prurient tastes.

Many of popular cinema's critics denounce it as a purely escapist form of mass entertainment. Much of Tamil cinema's negative reputation does indeed derive from its association with the masses (i.e. the urban and rural poor), who make up the overwhelming majority of viewers.[6] Lower class people themselves generally share this view of cinema, but attend films regularly despite it. Their enthusiasm for cinema has also had effects away from the box office, playing a significant role, for example, in the rise to power of the parties that have dominated state politics since the 1960s, led by stars of the "cine world" whose films deftly appealed to the hopes and frustrations of the poor.

Filmmakers and audiences belong, by and large, to groups or categories that I will argue can be considered distinct classes. When I began my research I knew that movies were patronized mostly by the poor, and was aware that consumers and producers might be distinguished by social and economic criteria, but did not particularly intend to carry out a class-oriented analysis. I have been insistently drawn to this perspective, however, by Tamils' own intentional and unintentional portrayal of various aspects of cinema as somehow marked by class associations. Filmgoing is seen – and disparaged – by all elements of the public as a largely lower class preoccupation; filmmaking is done by people who belong almost exclusively to the middle and upper classes. This is not to say that cinema participants are entirely restricted by socioeconomic status to specific roles; members of the middle and upper classes go to the theaters and watch movies on their VCRs, and the poor have some influence on the form and content of films. Nonetheless, the common image of cinema participation, accepted and promulgated at all social levels, is one of the poor watching and even demanding the unsavory, low-brow material of films. The generally unstated complement to this picture is the provision by middle and upper class filmmakers of this devalued material. Class, it is clear, plays an important role not only in influencing public perception of cinema, but also in the reception and creation of the movies.

Much of the meaning derived from cinema has to do with the socially, culturally, and economically subordinate position of the urban poor, and issues of class, power, and dominance are central to understanding the relationship of viewers to the medium. Class is essential to urban residents' identity; when Madurai residents talk about "people like us," they are much more likely to be identifying themselves with a socioeconomic category such as "poor people" than with forms of identity that have historically received more frequent consideration by analysts, such as caste or religion. As other observers have noted (e.g. L. Caplan 1987: 10; Holmström 1984: 282ff; Driver and Driver 1987; Omvedt 1989), social class and caste comprise separate but interacting forms of hierarchy. Class often proves the more effective frame of reference for determining hierarchically based behavior in South Indian cities, because it is more easily observed by both strangers and acquaintances than is caste identity.

The people I refer to as the "urban poor" in this work include skilled and unskilled laborers or low-level office workers, and their household members, who possess or control little in the way of land and other property and endure a general lack of economic security. Those I spoke

1. An autorickshaw driver and his auto decorated with a Vijaykanth decal. 1991.

with who had paid occupations worked, for example, as rickshaw drivers, construction workers, domestic servants, office "peons," flower and vegetable sellers, small shopkeepers, municipally employed street and latrine cleaners, leatherworkers, shop clerks, woodworkers, bicycle and motorbike repairmen, Brahman and non-Brahman small-temple priests. They worked in both the organized and unorganized sectors, public and private, and a few were members of unions; very few, however, worked in factories. Almost all had incomes at or near the Indian poverty line.[7] All were by their own standards clearly poor and financially insecure, although some were on the verge of attaining greater security, thanks to job promotions or the addition of a new wage-earner to the family. Economic security could also fluctuate downward – jobs could disappear, or a wage-earner be lost to the family when a child married; thus financial security was linked both to the larger economy and to stages in the domestic cycle. It is important to note that at the time of this fieldwork I did not get to know many of the poorest poor, people who in Madurai live in insubstantial shelters, usually on the banks of canals and rivers or on the sidewalks and streets. Nothing I observed then or thereafter, however, has led me to believe that their reactions to cinema would have differed significantly from those of other urban poor residents.

The preceding description suggests, rightly, that the category "urban poor" includes people who vary widely in such features as occupation and income. The term is nonetheless a useful one for a number of reasons. First, it corresponds to the category of people that Tamils lump at the bottom of the socioeconomic hierarchy, and to the self-ascribed identity of people in this position. Such people refer to themselves as "poor people," *eezhai makkaḷ* (or "laborers," *tozhilaaḷikaḷ*; "people who suffer," *kashṭappaṭṭavarkaḷ*; or "people who have nothing," *illaatavarkaḷ*), and are referred to as "the lower class" or "the mass" (usually in English) by members of higher classes.[8]

The poor lump all more privileged people together as "rich people," *paṇakkaararkaḷ*, or "big people," *periyavarkaḷ*, using essentially the same socioeconomic criteria as I have. These wealthier people, on the other hand, tend to identify themselves (in English) as "middle class" or "upper class" people. While there are indeed differences between those who identify themselves as middle or upper class in terms of lifestyle and values, in this work I adhere to the model cited by the poor in considering the relatively wealthy in largely undifferentiated opposition to the poor because they share significant attributes for the purpose of this analysis. Both the middle and the upper classes can be distinguished from the poor by their awareness and expectation of personal opportunities in education and employment, a sense of hope and potential much unlike the resignation expressed by the urban poor – who are often struggling to maintain a grasp on what they have rather than expecting or achieving improvement. Both hold a common view of the poor as short-sighted, narrow-minded, and often morally misguided. Members of both higher classes tend to receive substantial education (at least through secondary school) and share values that become significant in the analysis of filmgoers' reactions to their own position in the socioeconomic hierarchy and of the role those reactions play in responses to cinema.

Second, I have avoided imposing a more precise class label, such as the classical Marxist terms familiar to students of western capitalist societies, because the application of these categories in India is fraught with difficulties. These difficulties derive from variations in social and economic structures. Marxist categories rarely correspond to the most meaningful local divisions in India, even when such criteria as the mode of and relations to means of production are taken into account. As Lionel Caplan argues,

Students of Western societies are, even now, not in agreement on the criteria for identifying the major protagonists in late capitalist formations. How much more complex, then, are these questions where such systems are comparatively new and shaped by a range of quite special historical conditions. (1987: 10; see also Beteille 1974: 43, 117–19 and Kohli 1987: 237n)

Even where a relatively precise class can be identified, as in Holmström's study of the working class in Bangalore, the people it encompasses are hardly uniform in type or security of work, values, lifestyle, or identity (Holmström 1984). Moreover, little organized class consciousness or collective action is found among those who might otherwise technically be identified as members of a single class (Kohli 1987: 150, 240; Beteille 1974: 52; Sharma 1987: 11–12; L. Caplan 1987: 164). Compounding this difficulty of fit is the paucity of detailed and empirically based studies of the meanings and boundaries of class divisions in India. Most of the small but growing number of works have focussed on agrarian systems (Thorner 1956; Beteille 1974; Sharma 1978; Gough 1981; Omvedt 1989);[9] many of them emphasize indigenous categories rather than applying strict Marxist, Weberian or other forms.

All of these obstacles, it should be noted, apply to dominant as well as subordinate classes. It has been argued that no single dominant class can be identified in India, due to the fragmentation or pluralism of elite groups (Kohli 1987: 241; see Lele 1981), and to the divergence of the lines of their formation from those of dominant class formations in western capitalist societies. Kohli, for example, contends that there is rarely a single dominant class in India "capable of imposing hegemonic rule in the Gramscian sense" (ibid.), and Caplan points out that in urban areas, "ownership of the means of production resides principally with the state or multinational corporations, so that the indigenous capitalist class is only a tiny, highly compact, and barely visible minority" (L. Caplan 1987: 13–14). (See Ganguli 1977: 29 for a contrasting point of view.) Nor do most analysts believe that elites collectively possess a unified dominant ideology.

Should we avoid any reference to class under such circumstances? I would argue not. In particular, attempts to invalidate the "applicability of class analysis" to India based on a lack of class consciousness threaten, as Beteille has pointed out, to "define classes out of existence" (1974: 52). Even without an organized form of consciousness there is certainly, as others have noted among residents of Madras (Wiebe 1981; P. Caplan 1985; L. Caplan 1987: 147), an *awareness* of class. I suggest, following Lloyd (1982: 40), that this awareness constitutes a minimal level of class consciousness. Categories of class constitute a form of hierarchy that is consciously recognized, cognitively salient, experientially real, and behaviorally motivating (and, incidentally, remains distinguished from caste). I will also argue that to the extent we can speak of the existence of classes, we can also speak of the existence of class ideologies, a collection of beliefs and values conditioned by perceptions of experience, hierarchical position, and relationship to other categories in the hierarchy.

Thus I have chosen the phrase "urban poor" because it corresponds to the most prominent local subdivision of people made on a socioeconomic basis, while terms such as "working class" or "proletariat" would not; it is also more descriptive and precisely defined than the usually vague "lower class" (a term that will occasionally be used in this work – especially when it is appropriate to the indigenous context, e.g. where judgments are made about the value of "lower" and "higher" class aesthetics – as a synonym for the poor). It refers to a category of people who in some minimal ways, I argue, can be considered a class. The final reason for defining the people who form the primary focus of this book as I have is that, despite the term's broadness, it remains a useful category of analysis. Those whom I describe and who would describe themselves in this way share the features mentioned above, most notably poverty, a persistent sense of financial insecurity, and lack of sociopolitical power. Few if any meaningful class-related subdivisions could be made, aside perhaps from occupation, and the resulting groups would be too small and numerous to be of use here; moreover the shared identity based on insecurity creates a sense of commonality that is often stronger than the sense of identity shared with members of smaller categories or groups (cf. Sharma 1978: 167).

Thus, this study is a class-based analysis to the extent that filmgoers and filmmakers (and others like them) perceive and portray themselves as distinct from (and, more than incidentally, in opposition to) one another, based on economic, social, cultural, and political factors. Such an approach to class, while necessarily divested of the specificity gained from a stricter definition, provides other advantages by making sociocultural factors as fundamental as economic and political ones. As Lionel Caplan has pointed out, such a model

takes us away from the static and sterile notion of class as an occupational or income category, or even a set of people standing in a particular relation to the means of production. It invites us, rather, to regard class as a cultural as well as an economic formation. This enables us to treat class struggle as being every bit as much about definitive meaning systems or appropriate religious views and observances as about material means, scarce jobs, or the control of property. (1987:14)

In the approach taken here, then, opposition between classes has equally to do with values and aesthetics as with economic inequalities and relationships.

Class identity bears strongly on viewers' participation in Tamil cinema, and issues of class, elite cultures, and subordinate cultures are highly significant in understanding the relationship between film producers and consumers. This configuration is of course not limited to southern India, and the last decade has produced a growing scholarly awareness of the subcultural aspects of expressive forms in various societies. Much of this work has occurred in reaction to the position of the Frankfurt School, which extolled the enlightening aspects of high art or culture while deploring mass culture as an instrument of capitalist hegemony that created false needs and desires (cf. Adorno 1941; Horkheimer 1941). Implicit (at least) in this perspective is the assumption that mass culture is molded by the dominant ideology of a society and that its consumers absorb this ideology obediently and straightforwardly. Many Indian film critics have their ideological precursors in these views.

Much of the recent work questioning the monolithic nature of culture and mass media can be traced back to Raymond Williams (1977, 1982). Combining theory with ethnography, Williams and his colleagues began in the 1970s to investigate the potential for the expression of subaltern resistance within mass and popular culture. The first phase of this movement focussed on youth subcultures in Britain. Rather than viewing expressive cultural forms as mesmerizing consumers into submission, these authors saw scope within certain of these forms – including fashion, music, and rhetoric – for negotiation with the dominant culture and for some appropriation of it on the terms of the subordinates (see Hebdige 1979; Hall and Jefferson 1976; Jameson 1979 and Enzensberger 1982 also challenged previous assumptions). Others, building on this work, have investigated the potential for contestation, compensation, and empowerment in folklore, joking and word play, romance novels, rock music, and soccer (see Lombardi-Satriani 1974; Limón 1982, 1989; Radway 1984; Grossberg 1984; Lever 1983). Still others have demonstrated that the effects of a particular medium are not homogeneous, but depend on the experiences and statuses that individual audience members bring in as "active subjects" (Walsh 1989: 74; Gledhill 1988; Bobo 1988; Modleski 1986: xi).

Some who are largely sympathetic to this body of work have nonetheless begun to warn its proponents against perceiving subordinate resistance where it does not exist. Modleski, for example, argues that while Frankfurt School members were too far outside the culture they criticized, today's critics may be too close: "immersed in their culture, half in love with their subject, they sometimes seem unable to achieve the proper critical distance from it." She warns that we may unwittingly end up "writing apologias for mass culture and embracing its ideology" (1986: xi–xii). Some see in this dialectical response a balance closer to reality than the previous extremes. Stam has recently called for a "synthesis which eschews both the elitist pessimism of manipulation theory and the naive affirmative celebrations of the uncritical apologists for mass-mediated culture" (1988: 118). This synthesis becomes more easily realized when the production and consumption of mass media are viewed as processes of negotiation rather than of either unimpeded imposition or unhindered appropriation (cf. Gledhill 1988).

Studies in the field of cultural performance comprise another body of work that frequently takes into account the uses that audiences make of material. Beginning with Singer (1959, 1972), this approach has encouraged viewing "performance" as a whole – attending to audiences, performers, and creators as well as the place, style, and text of the performance. It also attends closely to the ways in which consumers and producers communicate images of themselves to themselves and others. These images cannot always be read straightforwardly, as Turner (1984, 1986) and Geertz (1973) point out. In MacAloon's words, performances are "occasions in which as a culture or society we reflect upon and define ourselves, dramatize our collective myths and histories, present ourselves with alternatives, and eventually change in some ways while remaining the same in others" (1984a: 1). Other works that address the presentation of images of self and others through media include Nowell-Smith (1985) on film melodrama, Enzensberger (1982) on the mass media, and Debord (1983) on spectacle.

Despite the recent attention paid to the meanings audiences find in entertainment, however, one element of audience experience that has received little consideration is pleasure. Within the debate on subordinate appropriations of media, some discourse has developed around the nature or construction of pleasure and escape, particularly with regard to cinema and television (e.g. Mulvey 1989a, 1989b; Ang 1985; Morley 1986; Gledhill 1987, 1988; Schrøder 1988), but it remains limited. Sometimes even writing on mass culture has shown a reluctance to acknowledge, let alone examine, the pleasure that these forms bring to their consumers. When addressed at all, pleasure has often been seen as reason for despair; in the eyes of the Frankfurt School, it was a mechanism for manipulating the masses. Just as often, analysts have refused to consider observers' pleasure altogether. Stuart Hall explains this in political terms. "The project of the left," he contends, "is directed at the future, at the socialism that has still to come, and that is at odds with the direct experience of pleasure here and now" (Ang and Simons 1982: 13, cited in Ang 1985: 18).

Writers who have begun to examine these issues contend that entertainment is anything but "mere" escape or pleasure. As Ang argues in her study of *Dallas* viewers in Holland, to associate entertainment with simple, uncomplicated pleasure is

to evade the obligation to investigate which mechanisms lie at the basis of that pleasure, how that pleasure is produced and how it works – as though the pleasure were something natural and automatic. Nothing is less true, however. (1985: 19)

Much of the dismissal of Indian cinema involves this refusal to ask why viewers find pleasure in movies, let alone to consider how pleasure and escape are constructed. Thomas castigates these critics by pointing out that "such supercilious criticism does no more than wish the films away." She argues,

Dismissing them as 'escapism' neither explains them in any useful way, nor offers any basis for political strategy, for it allows no space for questions about the specifics of the audiences' relationship to their so-called "escapist" fare. What seems to be needed is an analysis which takes seriously both the films and the pleasures they offer, and which attempts to unravel their mode of operation. (1985: 120)

Approaching filmwatching as a process of negotiation opens possibilities for a fuller appreciation of the meaning of cinema, allowing as it does "space to the subjectivities, identities and pleasures of audiences" (Gledhill 1988: 72). The appeal of Tamil cinema is indeed based to some degree on escape, yet if this constitutes the limit of our analysis we have explained very little. How do films and filmmakers create escape? From what and to what is the escape offered? Do audiences view themselves as seeking escape, and if so, what do they make of this? How do they view the effects of film in general? Questions such as these allow us to identify the significance and construction of pleasure and escape in cinema.

This work reflects a mix of my own and native perceptions of the entire performance that both of us have lumped under the term "cinema": the movies, the participants – including viewers, filmmakers, critics, and censors – and the activities – including filmwatching, filmmaking, censorship, formal and informal film criticism, and fan club and political activities. A number of these aspects of Tamil cinema are considered, all with an eye to determining cinema's meaning for viewers and the uses they make of it – what, to put it most broadly, it has to do with their lives.

In the remaining chapters of Part I, I describe a variety of contexts for situating the material that follows. These include social life in urban South India, my fieldwork and introduction to the field, the neighborhoods in which and people with whom this work was done, and the experiences, activities, and attitudes connected with cinema.

Part II presents Tamil cinema from several angles and begins an analysis of its appeal. The history of Tamil film, the elements and aesthetic canons of movies are described. Three film stories are presented and analyzed, and the models of utopia found in films are introduced.

Part III addresses the participants in film activities and their influence on film, as well as cinema's meaning in their lives. The chapters examine filmmakers' roles and views on filmmaking and audiences; viewers' and filmmakers' impressions of the relationship between cinema and real life, and of perceived reasons for and effects of filmgoing; and the significance of fan clubs and political activities for cinema. The concluding chapter returns to the appeal of Tamil cinema overall, linking contradictions in the utopian formulas that appear in different aspects and their significance for the meaning created through cinema.

2

Lives in Madurai

My research centered on Madurai, a city of about a million people in Tamil Nadu, the southernmost state of India. Despite the great variability in the lives of Madurai's poor residents, numerous shared social and cultural understandings are brought to bear when individuals respond to cinema. Here I concentrate on the issues most pertinent to filmwatching, including the forms of identity, social relations, and cultural practices most prevalent in daily life, and describe my fieldwork and the neighborhoods in which I worked.

Social life in urban South India
The division of forms and practices made in this description of social life is essentially an artificial one, in that these forms and practices normally interact with one another and may even be indistinguishable in behavior and experience. It is used here for ease of explication, especially for the sake of readers unfamiliar with South Asia. The lives and experiences of Madurai's residents are exceedingly diverse, and while that complexity cannot be approximated in a brief overview, I attempt to note where cultural practices are either more or less shared across such social distinctions as class, caste, and gender. Most of what is described here is characteristic of life in other South Indian cities as well, but where not, these exceptions are also noted.

Class and power
Of all the forms of identity in urban South India, socioeconomic class is one of the most salient. Poor Madurai residents speak often, with much resignation, of the difficulties of being poor. In Madurai, as in the rest of India, wealth bestows social and political power (closely related to the

amount spent on gaining and giving favors). Higher class persons are addressed respectfully, and expect deference. The wealthy will occasionally try to "do something" for their less advantaged fellows, accompanying their charitable acts by lectures on how to improve one's life. On such occasions, I have seen lower class people listen to the advice of their "betters," but with the general attitude that while wealthier people are free to do things their own way they have no idea of what poorer people's lives are really like. (Also see P. Caplan 1985.) While a few people seem to accept the terms of hierarchy – urging their children, for example, to respect the wealthy – in general a surface acquiescence to the upper class conceals actual resistance to its values and charitable gestures, and a questioning of the worth of the upper class lifestyle. There are still frequent fantasies of an easier and more genteel life, however, and cinema both plays on these fantasies and verifies the inner worth and righteous character of the lower classes.

A pervasive feature of the lives of the urban poor is a sense of social and economic insecurity. Jobs are dependent on an employer's whim or on an unreliable climate; house rent can be raised beyond reach at any moment; food and commodity prices often jump without warning. Uncertainties

2. Movie billboards lining the road across from the main bus stand in Madurai. 1986.

abound in social relationships as well. Grown children neglect the care of aged parents; a husband may die or abandon wife and children; siblings refuse to honor their responsibilities to one another at children's marriages. Madurai residents often complained to me that life was once easier, and that the social and economic insecurity they now experience is increasing.[1]

They are also frustrated because they cannot change the circumstances that make life insecure. Yet weakness and powerlessness do not characterize most of the daily experiences and expressions of poor residents in Madurai. Life is not pervaded by futility and resignation to the extent that people stop trying to find better or more regular work, to send their children to a better school, or to arrange for them the best marriages they can. They try to improve things in any small way possible; and the frustrations of life notwithstanding, they take pleasure in their successes.

Nonetheless the urban poor lack most of the resources to take effective action in the larger society. Power comes from wealth, prestige, and political connections. When poor people are faced with difficult or unfair circumstances – such as demolition of squatter colonies or reduction of water supply – they can do little in the face of entrenched bureaucracy, police coercion or political corruption. One of the few effective responses is mass action, either through the ballot box or in organized protests. Since the poor themselves rarely come to power through these processes, however – at best instructing their more powerful representatives to work in their interests – neither of these routes is a sure one.

The urban poor are sharply aware of their lack of power. They are convinced that virtually all efforts to combat unjust circumstances are futile. It is in this sense, then, that they feel ineffectual and powerless. When combined with a perceived increase in economic and social uncertainties, such feelings create a permeating sense of insecurity and helplessness. Such uncertainty and anxiety are an integral backdrop to the reactions that many viewers have to cinema.

Caste

Another social division in Madurai is that of caste. Caste, or *jati* (literally "genus," a classificatory device applied to non-human as well as human beings), refers here to the hereditary, endogamous, hierarchically ranked, and often occupationally specific units to which all Hindus belong (as do, to an arguable degree, Indian Muslims, Christians, Jains, Parsis, Sikhs, and everyone else).[2] Caste is significant to an individual's identity in part because, as this definition suggests, it helps determine who one can marry, where one's place is in a social and ritual hierarchy, and sometimes what work one does. It affects individuals in other basic ways as well; domestic rituals, founding myths, goals for education, and rules about gendered behavior often vary by caste. Nonetheless, caste is only one factor of identity, and cannot be assumed to be the ultimate or most "encompassing" determinant of behavior, as some analysts (primarily Dumont 1970) have suggested.

Caste is probably the aspect of Indian society most frequently noted by outside observers,[3] yet is cited less frequently by residents than many other principles of association.[4] When Madurai residents talk about "people like us," they are much more likely to be identifying themselves with a socioeconomic category ("poor people") or by gender. A person's friends are more likely to be drawn from the surrounding neighborhood than strictly from that person's own *jati*. Friends also come from school and work. Of course, many of the people visited most often are relatives, who are always of the same caste, and if a friend in the neighborhood or at school happens to be of one's own *jati*, this shared identity will usually strengthen the relationship.

Caste is important in determining social behavior in rural South India (where divisions are especially rigid between scheduled castes and other Hindus), but less so in the cities, at least on the surface of social relations. While caste considerations in the city are present, they are frequently submerged. Most people have absorbed the government denunciation of caste discrimination to the extent that they know they are supposed to believe caste is not socially significant. Children are taught this in school, and many adults remember Mahatma Gandhi's campaigns against caste prejudice. (The woman who cooked for me, who was about forty and belonged to a high caste, claimed not to know the *jati* of two scheduled caste women who were casual friends of hers and also cooked for Americans. "We can't ask those questions," she said; "people would take offense.") Moreover, the crowding and anonymity of city life make adherence to strict rules of hierarchy impossible. Members of lower castes are aware – sometimes militantly so – of their legal rights to equality. All of these factors make it difficult for residents of urban caste-integrated neighborhoods to practice open discrimination, or to give caste any marked importance in public.

While the importance of caste is attenuated and modified in today's urban areas, it has neither disappeared nor become irrelevant. It remains highly significant in some social arenas, and may be called upon in political alliances. While city neighborhoods are usually composed of different *jati*s, those in any given area are often of roughly equal social and ritual standing. There is also still a strong sense of "watching out" for one's fellow caste members, and in independent businesses people are more likely to hire someone of their own caste. Moreover, Indian government policies that list all *jati*s as either scheduled, backward, or forward encourage caste identification and divisiveness. These classifications are supposed to be based on social and economic factors, but are sometimes more closely tied to political considerations. Scheduled caste or backward "class" status (held by well over half of Tamil Nadu's population) confers benefits in education, political office, and government jobs. This highly entrenched system of protective discrimination, once intended to "level out" all castes, actually makes the divisions between castes stronger by officially and repeatedly defining social categories by caste, and by increasing the resentment of those who are ineligible for benefits against those who receive them (Washbrook 1989: 207; Dushkin 1972: 213).[5]

Beliefs and prejudices about caste may surface in certain situations where people of different castes come into close contact, especially where food exchanges are involved.[6] A Brahman schoolteacher joked that an Untouchable family and a high caste family could live next to each other and exchange sweets on holidays as if caste were nothing, but the high caste neighbors would throw the sweets away as soon as they were alone. One of my research assistants, a poor man of a lower middle caste who considered himself "modern" in outlook, refused food in the house of some scheduled caste friends of mine whom he too knew well. He told me afterward that he had drunk the water they offered in order not to offend them, but that even that had caused him "grief of the heart" (*manacu kashṭam*). In his native village, he said, he would not have faced this situation because Harijans there would never offer food or water; instead, they would buy the higher caste visitor a bottle of soda.

While overt expressions of caste concerns appear less frequently in the city – relative to more rural areas, to earlier urban areas (especially prior to Independence), and to western expectations of their appearance – these concerns nonetheless remain salient to Madurai residents. They are submerged but far from insignificant.

Religion

Most Madurai residents are Hindu. Religious activity is focussed on temples and shrines, of which there are many. Judging simply by the number of small shrines that dotted the streets – there were more than fifteen active ones within half a block of my residence – Madurai appears to be a very "religious" city. Shrines are often located inside the home as well as outside, and most Hindu households set aside one wall for brightly colored pictures of the deities worshipped most often. Neighborhood shrines, usually small enclosures housing an image or emblem of a deity, are very popular. Neighborhood residents provide the image with clothing, flowers, and devotional powders. Many of these shrines have annual festivals, in which the shrine is freshly painted, an image of the deity is paraded around the city streets on a small temple car, animal or other sacrifices are made, music is played, and food is served to participants. These festivals usually last several days, and neighborhood people of all ages become involved in the preparations and celebration.

There are many temples in the city, distinguished from shrines by their larger size and the greater area from which worshippers are drawn. Active temples are served by priests. (A few "inactive" temples have fallen out of favor with residents because their deities no longer demonstrate sufficient power to grant requests.) Within two blocks of my apartment there were seven major active temples, including the central Minakshi Temple.

There are no set days for temple attendance, as there are in churches or mosques, although Tuesdays and Fridays are the holiest days in Shaivite temples, and Saturdays in Vaishnavite temples, and people may make an extra effort to worship on those days. Generally, people attend the temple according to their own desires to pray and to show devotion – either because they have a request to make of the deity, wish to thank the god for a request granted or other good fortune, or simply because they wish to pay their respects. Some people rarely if ever visit temples, but many others – adults and children, women and men – visit frequently. Even small children can be seen going to a neighborhood temple by themselves.

While Madurai is more dominantly and visibly Hindu than some other southern cities (Hyderabad, for example, has a large Muslim population, and Kerala cities have sizable populations of Muslims and Christians), it also includes Christian and Muslim groups. Most Christians belong to either the CSI (Church of South India, a coalition of several Protestant denominations) or the Roman Catholic church. Almost all come from families converted to Christianity from Hinduism within the last several generations, and many still identify themselves by their previously Hindu *jati* names. Most Christians have pictures of Christ hanging on their walls, and sometimes of Mary or certain saints (as do some Hindus).

There are several distinct groups of Muslims in Madurai, who distinguish among themselves primarily by the language they speak at home (Urdu or Tamil) and by the strictness with which women are segregated from men in the family and from the general public. Some Muslims require that post-pubescent women remain in the house, separated from adult men including those of the household, at almost all times. Most, however, allow women to leave the household for shopping, and sometimes to go to the cinema; a very few Muslim women hold jobs as teachers or nurses.

I knew of no cases of group or individual conflict over religious differences occurring when I was first in Madurai. Pro-Hindu organizations (such as the Hindu Munnani) are now experiencing something of a resurgence, and violent protests have recently been staged in reaction to renaming a neighboring district after a Muslim leader, but historically such occurrences are rare in Tamil Nadu.

Language and politics
Similarly, despite the fact that a substantial number of people in Madurai speak something besides Tamil as their mother tongue (usually Telugu or Saurashtrian[7]), I was not aware of any instances of language conflict among city residents.[8] But language is nonetheless a volatile issue for Tamils, with frequent flare-ups in response to perceived "Hindi dominance" – appearing most reliably whenever the Central Government threatens to institute a long-delayed plan making Hindi the only official language, requiring it to be used in government offices and taught in schools.

Tamil chauvinism has been a part of the ethnic Dravidian political movement since that movement's inception at the turn of the century.[9] Its focus extends beyond language to wider Tamil culture. The movement grew out of upper-caste non-Brahmans' resentment of Brahmans' increasing social dominance at the end of the nineteenth century. Fueled by an inability to break "the almost exclusive control of government jobs and political life by Brahmans" (Irschick 1969: 17) and by suggestions of contemporary historians (most of them European missionaries) that the Aryan conquerors – northern Indians, with whom Brahmans were identified – had long ago enslaved the Dravidians and destroyed their proud and ancient civilization (Hardgrave 1965b: 9–10; Sastri 1966: 68–70, 74), non-Brahman resentment began to receive organized political expression at the beginning of the twentieth century.[10]

The political parties, ideologies, and rhetoric that now dominate Tamil Nadu politics grew out of this non-Brahman movement. The forerunner of the present Dravidian parties was the South Indian Liberal Federation, commonly known as the Justice Party, formed in 1916 and made up almost entirely of elite non-Brahmans. It contested elections with varying success. In the mid-1930s, with its fortunes at their lowest, the party was taken over by the radical activist E. V. Ramasamy (EVR, often known as "Periyar," "Great One"). EVR and his dramatic anti-Brahman protests put new life into the party. In 1944 EVR reorganized the Justice Party into the Dravida Kazhagam (DK), the Dravidian Federation, and launched a Tamil "cultural offensive," including theatrical productions that attacked or inverted Hindu and Brahman texts and ideals (Hardgrave 1965a: 400). However, despite such attempts at mass propaganda, the party's membership continued to be drawn from the elite.

In 1949, prominent members of the DK including C. N. Annadurai and Mu. Karunanidhi (both of them playwrights and screenwriters) broke with the party to form the Dravida Munnetra Kazhagam (DMK), the Dravidian Progressive Federation, for which they sought mass membership. Their early platform stressed the creation of a separate and united Dravidian state and the promotion of a "Dravidian" ideology. In the 1950s, dramatic and violent agitations were instituted by the DK and DMK against "Northern imperialism" (portrayed as both a cultural and an economic domination), including picketing northerners' shops, burning Hindi books, and assaulting Brahmans.[11] In the 1960s, after the Tamil-language state of Madras (now Tamil Nadu) had been formed and the goal of a Dravidian state thereby undermined and abandoned, party leaders turned from linguistic and ethnic separatist issues to more typical bread-and-butter political issues: wages, high prices, and food shortages. Most importantly, the principal focus was now on the "common people" and their neglected concerns. One of Annadurai's more effective means of attracting the masses was to include movie stars in party rallies. He also sought to use films as a medium of politicization and mobilization. His timing was ideal: a rural electrification program initiated in the late 1940s allowed the widespread construction of cinema halls, coinciding fortuitously with the DMK's initial use of film as a political medium (see Sivathamby 1981: 25).

The DMK became highly successful in state politics, attaining a majority in the legislature and control over the state in 1967. The DMK and the ADMK (Annadurai-DMK), a splinter party created by the movie star M. G. Ramachandran (popularly known as MGR) in 1972, have dominated state politics continuously since the 1960s. Their platforms have been strikingly similar, and while both are far more centrist than the parent DK, they will frequently refer back to issues of Dravidian (now Tamil) pride and chauvinism, particularly linguistic issues.

This chauvinism is fanned at regular intervals by politicians who recognize it as a passionate electoral issue and take up the banner whenever they think it will hurt an opposing party. In addition to the emotional appeal of language as a "primordial attachment" (Geertz 1963: 109), pragmatic concerns are involved. If Hindi were to become a truly national language, native Hindi speakers would have a great advantage in getting jobs. (At present, English holds that position *de facto*. Far fewer Indians speak English than Hindi, but their distribution is nationwide rather than restricted to a distinct geographical area. Tamils, on the other hand, are more likely to speak English than Hindi, though relatively few people in Tamil Nadu speak either language.) Usually, however, opposition to Hindi is framed in terms of a fear that its use at the expense of Tamil would result in widespread "cultural dominance" by northerners and destruction of a "Tamil culture."

Political passions such as these are regularly inflamed at election time. All Indians aged eighteen or older have the right to vote. Many of the people I knew exercised this right, and almost all of them held strong political opinions. Women usually accede to men (either their husbands or fathers) in their expressed opinions and party allegiance; many married women say that they leave those choices up to their husband. Most people are aware of at least some of the main policies of the party they vote for – in 1985–87, many cited, for example, MGR's school lunch and uniforms program as evidence that "he helps people like us" – but few have in-depth knowledge of the party's past or present political record. Political gatherings for a party or an individual minister or other politician are frequent, and speeches – made in a flowery literary Tamil – can draw large crowds. The largest gatherings during my first stay were for MGR, then the Chief Minister of Tamil Nadu. When the Second All-World International MGR Fan Club Conference was held in Madurai in 1986 – a political event despite its cinema-related title – it was inaugurated by a two-mile procession that began at 7 a.m.; by 11 p.m., many people were still waiting their turn to cross the starting line.

Work, education, and leisure
Work is an issue of frequent concern to the urban poor, and many are underemployed or, more rarely, unemployed. Those with full-time paid employment work at least ten hours a day, often more, but rarely express resentment of drudgery or tedium; work is scarce enough to make most workers grateful to have any job that matches their education and social standing.

Labor is divided by gender. Household work is done by women; this includes cooking, cleaning, washing clothes, buying food, carrying water, and childcare. Most jobs outside the house are reserved for men, whether in labor, service, administrative, or executive posts. There are many exceptions to this general division, although women are more likely to work outside the home – usually in addition to their domestic chores – than are men to work in the home. Educated women may hold positions as clerks in banks or government offices, or as schoolteachers. Poor women may support families or supplement household income by doing piece-work at home, or by selling fruits and vegetables in the open markets or door-to-door in neighborhood lanes; others work as manual laborers in construction, sweep the streets and collect garbage, or labor in fields on the outskirts of town. In general, families prefer not to have women take part in paid employment unless it is necessary for economic reasons (a choice often made to ensure survival among the poor or, much less often but with increasing frequency among the middle class, to support a certain standard of living).

Education is a major determinant of employment options. Most of the adults I knew had not completed the tenth standard, and many lower caste women (and a very few men) had not studied at all. Most, however, hoped to have their children complete secondary school, since this greatly enhances employment prospects. Nonetheless, a girl who has a marriage prospect will almost always be removed from school, since her security will come from marriage rather than from her employment. Those lower class girls and women who take on paid employment after their schooling – including those with college degrees – almost always quit their jobs at marriage.

Most of the people with whom I lived managed to send their children to school for a time. Private schools (especially English-language medium) are favored for the higher quality of their education and the edge they give children in standardized examinations, but most children of poor families attend public schools because their families cannot afford private fees. Even public schools are not free; parents pay for children's uniforms, books, notebooks, pens, and exam fees. There are some government welfare programs that help defray the cost of schooling, especially through the provision of uniforms; poor schoolchildren are also eligible for a free noon-meals program.

Boys in many families are encouraged to study further than girls, but the gap seems to be lessening. Children of wealthier families tend to stay in school longer than those of poorer families, and – although this correlation appeared to have greater exceptions – higher castes support greater education than do lower castes. Children may stop studying because they no longer want to attend school, but many if not most who leave do so because their parents can no longer afford to pay the school expenses and forfeit the income children can earn, or occasionally because parents decide it is time for their children to marry. Schooling can start as early as age three, when children can attend LKG and then UKG (Lower and Upper Kindergarten). They then enter the first through tenth standards; at the end of the tenth, a final exam is taken for the SSLC (Secondary School Leaving Certificate), the equivalent of a high school diploma. Those who study further can either enter a "polytechnic" institution directly or study two more years at the secondary level and then enter a bachelor's degree college or university program (usually a three-year course). Master's and doctorate degrees can follow, but are very rare. Completion of the tenth standard itself is a very significant and prestigious accomplishment, so much so that even those who fail the leaving exam may identify themselves with the title "SSLC Fail." The most esteemed of all degrees is the college or university credential from a foreign country.

Whatever their education or employment, the poor find little time for leisure. Men may visit a coffee stall in the early morning or evening, where they stand outside to drink their coffee and perhaps read a newspaper or listen to film tapes. If people have spare time in the afternoons, they take a nap, especially in the hot season. In the evenings, when household labor and outside work are over, and the final meal eaten, sitting and sharing conversation in doorways is a frequent pastime. The most common leisure activities are visits to temples or the cinema. Women, whose work overall is more time-consuming, may nonetheless have more flexible schedules than men, so they may be able to sneak in a cinema show in the morning.[12] (Morning show audiences are almost completely made up of women and their small children, while evening shows are usually filled with groups of men and some families.) Some people also belong to voluntary associations (*manram*s), such as religious devotional groups, movie star fan clubs, or political organizations, which meet occasionally.

Marriage, family, and gender

Marriage is one of the paramount events in a Tamil person's life. With very few exceptions, marriages are arranged by the parents or guardians of the couple rather than by the bride and groom themselves, a custom virtually unchanged by urbanization and modernization. About a year before they hope to hold the wedding, parents inform their relatives, fellow *jati* members, and friends, who oblige by scanning their own acquaintances for suitable partners. Matches must be made within the same *jati*, usually in the same sub-*jati*, and hopefully (especially in the case of a daughter) with someone living nearby. (Almost all inter-*jati* marriages, which are generally viewed with extreme disapproval by members of both *jati*s, are non-arranged marriages.) The preferred marriage partners for Hindus are cross cousins or mother's brother/sister's daughter, either genealogical or classificatory, although the majority of marriages do not follow these patterns.

Husbands should be taller, older, and better educated than their wives in order to protect what is supposed to be the man's unquestioned dominance. Future in-laws also consider the man's job, earning potential, and character. Parents looking for a daughter-in-law take into consideration a woman's attractiveness (including her build, face, skin color, and hair),[13] cooking ability and other homemaking skills, character, and occasionally musical or artistic ability. Nowadays a few men, most of them well educated and middle class, want the material benefits of two incomes, and will ask their parents to look for a wife who can work outside the home. Women are firmly expected to be virgins at marriage, but men's previous sexual experience is not usually a concern. Both sets of parents also take into account the other family's background and social prestige, the amount of dowry requested/offered, and almost always the compatibility of the children's horoscopes. Women are generally between the ages of sixteen and twenty-five at marriage, men eighteen to thirty. And despite the fact that few children have direct say in their choice of spouses, many parents listen to their children's preferences, at least to the extent of giving them veto power over a prospective mate.

Some young adults go against their parents' wishes and enter into a "love marriage." Except in the most educated circles with broad exposure to other cultural practices, however, the social pressures against this are strong and effective. Children who select their own marriage partners, whether before or after their parents have selected a spouse for them, can expect to be ostracized by both families. This makes their lives difficult since their families no longer give them either financial assistance or access to the important connections necessary for finding a job, and since Tamils' closest social and emotional ties are usually with close relatives. Love marriages rarely involve dowry, adding to the husband's (and perhaps even the wife's) parents' disapproval. Such censure may be softened by the birth of a child to the couple.

The majority of arranged marriages include a "dowry" in cash and kind. In Indian popular usage this term includes two different kinds of marriage prestations made by the bride's family: one a gift of gold jewelry, cooking vessels, and other household items for the daughter, and the other a payment of cash, other gold items, and sometimes land, a car or motorcycle, and job offers for the new son-in-law, bestowed on the groom and/or his family. The latter type of "gift" – which is sometimes referred to by itself as the dowry – is illegal in India, but the practice has become increasingly widespread rather than less so, and is now found in almost all religious and caste communities (see e.g. L. Caplan 1984). The marriage settlements often rise proportionately with the husband's level of education and employment, and generally correlate with (and are interpreted as a sign of) the social status of both families.[14] Relatives usually ask for smaller dowries than do strangers; this, along with the fact that parents feel their daughters are likely to be treated better in a relative's house, partly explains the preference for contracting marriages with relatives. Even in arrangements where "a dowry" is explicitly not requested or given, the bride comes to the marriage with as much gold jewelry as her family can afford, kitchen utensils, clothing, and sometimes land. Dowries are often devastatingly expensive for the bride's family, and parents may openly bemoan the birth of a daughter.[15]

Most newlyweds have seen each other only once or twice before the wedding, if at all. The two partners often appear shy at first (although in some cases this is only adherence to cultural expectations), but it is expected that love and fondness will grow with the marriage, and this does occur in many cases. Nonetheless, any such affection is rarely given public expression, and even in private love is expressed indirectly if at all. Trawick notes that "spouses, who were supposed to love each other most and to focus their sexual feeling entirely upon each other, were expected to keep both feelings hidden" (1990: 94). Real relationships contain little of the overt romantic love seen in every movie and idealized in film songs and folk songs alike.

Wives should be obedient and submissive and respectful toward their husbands. No matter how great a scope they are allowed (or take) for expressing their opinions, they are expected ultimately to follow their husband's will. Women possess a great amount of inherent power (*cakti*) – greater than men – but if this power is not limited and directed by a father, husband or brother it will lead to harmful events (such as illicit sexual liaisons) destructive to the woman's kin group and even to the fruitfulness of the land they live on (Wadley 1980; Reynolds 1980).

But this is not the only way to explain or argue for patterns of gender relations. S. B. Daniel (1980) describes two other mutually exclusive but culturally provided explanations for husbands' and wives' behavior. In one, women's greater *cakti* makes them morally superior to men and therefore responsible for curbing male irresponsibility and making those decisions that affect the family's well-being (although modesty and regard for social sanction require that the wife appear submissive to her husband). In the other explanation neither husband nor wife is thought to be superior, a balance between their strengths and weaknesses being sought instead. Generally, popular ideology corresponds to the first model, in which a woman must be bound by her husband (for which she is seen to be grateful, because without his gift of marriage she is an inauspicious being). Non-public behavior often correlates more closely with the second or third.

Young people look forward to marriage in an idealized way, and openly fantasize about future spouses with friends and schoolmates. Despite their lack of control over choice of partner, they dream romantically of handsome and beautiful mates. This seems to be especially the case with young women, for whom the wedding – specifically, for Hindu women, the essential act within it of tying the thali[16] – is the central event of their lives. The thali tying both represents and accomplishes the binding of a woman's potent but unreliable *cakti* by her husband.[17] The thali is a powerful emblem for a woman. It symbolizes her status as a *cumankali*, a woman who is auspicious because she is married (even more so when she has children) – auspicious because she uses her *cakti* to protect her family and prolong her husband's life. A woman is thought to have this ability when she is chaste – that is, when she controls her thoughts and deeds, and in addition is controlled by her husband, thus ensuring her *cakti* will be channeled toward the good of the family – and is honored when her husband lives a long life. A widow, however, is often regarded as a woman who because of a lack of chastity has failed to support her husband's life, and she is the most inauspicious of all women.

Children are expected to follow soon after the marriage. Children are welcomed, especially by women. A woman who fails to bear children who live past their first few years is considered highly inauspicious. Male children are valued highly, and often, especially among the poor, the new mother of a female baby is likely to be consoled rather than congratulated. Women do most of the childcare. Men are also involved, however, and proud of their children, and it is not uncommon to see a man walking with a child in his arms. Children are generally indulged. Boys are praised for having a streak of devilry in them; girls are encouraged to be modest and polite, especially as they grow older. Both are given a greater scope of movement at a young age than are most children in the US; it is not unusual to see a four-year-old walking alone to buy the family coffee in the morning. Both boys and girls are expected to help with household chores, such as carrying water and cleaning the house, but these jobs become more segregated by gender as children grow older. By the time they are teenagers, girls usually know how to cook, clean, and do laundry, but few boys are adept at such tasks.

A girl's life begins a new stage at puberty. This is marked by an often elaborate coming of age ceremony designed to initiate the binding of her *cakti* so that her power can be channeled for the benefit of her family and others (see Reynolds 1980: 40–42). Between the onset of puberty and marriage, a girl's behavior must be closely watched by her family in order to guard her reputation, the honor of the family, and consequently the girl's chances for marriage. Generally, the higher her caste, the stricter the constraints she faces. In some families this means that she will not be allowed outside the household except for school or work or to carry out household tasks. In most poor families, however, teenage girls are allowed to visit nearby friends in their homes or go on occasional outings if chaperoned by men from their own or neighboring families. If they do not go to school or to an outside job, most girls spend their time helping in the house.

Teenage boys have fewer restrictions. Their behavior does not reflect as strongly on family honor, nor are their marriage chances hurt by a little wild behavior or even premarital sexual involvement. Boys between about fifteen and twenty are expected to be restless, and indeed it seemed that many of them were. Most have left school by this age, and are looking for a trade or job that may turn into relatively permanent employment. Often they work only part-time. After work they have few if any household responsibilities, and are free to spend time with friends, often socializing in groups on the street. They have neither the prestige and authority nor the responsibilities accorded to married men, and this position seemed to spark many young men to search for something that gave them a social place – be it a fan club, political work, or a noisy band of "rowdy" friends.

Madurai: fieldwork and the field
Most of my research was done among poor residents of Madurai. I also carried out interviews with directors, producers, and actors in Madras, the state capital and center of the Tamil- and Telugu-language film industries.

The bulk of the research took place between October 1985 and January 1987. This material was updated during a six-week visit in May and June of 1990. Throughout both stays I watched movies, listened to conversations about cinema, and spoke with movie industry members (generically called "artistes"). What could now be represented as a more or less intentional period of fieldwork, however, took shape as much through the broader experiences of my days in South India as through these focussed activities.

When I arrived in Madurai in 1985 with my husband Ted Adams, my first concern was to choose a neighborhood to live and work in. I concentrated on the city's center, near the Minakshi Temple, an area that offers lively activity, densely settled neighborhoods with a mix of ethnic, caste and income groups, and convenient access to other parts of the city. We found a third-story apartment on a well traveled lane in a lower class neighborhood. With two rooms and a kitchen, the apartment offered generous space in this crowded section of town.

Getting to know people in our new neighborhood took time. The two floors below us were empty, since the landlord's family had recently vacated the house and it was now the Hindu month of Margali, an inauspicious time to change residences. Though the streets and stoops

3. A street in downtown Madurai viewed from a bus window. 1992.

outside were full of people, many of whom watched us pass by and occasionally greeted us, it was difficult to find a comfortable way to break the mutual reserve.

One day a couple of weeks after moving in, I was up early and walking down the adjoining lane. Margali month is a time for making elaborate *kolam*s – geometric or pictorial figures drawn at the entrance of Hindu houses to welcome the goddess – and the street was decorated with intricate figures. I stopped to admire a large and particularly inventive *kolam*, and a teenager who had been combing her hair came to the doorway to ask what I thought of it. The next morning when I went past a number of people came out. I asked if I could return to take a photograph, and when I did, twenty people emerged from the doorway to have their picture taken around the *kolam*. They invited me in, and what I had thought to be one family's house turned out to be a compound of seven unrelated households, each occupying a single dark room with access to an open central courtyard. The family of the girl I had first spoken with soon became my closest contacts. They listened patiently to my uncertain Tamil, translated it among themselves, and phrased their responses in as many ways as necessary to make me understand.

I quickly came to know several families on the lane and elsewhere. Besides our neighbors, there were also our landlord's family, the people who rented furniture to us, old friends of my husband from his previous stays in Madurai, people who worked with and for the Americans I met when we first came to the city, and the vegetable sellers that my cook and I patronized. Each of these acquaintances led to new contacts. With this spreading network came an awareness of other parts of the city, and I was soon able to choose two additional neighborhoods for future visits and interviews.

Most of what I learned in Madurai came from observing and participating in life in these three neighborhoods, from conversations and interviews with their residents, and from watching many movies. As noted above, I first expected that cinema's popularity would make it an easy topic to discuss with people. I soon found, however, that the public stigma attached to cinema caused most people to deny any interest in it until we knew each other well. This meant that I could not use anything approximating a random sample of informants. Instead I got to know as wide a variety of people as possible and talked to them about movies. I interviewed them about movie-going, favorite actors and actresses, and political matters, and later I conducted a survey on similar topics; but much of my information came from talking about movies with people during the normal course of the day, as we worked together in the mornings or relaxed in the evenings.

When we first arrived in Madurai I intended to investigate the effects that frequent filmgoing and other cinema-related activities had on the urban poor. My thoughts were pointed toward behavior and values. Soon, however, the difficulty of disentangling the consequences of film-watching from those originating in other expressive media became very clear. Moreover, movies seemed to reinforce some traditional values and behaviors while at the same time encouraging others that were new and often contradictory; and the idea of tracing the path of cinema's influence separately from that of the multiple and interwoven messages learned from such other media as recitations of religious literature, stories told by grandmothers, and gossip shared on stoops in the evenings quickly appeared ill-conceived. For a time I questioned the entire project: did the mere popularity of a medium imply cultural or social influence?[18] Surely, I thought, audiences must have far more sway over the shape of films than films have over them.

This disillusionment fortunately did not last (although the questions that generated it still seem valid). As I continued to observe people going to the movies, talking about them, watching fan club dances and flocking to rallies for actors and actor–politicians, I soon regained confidence in my original question, albeit rephrased. Given the tremendous amount of physical, mental, and emotional energy devoted to films, what is it about Tamil cinema that makes it so appealing to its viewers?

This question guided my research. Three different research assistants helped me in different parts of the project. In the beginning, when my Tamil speech and comprehension were halting, I wanted an assistant to accompany me to interviews to fill whatever communication gaps the respondents and I could not overcome ourselves. It was important that this assistant be a woman, especially in the early stages, because it would have struck most people as unseemly for me, a young woman, to move about by myself with an unrelated male. It was difficult, however, to find a woman who was able and willing to do this work,[19] but finally I was fortunate enough to meet an unmarried social worker of my own age who had worked in low-income areas before and whose parents allowed her to accompany me (until, that is, she became engaged four months later). This woman had a rare gift: she was able to attend an interview and provide assistance when misunderstandings arose, but repress commenting on the many other mistakes she must have noticed, or asking questions of her own, until the interview was over. She also taught me, by example, how to impose politely on the time of busy people.

Another assistant, a young man, spoke no English but was a master of circumlocution in Tamil. He knew the city inside out and enabled me to meet many people I could not otherwise have found. He too was about my age, was from a lower caste and had studied through the eighth standard. He accompanied me to interviews with fan club members – when it was important I have a male companion – and worked in the same perceptive manner that my female assistant did. He also taped speeches at certain political meetings where my attendance would have been inappropriate, and carried out a questionnaire survey of over 550 households.

Another young man, an officer in a fan club, helped by scouting out numerous fan clubs of a certain star in order to ease my access to them. He also provided a wealth of information on his own club, and introduced me to the city leaders of his association.

In addition to conversations and interviews with neighborhood residents and fan club members in Madurai, I interviewed movie actors, directors, producers, censors, critics, and other industry personnel during several trips to Madras. There I was given crucial assistance by a film critic (a man who also publishes and edits a monthly journal), who accompanied me to all these interviews and made them possible through his contacts and estimable reputation in film circles. We were both aided by another man, a highly respected film historian and public relations agent for several stars, who also accompanied us on some interviews and made several of them possible.

Despite sojourns in Madras, Madurai remained the focus of my research. Madurai is an ancient city, said to be the oldest inhabited city in India. It is built around the Minakshi Temple, one of the most famous Hindu temples in the country. The plan of the ancient city is visible in the present downtown area, where four concentric roads ring the huge walled temple complex. The area within the outermost road covers about one and a half square miles. The old city's social geography can still be seen from some of the street names in this area, such as Flower Sellers Lane, Idol Caretakers Road, and Vestment Weavers Road.

Despite its size, Madurai has more of the feel of a town than a city. It is not highly industrialized, and, aside from the temple towers, the tallest structures at the time of my first research were no more than three to five stories high. The ancient part of the city now comprises most of the downtown area, its streets packed tightly with pedestrians, bicycle riders, and rickshaws, plus buses, a few motorbikes, and cars. The Vaigai River flows – when there is water – on the northern edge of the old city, bisecting the present metropolitan area. Madurai is a religious and trade center for the surrounding rural district. The nearest cities are about four hours by "express" bus; Madras is a ten- to twelve-hour bus or train trip.

Most neighborhoods in Madurai are not integrated by income level, although even the poorest neighborhoods tend to have one or two "big houses" with relatively wealthy residents. A few neighborhoods are also segregated by caste or religion, their residents usually Muslim, scheduled caste, or Anglo-Indian (the latter of mixed Indian and British ancestry). Some other neighborhoods are dominated by workers in a single trade (and thus often caste or ethnic group), such as weaving.

Of the three neighborhoods I worked in, one was downtown in the center of the city, where my husband and I resided during my first trip; the second was on the western outskirts of town; and the third was far northeast of the center and, although once on the outskirts, had recently been surrounded by a large and wealthy suburb. While all were lower class neighborhoods, each differed in the social makeup of its residents.

I lived in our downtown apartment for fourteen months. The lane running past it includes a school, many small shrines, and two small stores selling household needs, and at one end is crowded with milk cows and calves. Residents here had the highest overall income level of the three neighborhoods; nonetheless, most would qualify as lower class, a few who own small shops or work as office clerks reaching into the lower middle class. There is a large variety of *jati*s; most people belong to middle or upper middle castes, including Mutaliyar, Naidu, Saurashtrian, and Chettiar. There are only a few Muslims and Brahmans. The majority of residents work as laborers and include rickshaw drivers, construction workers, tailors, and small-machine repairmen. Others work as office "peons" and petty clerks, as priests, or as businesspeople owning small shops or a few milk cows. Total household incomes ranged between Rs. 400 and Rs. 1,000 per month (about $30 to $80 at 1986 international exchange rates, but much closer to $400 to $1,000 in buying power); per capita monthly income in most households was Rs. 50 to Rs. 110.[20] Housing is very dense, as in the rest of downtown. Most residents rent their one- or two-room homes, usually located in compounds with shared baths, and few have any sense of economic security. Two or three households in the neighborhood, however, were solidly middle class, with incomes up to Rs. 3,000 per month and possession of such enviable items as ceiling fans, television sets, and even refrigerators and bore wells.

I also spent a great deal of time with residents in the two other neighborhoods. These were poorer than our own neighborhood, and all residents were lower class. In one of these neighborhoods, Lakshmipuram, household income varied from Rs. 100 to Rs. 900 per month (ranging from Rs. 35 to Rs. 100 per person per month, with most households in the Rs. 50 to Rs. 80 range). Many of the residents are scheduled caste, either Paraiyar or Pallar; others belong to lower and lower middle *jati*s including Nadar, Thevar, and Konar. Lakshmipuram is on the western edge of town, and is much less densely populated than Madurai's city center. It is bordered by fields on two sides, and despite its substantial distance from such conveniences as vegetable markets and commodity stores, residents say they prefer it for its breeze and relative peacefulness. Most houses are individual one- or two-room units, built of brick and plaster or mud walls, and covered with either metal roofs or thatch. All toilet facilities are shared, usually among groups of four to eight households. There are fewer city water pumps per household here than downtown, and by the time the water arrives at about noon there is always a snaking line of hundreds of brass, stainless steel, and plastic water pots waiting by each pump.

The other area, Tholilpatti, is a slum referred to by residents and non-residents alike as the "Low Caste Colony." Almost all residents are of scheduled castes. The colony is divided down the middle by its main footroad, on one side of which are "pakka" houses of brick and plaster built by the government, while on the other are squatters' densely packed homes of mud and thatch. Almost all of my research was done on the "unofficial" side of the colony. Most of the squatters rent their homes from people who built the houses on land to which they had no legal rights. Because the houses cannot legally be there, most have no electricity. This area has the lowest availability of toilets and water supplies of all three areas.

Living and studying in these neighborhoods, I found that poor residents of Madurai share a sense of identity based on common insecurities, but this is far from the only way in which individuals identify themselves. All of the issues covered early in this chapter are relevant to the ways people see themselves, and are salient in their daily lives. Many aspects of these lives are represented in Tamil cinema, yet as we will see neither the representation nor the resolution of their difficulties is straightforward. Before discussing the particulars of the relationship between life and cinema, I turn to a description of the activities and attitudes connected with cinema in South India.

3

Activities and attitudes

Watching a movie in Madurai

Most adults I knew went to movies three or four times a month (in a survey I administered, 92 percent of respondents reported attending films, and of these 63 percent went at least three times per month). Generally, the occasion is conceived of as "seeing *a* movie" – that is, people are willing to see any movie that is worth seeing (and to most people, this means almost any film), and do not think of it as a chance to see a particular chosen film. When a family or group of friends has made plans to go to a movie, they may change their minds several times about just which film they intend to see, but the plan to go is rarely cancelled. There are exceptions to this, especially among people who see only a few films of a specific type – older people, for example, who restrict their viewing to religious films, or children whose parents accept only an occasional movie as suitable for children's viewing.

No matter how often a person goes to films, the decision to attend a certain one is usually made by listening to the reports of others who have seen it, or who know someone else who has. Decisions may also be made exclusively on the basis of subject matter (especially movies about deities), the actors or actresses, or songs. People almost never consult reviews in newspapers or magazines, relying instead on the opinions of acquaintances.

Viewers usually attend films with family members and other relatives, and also frequently with friends. Men occasionally go alone.[1] Young children are allowed to go to movies only with family or neighbors, but teenagers sometimes attend in same-sex groups, usually with one or two adults. Groups of male and female college students may see movies together. Recently married couples seem to go to movies often, but attend less frequently once their children are born, and husbands and wives tend to start seeing movies separately with their own friends as time goes on. (There is great variation in the latter pattern, but one of the most frequently mentioned grievances of husbands against their wives is the wives' attendance at cinema in the mornings, while women often complain that their husbands do not take them to the movies. Cases like these prompt claims that cinema divides families – see below.)

Most of the people I knew went to cinemas that they could reach on foot; occasionally they took a bus. Most theaters have three weekday shows: morning (starting 9 a.m. or 10 a.m.), afternoon matinee (1 p.m. or 2 p.m.) and evening (about 6 p.m.). Weekends add another evening show that begins at 10 p.m. or later, and on some holidays theaters will crowd in five shows.

Theaters vary greatly in the comfort of their accommodations, and ticket prices range accordingly. There is a hierarchy of tickets and seats within most theaters as well. The standard theater has four classes of seats, with ticket prices in 1987 ranging from about 85 paise to Rs. 1.10 for IV class to Rs. 3.50 to Rs. 4.25 or so for I class; by 1990, ticket prices in Madurai had doubled. Class IV seating begins directly in front of the screen. Seating is on backless wooden benches, which are packed with people when the theater is full. The only electric fans in this section stick out from the walls on either side of the very wide theater. Madurai is always very warm, and the open sides of the theater building are covered with heavy tarpaulins during the show, allowing for little breeze except what the fans provide. Further back, III class is substantially more comfortable since there are usually ceiling fans above all the benches. Classes III and IV both have one great advantage over the more luxurious padded seats above them: their wooden benches have no bedbugs. In standard Madurai theaters the I and II class seats, padded and covered with vinyl, are (in my experience) invariably host to what Tamils call red bugs (*civappu puuccikaḷ*). Class I is at the far back of the theater, in the balcony, and the II class seats are in front of them. Both have plenty of ceiling fans (and because of the balcony are much closer to them than are the seats below), and except that the more expensive seats are at the very back, the two classes are virtually identical. The different classes of seats in the theater are separated by dividers and have separate entrances.

Fancy cinemas, especially the AC (air-conditioned) theaters, have nicer seats and higher prices. During the 1986 hot season, tickets started at about Rs. 2 and went to Rs. 5; these too had doubled, or nearly so, by 1990. Prices are lower when temperatures do not demand air conditioning. (Even when it is used, however, there are frequent complaints about theaters that turn off the air conditioning shortly after the show begins. The only time I attended an AC theater in the hot season, the air conditioning continued working for some time, but stopped when the electric supply failed – which happens frequently in Madurai. Generators turned on the fans in the enclosed theater, but could not operate the air conditioning.) All of the seats in these theaters are padded. There are only a few such deluxe cinemas in Madurai, and they comprise most of the prestigious group of theaters which distributors compete to acquire for their new releases.

At the opposite end of price and luxury are the "temporary" cinemas in outlying areas, thatched roof structures that are really settled touring talkies. These theaters qualify for tax breaks, and offer seating at much lower prices. Often tickets will be only half a rupee each. There is only one class of tickets, though seating is still divided: women sit on the floor in front, and men stand or squat behind. Sometimes double features can be seen for a single ticket. These theaters usually have only evening shows, and since thatch is a good insulator, the building is fairly cool even without fans.

Seats at most theaters can be reserved by buying tickets ahead of time.

4. Men lining up before a ticket booth in front of a Madras film theater. 1991.

People will do this if they are afraid that the movie (or their favorite class of seats) will be sold out, or if they do not want to have to arrive early and stand in line for a ticket at showtime. Most people, however, do not reserve tickets, and try to arrive at least half an hour to an hour early to be assured of getting a seat. For a popular movie viewers may arrive hours early, and sit or squat in queues, chewing betel, eating snacks, talking with people nearby, waiting for the ticket booths to open. There are two booths for each class of ticket, one each for the men's and women's queues. The longest lines are always for III and IV class seats, and the ticket booths are fronted by long, narrow enclosures for the waiting lines. When the booths open about one-half hour prior to showtime, the neat, patient queues suddenly become a crush of people pushing past one another in the narrow aisle. Class I and II ticket booths do not have these covered waiting aisles, which means that daytime buyers usually stand in the sun, and occasionally some of them will faint.

Once the tickets are purchased, the group joins the crowd standing outside or in the lobby. Inside the lobby are stills of the current movie and coming attractions. The waiting area is usually quite congested. Ticket-takers at each entrance ensure that viewers sit in the right area. Sometimes most or all of a section will have been reserved by people who bought tickets early, and remains empty until shortly before the feature. This happens most frequently with II and III class seats, which are thought to give the best combination of comfort and price.

Audience makeup varies throughout the day. Weekday morning shows are filled almost entirely with women and their young children. Afternoon audiences are more mixed – still a substantial percentage of women, but also older men, some children, and teenagers. In the evenings there are a number of families, groups of college students (often young men and women together), and many groups of male friends. The women in the family groups are often dressed up, with nice saris, extra jewelry, and flowers in their hair. College students are fashionably dressed. Weekend and holiday audiences are more mixed, with a larger percentage of men and schoolchildren on leave from work or school.

Shows rarely begin when scheduled, and people talk (and walk about, if the theater is not crowded) until eventually the side tarpaulins are dropped and the lights dimmed. The feature is generally preceded by advertisements and a newsreel, although these may not be shown at morning or afternoon shows. The advertisements are like television commercials. Most people in the audience pay attention to the ads, which are bright and glossy and show happy upper-middle-class families. Most advertisements are for household and personal products: coffee and tea, laundry powders, facial soap, skin lightening cream. Five to twenty-five commercials may be shown. There is also the ten-minute newsreel, in color or black and white, which as often as not is ignored by viewers. Newsreels, approved and distributed by the Films Division of the Ministry of Information and Broadcasting (often made by a Films Division branch in Tamil Nadu), usually concern current events on either the national or state level. At the time of my first fieldwork, these included many shots of Rajiv Gandhi or MGR at important state or cultural functions. Sometimes documentaries portray the geography and lifestyles of other areas in India. Audiences in 1985–87 were most attentive to newsreels of MGR, especially when they depicted recent familiar events.

Finally the feature begins. First its censor certificate is flashed on the screen, and people watch carefully for this because it tells how many reels long the movie is. Each reel plays ten minutes, and most movies are fourteen to fifteen reels. (Older movies were usually eighteen to twenty reels long.) Often the credits are shown at the very beginning of the movie. The stars', director's and producer's names are given some time on the screen, and then the rest of the numerous credits fly by.

The audience participates throughout the movie. If fan clubs are present, they cheer and throw confetti when their star appears. The dialogue may be drowned out by the cheers, but this is not an annoyance to other viewers when the show is an old MGR or Shivaji movie, since most people have seen the movie before and many know the important bits by heart. Viewers may boo the villains and cheer the heroes, especially in older movies; young men may hoot or whistle at love scenes. Audiences may also applaud outstanding moments in films. In religious movies, some viewers sing quietly and tap their fingers during devotional songs. Bharati (1977: 263) reports that audience members prostrate themselves when a deity's image appears on screen, and informants told me that this sometimes still happens in rural areas, but I never witnessed it in Madurai. I was, however, told by one viewer that she could no longer go to *amman* (goddess) films because she would become possessed when she saw the goddess's image.

The film always includes a ten-minute intermission. People get up from their seats and walk around, and buy soft drinks and "ice" – soft chemical-flavored ice cream – from a stand inside the theater compound. Drinking water and restrooms are also available on the premises.

By the time the movie ends, the whole excursion, from ticket line to end of show, can easily have taken five or more hours. Afterward most people

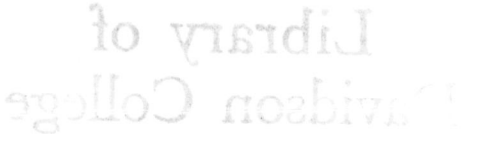

go directly home, without stopping to visit in the households of any of their movie companions. But once home, or at least the next day, other family members and neighbors will be eager to hear the movie story, and how the viewers rate it. Stories are told and retold in detail, and are often a favored topic with household visitors.

Cinema activities and attitudes
While studies of cinema generally focus on films – i.e. the texts, or perhaps the performers and directors – and occasionally consider audience responses as well, the scope of cinema is wider than this, and any consideration of its social or cultural significance should look outside these boundaries to the other activities, physical and mental and emotional, that inevitably are connected. Speaking of South India, Hardgrave has aptly referred to the "vast system of popular beliefs and behavior" surrounding film as a "folk culture of cinema" (1975: 2). There is indeed a vast system of popular literature, greeting cards and posters, clothing fashions, gossip and legends, memories, opinions (publicly acceptable or unacceptable), and activities supporting the stars. All of these features and others are part of the complex cinematic environment, but certain ones stand out as particularly significant both for the viewers

5. A vendor selling film star photos, buttons, greeting cards and other paraphernalia. 1991.

themselves and for our understanding of what cinema means to them. Fan clubs, political activities, and popular opinions about cinema are most noteworthy. I introduce them here as part of the background for the discussion of films in Part II, then examine them in detail in later chapters.

Fan clubs (*racikar manrams*) are active and popular organizations in Madurai. Most support male actors, and almost all club members are young men. These groups vary greatly in size, level of organization, and administration, and engage in a variety of activities as well, all intended to support the star in some fashion. Some groups are concerned only with attending and supporting films. In addition to a wide range of film-related activities, however, most groups are also active in other ways, staging celebrations, carrying out various social service activities, and sometimes – where the movie star has entered politics – engaging in political activities. The actor–politicians such clubs support have almost all been heroes of the lower class, the most notable example being the late MGR, whose fan organizations have remained active since his death in 1987. These heroes have been able to rely on cinema to help their campaign efforts not only through the fan clubs, whose members in these cases act as political cadres, but also through their ability to create a widely recognized, attractive image in a region where no other mass medium can accomplish this. Voters' tendency to prefer attractive "personalities" over service record or political platform has made cinema an especially powerful tool (see Dickey 1993).

The prevalence of cinema in many areas of urban life does not make it "popular" in all respects. Madurai residents see movies frequently; they are surrounded by visual artifacts of cinema; they fantasize about actors and acting and leading a performer's glamorous life. But they do not necessarily like cinema, nor think that it is a good thing. Cinema in Tamil Nadu has a place similar to soap operas in the US – a great many people watch them with real interest and enjoyment, yet few admit to doing so. (This is true of the generally scornful middle and upper classes as well, many of whom evince a fascination with cinema that varies from frequent discussions of the depravity of cinema, to attendance at private film screenings, to sponsorship of gala events for film stars [cf. Kakar 1981].) Fifty-eight percent of respondents to a survey carried out in poor Madurai neighborhoods said that they believed most people wanted to get into the cinema field, but 84 percent said that they themselves had no interest in doing so. I found early on that, despite the fact that most people I knew went to the movies at every opportunity, almost no one would admit to liking cinema if they were asked about it in any formal way, especially if people of authority (parents, husbands, mothers-in-law) were present.

Disdain for the dramatic arts is not uncommon in other areas of the world. It has been present, for example, in Britain and the US during parts of the nineteenth and twentieth centuries. The social censure of Tamil cinema derives partly from the stigma attached to the prostitutes and dramatists who were some of its early performers (see chapter 4), but also from other sources as well. Cinema has a reputation for corrupting the morals of the young by depicting illicit romantic liaisons and ridiculing religion; it is also thought to promote violence and crime. The mere existence of the movies – the seductive lure of the next glittering show – allegedly keeps children from attending school, men from going to work, and women from doing their housework and caring for their families.

Aside from the general feeling that cinema is not good or respectable, people also hold strong opinions about cinema's specific effects on individuals. It is thought to have both negative and positive effects within families (causing fights, for example, or inspiring greater cooperation), and within the community (usually by inciting crime). Most of all, fans and detractors of cinema alike point out the effect it has had on politics, embodied in the rise of MGR. People may applaud the role of films in showing MGR's true character to society, or they may disparage the intelligence of the poor and uneducated viewers who believed MGR would govern in real life as he acted in his films. In either case they recognize that cinema has been of direct importance in shaping this aspect of their lives and society.

Cinema not only has a strikingly visible place in the South Indian urban landscape, it also occupies a prominent space in the attention and emotions of urban residents. This includes those who love the medium and those who hate it; very few have no opinion at all, just as very few avoid its influence entirely.

PART II

4

History of Tamil cinema[1]

Tamil cinema has common roots with and borrows from other national and regional cinema traditions, and thus shares some characteristics with those traditions. It also, however, draws from an aesthetic history specific to India and its southern regions, and has developed formal and narrative conventions of its own.

Films have been shown in India since July 1896, when the Lumière brothers introduced their cinematographe six months after its original unveiling in Paris. Production of Indian films began shortly thereafter. Indian movies have retained some foreign influences since those first days, but have also developed a style and format that are unique. The indigenous characteristics of popular cinema that seem most notable to the western viewer include the obligatory inclusion of songs, dances, and fight scenes, the emphasis on melodrama, and the apparent focus on these elements at the expense of narrative and verisimilitude.

Many of the aesthetic conventions of Tamil and other Indian cinema appear to derive from the various folk and classical dramatic performances that preceded film. The search for motivations of present-day forms in those of previous ones can be risky and even arbitrary, however, and I concur with Thomas in cautioning against too heavy a reliance on "tradition" as explanation of contemporary form – in part because South Asian traditions are heterogeneous enough to account for almost anything, and in part because of the danger inherent in such explanations of romanticising the exotic and ignoring other influences (Thomas 1985: 130). Nonetheless attention to traditional roots does allow us to note the presence of longstanding indigenous aesthetic conventions that are distinct from those of the west, and prevents the all too frequent assumption that intelligent viewers will expect canons of the western type. A few examples of dramatic forms seem particularly noteworthy in this regard.

What might be called "classical" – elite, as opposed to "folk" – Indian drama was staged largely in temples or courts. Dance dramas were held at temple festivals (performed primarily by *devadasis*, female "servants of the god"). These were not organized commercially and reached only a small part of the population, since many individuals were prevented from attendance by caste or class restrictions (Baskaran 1981: 21).[2] Another type of performance, classical Sanskrit dramas, included dance, music, and song, and were performed in royal courts. The classical Sanskrit theater reached its height in the fourth and fifth centuries AD, but declined afterward and was later abolished by Muslim invaders. Plays continued to be written as a scholastic exercise, but were not performed for another 800 years (Barnouw and Krishnaswamy 1980: 70). Folk drama, however – such as the Bengali *jatra*, the Tamil *terukkuuttu* and the *kathakali* of Kerala – continued to flourish in village festivals. These dramas were always musical and often included dance.

Both classical and folk drama influenced the new Indian theater that appeared in the nineteenth century under the British. As Baskaran points out, the familiar modern drama – which he describes as theater with "divisions of acts and scenes, scenography of painted settings and a concealed orchestra" – has existed in South India for only about 100 years (1981: 21). The first of these plays were copies of European theater, but they soon re-incorporated the "ancient usage" of song and dance (Barnouw and Krishnaswamy 1980: 71). While modern Indian drama has developed contemporaneously with cinema, it nonetheless retained its own separate style and set of performers for many years, and had little influence on the early decades of film.

The emphatically musical nature of the older dramatic forms was to have little impact on films until the advent of sound, but other aspects of these forms appeared in cinema from the beginning. A reliance on histrionics and strong expression of emotions, for example, are typical of Indian dramas and have long been a part of popular Indian cinema. Some authors have suggested that other expressive forms also have influenced film. Sarkar, for instance, credits the Indian epic tradition with several influences, arguing that it has encouraged

the tendency to exaggerate reality, the extravagant speeches and sentiments, the mixture of conflicting emotions and the slow deliberately paced exposition of a major theme (with endless distractions from minor sources, each complete in itself), [and] the black and white characterisation.

She even attributes the great length of feature movies to the model of the epics, and contends that more recent literary traditions have supplied movies with "the markedly melodramatic strain, the exacerbation of sentiment and accumulation of coincidence" (1975: 14, 15).

Silent cinema

The first Indians to watch the Lumière brothers' moving pictures were the social elite of Bombay. Their response was enthusiastic enough to encourage the films' exhibitors to draw wider audiences with women's-only shows and graduated ticket prices. Lower prices created the "*Char-annawallah* class of movie audience,"[3] a segment of viewers who, according to Burra,

in the decades that followed shaped the growth of the film industry in India, determined the rise and fall of its stars, the shifting fortunes of the studios and to a large extent dictated (and dictates even today) the form and content of the commercial Indian film.

Nonetheless, most audience members in the early years were educated, upper class urban residents (Burra 1981: 10).

Moving pictures came to South India a year after they were introduced in Bombay, and regular showings began in 1900. The first Indian feature film was made in 1912 by the pioneer D. G. Phalke – coinciding with the beginning of feature filmmaking in the US – and the first South Indian-made features appeared a few years later (although documentaries and other shorts had already been produced for several years in the South) (Baskaran 1981: 70, 74–75).

Southerners had picked up training and equipment from early European exhibitors traveling through India and, occasionally, from trips to overseas production centers. Technical personnel were also imported from Bombay, where regular film production had begun earlier than in the South. Studios were enclosed spaces, usually roofless, and relied on natural light. Sometimes glass roofs were used for light diffusion, but more often light-colored perforated cloths were stretched overhead. Sets could be either natural or constructed, and film was processed by and in each production company's own laboratory.

Most silent movies were "mythological" stories. Earlier dramatic traditions had also drawn heavily from religious epics, but cinema could add its own special effects to these stories; Bahadur argues that

the miraculous and spectacular elements in the popular religious imagination of the Indian public [were] ready material for film stories; the medium could make this imagination visually palpable, sensuously perceivable! (1976: 91)

Serials and stunt films were also very popular, and were copied from the Hollywood movies exported to India (Bahadur 1976: 92, Baskaran 1981: 83). In the 1920s, the "historical" and the "social" (the latter referring to any story set in the present, possibly but not necessarily dealing with current social issues) made their first appearances.

One of the problems faced by early filmmakers was the difficulty of finding actresses. The stigma carried by dramatic performers (see Barnouw and Krishnaswamy 1980: 13) attached to cinema performers as well, and in particular to women. Baskaran (1981: 79) reports that women were also said to believe that exposure to the cinema lens would harm their health. (Moreover, the recruitment problem was compounded by theatrical performers' general reluctance to enter cinema since their stage talents relied heavily on singing and dancing to musical accompaniment, talents of little use in silent movies.) Different filmmakers overcame this problem in different ways: Phalke used a male actor to play the heroine in his first movie, and one southern director recruited a European actress, but many of the first women persuaded to act on screen were prostitutes. The shortage of actresses eased somewhat in the 1920s, when a number of Anglo-Indian women (of mixed British and Indian parentage) entered cinema (Baskaran 1981: 79; Barnouw and Krishnaswamy 1980: 169–70).

Several actresses became quite famous. So also did a few actors, who due to the popularity of stunt films were often chosen for their acrobatic ability. Overall, however, individual performers received little attention, and – in contrast to later years – filmmaking was largely controlled by the interests of directors (Baskaran 1981: 79).

The first movies to come to India had been foreign in more than one sense, and the early indigenous productions were well received by local audiences. As Barnouw and Krishnaswamy point out,

the slinky French heroine Protea, the Italian comedian Foolshead, and those American Keystone Kops were all amazing but might as well have come from Mars. In the Phalke films the figures of long-told stories took flesh and blood. The impact was overwhelming. When Rama appeared on the screen in *Lanka Dahan*, and when in *Krishna Janma* Lord Krishna himself at last appeared, men and women in the audience prostrated themselves before the screen. (1980: 15)

Yet while most Indians apparently preferred their own movies to those from overseas, western movies – especially those from the US – dominated the market. Baskaran (1981: 80) notes that even after the mid-1920s, when Madras had begun steady film production, most of the films shown in the Madras Presidency were North American. India-wide, foreign films (mainly American) comprised 85 percent of the films shown in 1926 (Barnouw and Krishnaswamy 1980: 298n).

US domination of the international film market had begun during the First World War, when most European industries were greatly curtailed by a scarcity of raw materials and other restrictions. Hollywood, by now firmly established as a production center, did not feel the same pinch, and set out to fill the new void in the market. By the time the war ended the Americans had gained an unbreakable hold on worldwide film distribution, mostly through their system of block-booking theaters. Block-booking required an exhibitor to take a production company's entire output, not just its most desirable films. This distribution system left little room anywhere for British, French, or Indian films. Even those Indian theater owners who preferred not to show any western films had a difficult time because American filmmakers, for whom overseas markets were pure profit, could offer movies for much lower prices than could Indian producers, who still had to recoup their production costs (Barnouw and Krishnaswamy 1980: 39–41).

Nonetheless, exhibitors were better off than producers. The number of permanent theaters – mostly tin-roofed structures with different classes of seating – rose from fourteen to forty-three between 1921 and 1927 in Madras city (Baskaran 1981: 81).[4] The Presidency also had twenty-three "touring" cinemas, which traveled to festivals and to rural areas without permanent cinemas. The exhibitors rented halls, set up viewing tents or constructed temporary thatched shelters for projection.[5] Since most audience members were illiterate, theaters employed narrators to read the title cards (which might be printed in two or three languages). Some narrators also added their own commentary and story embellishments; a few were popular enough to become actors themselves when sound came to cinema (ibid.).

The talkies

The arrival of sound in the early 1930s changed Indian films and the film industry dramatically. Previously, any movie could be shown throughout India with at most an addition of title cards in the regional language. Sound, however, made wide distribution much more difficult. It greatly increased the importance of "regional" cinema (the label given to films in any language besides Hindi or English) – in fact, it effectively converted all cinema in indigenous languages into regional productions[6] – and made the financial position of the Tamil production companies much more secure.[7] (Competition from the US and Bombay had forced all Madras production to cease by 1932 [Baskaran 1981: 99].) The first talkies reached Madras in 1931, the same year in which the first Indian sound feature, *Alam Ara* (Hindi), as well as the first Tamil sound shorts and feature, were produced in Bombay. By 1934 production of Tamil talkies had begun in Madras itself.

The switch to sound changed cinema in other ways as well. Sound allowed continuities with folk, classical, and modern drama traditions to be felt fully, and song and dance became a central part of all films.[8] Suddenly singing actors, songwriters, musicians and dancers were in demand, prompting a mass exodus of personnel from the theater.[9] Many of these stage artists had been involved with nationalist politics, and quickly injected their political concerns and social reformism into the new cinema. During the 1930s, a few Brahman women and others of "respectable families" had begun to star in screen roles (Baskaran 1981: 170). This, plus film's growing association with politics, resulted in an increased aura of respectability that persuaded several of the most famous classical singers of the day – including K. B. Sundarambal and M. S. Subbulakshmi – to act. For a time, in fact, heroes' and heroines' singing ability played a greater role in their success than did acting.

The importance of the singer-actor declined when, in the first step toward creating what could be termed "particulate" actors – the separate pieces of whose total performance are contributed by different individuals (see also chapter 7) – filmmakers began employing "playback singers" in the 1940s to dub over actors' singing parts.[10] The purpose of the substitution was, according to Sarkar (1975: 104), "to match an excellent voice with the most attractive possible image, which real life rarely provides." Unlike the western practice, in which, as Barnouw and Krishnaswamy put it, the playback singer's "very existence is kept secret, with the assumption that audiences must be persuaded that the star does the singing," Indian cinema "scorns this deception" (1980: 277).[11] Where songs are one of the most important elements of the film, the most successful playback singers and music directors have become as popular as – and generally more long-lived than – the favorite actors and actresses.

Nonetheless, throughout India, heroes and heroines have become very significant factors in a movie's success. Cult-like followings of actresses and actors began in the 1930s, when famous singers entered the cinema. After Independence, screen stars began appearing frequently on platforms with politicians. As the overall popularity of individual stars grew, so did their importance to a film's success, and their salaries. Since the 1950s, which saw the rise of superstars like Shivaji Ganesan and MGR –

History of Tamil cinema 53

and their increasing participation in politics – it has often been the star and not the director who has had greatest control in making a film. The stars' position has been further strengthened by growing networks of fan clubs, which first appeared in the mid-1950s. Fan club members engage in numerous activities in support of their idols, occasionally including political work.

Connections with politics have existed since the early years of Tamil cinema, but the type and extent of those connections have varied according to the political climate and trends in movie stories. While mythologicals continued to be popular during the early years of sound, the social film was quick to overcome them. This had much to do with the growing Indian nationalism of the 1930s and '40s, when even stunt films contained the "obligatory" nationalistic song (Baskaran 1981: 111, caption). Stage dramas had included direct and allegorical protests against British rule since the turn of the century, and stage presentations had been an important element of the Non-cooperation movement. The last years of silent movies had seen the occasional introduction of Gandhian social reform themes, including the prohibition of alcohol and the uplift of women and Harijans.

British censorship of all performed and written material tightened as nationalism gained popular support. Government officials began to invoke the Dramatic Performances Act of 1876 in southern India in 1919. This legislation, which had originally been drafted to control Bengali political theater, enabled officials to register and censor drama companies and their plays. Government control over performances increased as dramatists became involved in the Gandhian Non-cooperation movement through the 1920s. The Cinematograph Act of 1918, which created censor boards to review all films, was applied with increased rigor when cinema artists entered the Civil Disobedience movement of the 1930s and early '40s. Script- and songwriters became adept at indirect reference to Indian nationalism and British tyranny in their attempts to pass the censor boards. Songs became particularly important during this period, since they could be passed on by word of mouth and were much more difficult to censor than written materials (Baskaran 1981: 52). Censorship loosened when the Indian Congress government was formed in the Madras Presidency in the 1937 states' reorganization, and for over two years nationalist propaganda was allowed in movies and other mass media. The British immediately reintroduced strict censorship during the Second World War, however, when the Congress ministry resigned in protest against India's war involvement. The newly instructed censor boards strongly favored "war-effort" films. Indian nationalist propaganda more or less disappeared from Tamil movies, although social reform themes continued.

Cinema's close alignment with nationalist politics brought about its first ties with South Indian intellectuals, who previously had viewed cinema as "a cheap and contemptible popular art" (Baskaran 1981: 120; cf. Sivathamby 1981: 20). But Independence in 1947 put an end to Tamil film's brief association with the intelligentsia (Baskaran 1981: 124). Coincidentally the postwar period witnessed a number of changes in Tamil cinema, primary among them the swing toward spectacular and, according to Baskaran (1981: 150), "escapist" cinema. The initiator and foremost example of this new style was S. S. Vasan's dazzling *Chandralekha* (1948), an extravagant contrast to war-effort movies and the most expensive Indian film yet produced (Barnouw and Krishnaswamy 1980: 173). One distinguished film editor and former censor stated that *Chandralekha* was the first film to combine all the elements now seen as essential to box office hits – comedy, fights, songs, and dances (R. K. Ramachandran, interview, September 1986). It was certainly the most successful movie to date (Ramachandran and Rukmini 1985: 638). Vasan, who had recently established the important Gemini Studio in Madras, also produced his hit in Hindi for distribution in the north, where it was a similar success. This marked the postwar entry of Madras filmmakers into the northern market (Barnouw and Krishnaswamy 1980: 173–74).[12]

Another feature of postwar cinema in the South was an emphasis on Tamil linguistic pride, and the pro-Tamil, anti-Brahman, anti-North political sentiments that accompanied it. As before, movies became involved with politics because influential artistes were politically active. The first of these were leaders of the DMK (Dravida Munnetra Kazhagam) party, who in 1949 had broken off from the DK (Dravida Kazhagam) to establish an electoral party. C. N. Annadurai, the party's founder and chair, was a dramatist, occasional stage actor, and screenwriter. So also was Mu. Karunanidhi, another party leader. Such leaders found film an excellent vehicle for disseminating social commentary. In 1949, for example, Karunanidhi attacked social injustices and religious hypocrisy in his script for the film *Parasakthi*. An important new feature of these DMK and other films was "dialogue" – extended critical speeches delivered in formal alliterative Tamil. The new social movies and their dramatic rhetoric proved very popular; indeed, a number of people can still recite favorite dialogues memorized during a DMK movie's first run.

The importance of screenwriters had greatly increased with the rise of

Karunanidhi and Annadurai, but the actor too would soon gain in importance. Annadurai asked the young M. G. Ramachandran to star in one of his movies in the early 1950s. Ramachandran was a great success, and soon became a member of the DMK party. He and other movie stars were utilized to "decorate" party functions and draw crowds. MGR began to use the DMK colors of red and black in his movies (after the switch to color in the late 1950s) and made frequent allusions to party policy and rhetoric, much of it anti-Congress. Injections of political spice became very popular in the 1950s and '60s, and it was said that no movie could succeed without some references to the DMK. MGR, the main star allied with the DMK, gained a large and devoted following and soon controlled many aspects of his movies, using them to promote an image of himself as the savior of the poor. Shivaji, who had starred in *Parasakthi*, had left the DMK for Congress by this time, and although he retained some interest in and association with politics, for the most part he was not as thoroughly political as MGR became. When I left Tamil Nadu in 1987, he and MGR were still the top two stars, as they had been for thirty-five years – despite the fact that MGR had not made a movie in a decade.[13]

Another actor who appeared at rallies, but was not otherwise connected with the DMK, was the extremely popular N. S. Krishnan, a "brilliant comedian and satirist ... often compared with Chaplin" (Barnouw and Krishnaswamy 1980: 180–81). Krishnan and his wife T. A. Madhuram first appeared as a comedy team in 1936, and continued as favorites for twenty years. Krishnan performed his skits at DMK gatherings, often satirizing religious orthodoxy and poking fun at Brahmans.

As the popularity of the DMK's dialogue-laden socials increased, mythologicals were made less often, and the spectacles copied after *Chandralekha* disappeared by the mid-50s, apparently because dwindling profits could not justify expenses. In the 1960s, Bond-style thrillers featuring smugglers and spies appeared. (Even in these movies, such as *Rakaciya Pooliis* ["Secret Police"], secret agent MGR dressed in red and black.) Romantic melodramas – which by now had appropriated the "socials" label – grew in popularity. So too did the more sedate "family films," but in the 1970s and '80s even these required increasing amounts of violence and sex – though it is worth noting that neither was generally as explicit as in much of western cinema. There were numerous shots of lovers rolling in the grass and chasing around trees, yet kissing was banned by censors until 1986.

Politics largely disappeared from films after the 1960s, until a recent (and limited) reappearance in new forms.[14] Political allegories and propaganda have been replaced by attempts to appropriate MGR's charisma, either by paying direct homage or by copying plots and titles from his films. Since MGR's death there has been a rush among actors and directors to associate themselves with the former leader, even among those who previously supported other parties, in an attempt to gain popular support among audiences who remember MGR nostalgically. Another new type of "political" film specializes in stories of revenge against corrupt politicians (an image that reflects many viewers' opinions), a trend that began with *Puu Onru Puyalaanatu* ("A Blossom Became a Gale") in 1987.[15]

Today's Tamil films display some continuities with other entertainment and dramatic forms. The importance of music and dance are striking examples, as the next chapter discusses further. There are also continuities throughout the development of Tamil film itself, including the important presence of political ties, albeit in changing forms, and the continuing stigma attached to performers, at least to actresses. Other features have been less constant; mythologicals, which have been replaced by romances, now comprise only about 5 percent of Indian films annually (Dharap 1983: 83) (a figure that from my observation seems accurate for Tamil film), and graphic depictions of violence have increased. The following chapter turns from history to discuss the elements of contemporary films.

5
Films

The relationship between Tamil cinema's consumers and producers, and the impact of this relationship on cinematic content, is much as it is in popular entertainment everywhere. Producers of commercial entertainment generally find it necessary to respond to a modicum of the entertainment desires, both conscious and unconscious, of their paying audience. Speaking of North Indian movies, Kakar has portrayed popular cinema as "a collective fantasy containing unconscious material and the hidden wishes of a vast number of people" (1981: 12). While the makers of popular cinema may have different "unconscious" desires and needs than their audiences, he argues, they are nonetheless motivated to discover prospective viewers' own needs by the goal of financial success:

> The prospect of financial gain, like the opportunity for sexual liaison, does wonderful things for increasing the perception of the needs and desires of those who hold the key to these gratifications. The quest for the comforting sound of busy cash-registers at the box-office ensures that the film-makers develop a daydream which is not idiosyncratic. They must intuitively appeal to those concerns of the audience which are shared; if they do not, the film's appeal is bound to be disastrously limited. (Kakar 1981: 12–13)

The dependence of filmmakers on healthy financial returns ensures that they will try to fill their movies with the elements that viewers consciously and unconsciously seek from entertainment. However, the creation of a successful movie does not require satisfying *all* of a viewer's desires; rather, film creators must simply ensure on the one hand that the movie's content does not clash with any of these desires too strongly, and on the other that a sufficient number of them are met with adequate force. As Dyer points out, while entertainment "responds to real needs *created by society*," it simultaneously defines and delimits "what constitutes the legitimate needs of people in this society" (1985: 228; emphasis in original). As we will see, viewers' felt needs or concerns are not uniformly represented or expressed in popular movies. Producers and directors avoid some themes that might be of significant interest to audiences, while also imposing themes that are peripheral to viewers' interests. The relationship between this selective avoidance and imposition of material and the differences in viewers' and producers' class-based interests will be investigated further below.

The elements of a movie
It is said that all Indian movies must follow a certain formula for success: a star (or two), six songs, three dances. Noticeably missing from this formula is the story, which critics label merely an excuse to link the other elements. Nonetheless, the story, usually a romance, influences the popularity of a film. Other elements that may contribute to its success are fights and comedy. Often, each of these elements is written and/or directed separately, and they need never be entirely integrated within the movie. The audience – who expect a variety show – appreciate each segment for its individual merits, and the popularity of any single segment may be enough to ensure the success of the entire movie.

Songs, dances, fights, and laughs
Film music has a much more significant role in Tamil movies and daily life than we see in the west. The only comparable use of music in Hollywood movies occurs in musicals. No such separate genre is found in India; *all* commercial movies are musicals. Moreover, virtually all pop music in South India is movie music. Movie songs are sung and played constantly, over radios, on horn speakers in the streets, at weddings, and at temple festivals. Their popularity is such that they can turn an otherwise bad film into a success. Songs have been an essential element in film promotion since the early 1950s (Barnouw and Krishnaswamy 1980: 157), and are generally released several weeks ahead of a movie in the hope that at least one will have become a hit by the time the film opens. The songwriter, called a music director, is often more famous than movie's writer, director, or stars.

Nonetheless, film music is not highly regarded in sophisticated circles. It is a combination of Indian and western traditions – sounding foreign to purist fans of both – and is scorned as a "'hybrid' abomination" by its critics (Beeman 1981: 83). All India Radio (AIR) ceased airing movie songs in the early 1950s. They lost most of their listeners to Radio Ceylon, which had immediately taken over Indian film music broadcasts, and AIR's directors soon felt compelled to reinstate film music and did so in 1957 (Beeman 1981: 83; Chandavarkar 1985: 249).

Movie dancing is likewise disdained. Most of it is a variety of what Tamils call "disco" dancing (which draws from the western version but remains quite distinct; recently, adaptations of breakdancing have also appeared), and provides actors and actresses with an occasion to dress and approach one another in ways that would be highly immodest and inappropriate in the rest of the movie's settings. Occasionally the film dances are of a classical style, usually in the South Indian *bharatanatyam* tradition, and actresses and actors who are trained in traditional dance often find a way to incorporate it into their films. Dance is generally either "modern" or "classical," and not the combination of styles that typifies movie songs.

The songs and dances in Tamil movies, as in some western musicals, rarely fit into the straightforward flow of the movie story. Outsiders find them to be one of the most striking features of Indian cinema. As the story progresses, the hero and heroine suddenly find themselves singing and dancing in a scene whose location and meaning may appear to have nothing to do with the story. In fact, sometimes the song and dance sequences are merely a "vitamin injection" (Segal 1985: 256) and irrelevant to plot advancement (Sarkar 1975: 107).[1] More often, however, they contribute to the overall story by dramatizing feelings that cannot be stated directly – either tender or (as in the recent surge of "double-meaning" songs) not-so-tender sentiments – and in this way can provide "conventionalized substitutes for love-making and emotional crisis" (Barnouw and Krishnaswamy 1980: 155). This circumvents not only censor restrictions but also cultural proscriptions against the direct expression and display of passionate feelings. Often the scenes are shown as fantasies or dreams of the hero or heroine. Occasionally songs or dances will even act as essential elements of the narrative itself, as in *Sindhu Bairavi* ("Sindhu and Bairavi," 1985), a story of two Carnatic singers (see below), and *Calankai Oli* ("The Sound of Anklets," 1983), a film originally made in Telugu about a classical dancer who teaches his former lover's daughter to dance.

Fight scenes are also regarded as a separate ingredient of movies. Just as some actors are known for their dancing (such as Kamalhasan), other actors (never actresses) base their reputations on their fighting proficiency (including MGR and Rajnikanth).[2] Fights resemble those in Hollywood Westerns, but involve a wider array of instruments: sticks, poles, and swords, in addition to fists. Kung fu has also been popular. The fights are as well and as obviously choreographed as the dances, but the obviousness of the gestures is not at issue; as with acting, fans appreciate the expressiveness and the acrobatic ability of it all.

Comedy is often a separable piece of a movie. Most films include slapstick comedy scenes performed by comedy teams – actors and actresses other than the hero and heroine – which are only loosely connected to the main story. The team will appear for comic relief at various times during the film. The most famous of Tamil comedians was N. S. Krishnan, who for years was said to have been necessary to the success of a movie (Barnouw and Krishnaswamy 1980: 181). Today a few films incorporate humor into the main body of the film, making it a part of the regular performers' conversations and actions.

The story
Over the years several broad types of Tamil movies have appeared. These include socials, historicals, and mythologicals. Other categories can be cited – romance, suspense, and comedy, to name a few – but the basic Tamil "masala"[3] movie is such a combination of elements that it is largely impossible to categorize movies except in the widest sense. *All* stories involve romance, social conflict, suspense, and humor. The division that most Tamil filmgoers make is between religious movies (*caami paṭankaḷ*), family movies (*kuṭumpa paṭankaḷ*), and others (movies not considered wholesome enough to attend as a family). Even though religious movies also involve romantic elements, suspense (including a fight or two), and songs (usually devotional), it is thought to be more respectable to attend *caami* movies than other kinds, and many people claim to like only these films (a statement that does not usually correspond to actual filmgoing habits and, if it did, would make the present industry's survival perplexing since so few films fit this category). It could be noted here that, conversely, social movies also involve religious elements, ranging from the invocation shot of a deity's image that opens almost all films, to occasional scenes of religious practices (such as women performing domestic rituals), to the "mythological models" that underlie heroic and villainous characters (see Derné n.d.).[4] These religious aspects of social films are apparently too sparse, however, to bolster the films' respectability.

Tamil movie stories involve numerous subplots, and a greater amount of melodrama and unlikely coincidence than western audiences are accustomed to. The movies' length is due not only to the inclusion of song, dance, fight, and comedy sequences, but also to the numerous storylines.

Stories often introduce issues that are of concern to viewers, such as changing family relations, economic difficulties, and class relations, but instead of being addressed realistically they are resolved through acts of villainy or coincidence, thus giving the impression that all such troubles have happy endings.

Critics complain that the story in Tamil films is only a thread serving to link more profane elements, but viewers disagree. When I asked people to tell me about a movie (see chapter 8), they almost always focussed on the story and had little to say about songs or fights. In daily conversations people recount movie stories enthusiastically, and in great detail, to one another. Viewers will also remark that an occasional movie has "no story," indicating that they do think most films have a substantial story. Moreover, viewers' assessment that a film lacks a story is not necessarily a criticism, as it is in the case of critics. When I was in Madurai in 1990, the film *Karakaattakkaaran* celebrated its 365th day, a phenomenal success, and this was a film that numerous people told me "has no story, but the village songs and dances are wonderful."

Heroes and heroines

Actors and actresses generally have more audience draw than the director, screenwriter or any other personnel. Tamil actors and actresses are idolized, and filmgoers fantasize about living the stars' glamorous lives. At the same time, however, performers – especially actresses – are seen as "bad" or "loose" (*moocamaana*) people.[5]

The esteem in which actors and actresses are held is reflected in viewers' typical reference to them as "heroes" and "heroines." But, as one director pointed out, "anywhere in the world it is hero worship, not heroine worship" (K. Balaje, interview, September 1986). In Tamil Nadu the lack of regard for actresses derives from the great number of actresses available, the relative shortness of their careers, and the "aura of disgrace" that attaches to female performers in particular (Hardgrave 1975: 3). Careers are short because almost all actresses quit as soon as they marry (just as most other young women who hold jobs do). The stigma derives from associations with prostitution early in the history of cinema, and even before that from the rather low reputations of all dramatic performers, who tended to be members of itinerant low castes.

Male actors have largely lost this reputation. Its continued association with actresses appears to stem from two or three possible sources. One is the common belief that women who act must be in close physical contact with men (as during romantic song sequences), and therefore "go bad"

6. Rajnikanth featured in a shop signboard. Movie stars' images are often painted in signboards to help promote products; here, the actor wears eyeglasses outside an opticals shop. 1986.

keṭṭu pookum). A few viewers believe that aspiring actresses have to "do favors" for directors in order to gain movie roles – similar to popular belief in the US. The basis for the stigma attached to actresses, however, seems to be related primarily to the sentiment that no "good woman" would display herself in public. A girl of fourteen told me that she had written to several of her favorite actresses, some of whom had sent her back signed photographs, and talked enthusiastically about how much she liked them, especially Ambika and Revathi (both popular actresses in the mid-1980s). I asked her what they were like. "Good people (*nallavarkaḷ*)," she said. Then her cousin, a girl of the same age, said that they were really bad people (*moocamaanavarkaḷ*), and to my surprise the first girl agreed. When I asked, "But aren't those actresses good people?" she answered, "Only in their acting (*appaṭi cumaaka naṭippaarkaḷ*) [that is, they *portray* good people]." "Even Ambika? Even Revathi?" "Yes," she said, "They're *all* bad (*ellaarum moocam*)." This is obvious, she explained, from the fact that they act: nice women would not show themselves to the public, so these women must have been bad before they became actresses.

Despite the public disdain for the performers' occupation, there are many young people eager to take a place on the screen. Stories are still told of children running off to Madras to enter the movies (and I knew a couple of adults who had done so years ago – one to become a dancer and the other a makeup artist). Partly because they are so easily replaced, but primarily because audiences are seen as having fickle tastes, film artists will take on as many screen roles as possible in order to earn money and stay in the spotlight while they can. Hardgrave quotes one star as saying, "You must be prepared to hold the industry tight before it loses hold of you. You never know how long you will be popular. The audience can drop you as soon as they take you up" (1975: 2).

The problem of maintaining popularity also encourages many artists to promote public images that will appeal to audiences. MGR was by far the best example of this, choosing his screen roles with great care to contribute to his image as member and defender of the people and making large and widely publicized charitable contributions to popular causes. Shivaji Ganesan also makes publicized donations to charities, and in recent years has preferred roles of upright family men. Younger actors have chosen different routes. Kamalhasan is said to have once used the press to advertise his virility (Rao 1986: 10); more recently he has advertised the work of his fan clubs ("social welfare organizations") in establishing blood banks and eye banks. Most actors and actresses court their fan clubs, and see them as an important source of support. None of the top young stars is involved in politics as of this writing, but some with slipping careers have attached themselves to popular political issues – such as the problems of Sri Lankan Tamils – in order to bring their names back into the headlines.

The style of acting in Tamil movies tends to be more intensely histrionic than is appreciated in North American and European cinema. Gestures, makeup, facial expression, and dialogue delivery would all be considered overdone by most western filmgoers. Shivaji Ganesan, widely praised for his fine acting, once explained the reasons for using this style:

I am conscious of the fact that I overdo my parts sometimes. I do it rather deliberately ... While discerning connoisseurs and critics consider my performances loud, the large majority of fans in the districts think otherwise. Films are afterall made for the masses and I have therefore to shape my performance accordingly to their requirements. That doesn't mean I play to the gallery but I certainly take into due consideration the likes and dislikes of the patrons of the cinema.

While I wish to interpret my roles in a natural manner, I do attempt to make a compromise, so that my portrayal may create a far-reaching impact on a large section of moviegoers with little or less educational background. I myself belong to this cadre ... I have to perform as they expect me to do. After all, the taste of the public has not fully developed. (Hardgrave 1975: 7)

Later, in an interview done in 1986, Shivaji defended himself against criticisms of over-acting, revealing more of the thespian philosophy behind Tamil acting:

The moment one puts on make-up and stands before the camera, one begins acting. What is acting? It means doing something that is not natural. Something that is not normal. So then, where is the question of over-acting?

When your mother dies, what will you do? You will shout *amma* ['mother'], and cry, won't you? Anyone who loves his mother, that is. You will not sit quietly covering your eyes. Your instant reaction is to cry out loud. That is exactly the way I do it in my films. (Sunil 1986: 62–63)

Melodrama and popular entertainment

The form and content of Tamil cinema are highly melodramatic. Melodrama, a term that originally referred to a dramatic presentation interspersed with songs and music (a definition that still fits Tamil film), today is generally regarded as any expressive form characterized by the sensational portrayal of and appeal to heightened emotions. Elsaesser argues that the social functions of melodrama have varied historically according to sociopolitical conditions, with the genre's importance peaking during "periods of intense social and ideological crisis" (1985: 167). Thus, for example, French melodrama prior to the Revolution had "pointed to the arbitary way feudal institutions could ruin the individual unprotected by civil rights and liberties," but dramas of the Restoration "functioned more as a means of consolidating as an yet weak and incohert ideological position." While earlier melodramas were often tragic, those of the Restoration ended happily, reconciling "the suffering individual to his social position, by affirming an 'open society', where everything was possible" (Elsaessser 1985: 169).

The happy endings of these Restoration melodramas bear a significant resemblance to Tamil films, whose fortuitous resolutions may indicate an avoidance of the true conditions of most viewers' lives. Tamil cinema as a whole fits the category of "reactionary" cinema proposed by Wood (1985) in his critique of western horror movies. Wood differentiates between progressive films – those whose tragic endings deny any possible escape from the confining situation constructed in the movie – and reactionary ones, which are characterized by happy endings and, like the Restoration melodrama, offer hope to viewers. I would concur with Wood to the extent that his perspective suggests that the happy endings of most Tamil films allay the anxieties of viewers by implying that the problems and contradictions of their lives can be resolved without effort. Viewers' reactions to such resolution will be discussed below; for the moment I shall simply state that any overt or covert message along this line would be likely to suit the interests of middle and upper class filmmakers, who have a stake in viewers' acceptance of a comforting message that assists in the maintenance of the present social order. Thus, as Dyer suggests, the selective response of filmmakers to the entertainment needs and desires of their viewers helps to define the category of legitimate viewer needs as dictated and accepted by the dominant class.[6]

This is not to suggest that melodrama must always manifestly support the status quo. The melodrama is a highly popular genre throughout Asia (see Marchetti n.d.), and has been used to pose potentially revolutionary challenges to the dominant social order and the state. It can provide a forum for drawing suppressed desires and fears into the public arena (Gledhill 1987: 33). Yet even while criticizing social evils – such as, in the Indian case, political corruption, caste discrimination or bride burning – or portraying crises that resemble the everyday difficulties faced in viewers' own lives, the social or collective implications of these issues may be avoided. As Gledhill argues, melodrama "touches the socio-political only at that point where it triggers the psychic, and the absence of causal relations between them allows for a short-circuiting between melodramatic desire and the socially constructed world" (1987: 37). Melodrama makes public the anxieties repressed by individuals; but in then dramatizing current social problems in very personal terms, privatizing them in the unique circumstances of a particular family or other group (and, occasionally, a particular historical setting), it can avoid drawing wider social implications. Moreover, filmmakers – who provide both positive and purely individual solutions to crises – may reinforce the current social order by selecting themes that support or encourage resignation to it even as they appear to criticize it.

Both the criticism and the validation may be picked up by audiences. As Elsaesser points out, there is "a radical ambiguity attached to the melodrama ... Depending on whether the emphasis fell on the odyssey of suffering or the happy ending ... melodrama would appear to function either subversively or as escapism" (1985: 169). Whether a film encourages subversion or submission is dependent largely on whether and how the crises it portrays are resolved. The mechanisms of resolution seem to be typical of melodrama as a genre across contexts. Compare, for example, the mechanisms described for melodramas of the French Restoration and in contemporary Hindi cinema, which in both cases are strikingly similar to those of Tamil cinema. In the first case, Elsaesser reports,

complex social processes were simplified either by blaming the evil disposition of individuals or by manipulating the plots and engineering coincidences and other *dei ex machina*, such as the instant conversion of the villain, moved by the plight of his victim, or suddenly struck by Divine Grace on the steps of Nôtre-Dame. (1985: 169)

And by the conclusion of Hindi films, Kakar reports, "parents are generally happy and proud, the princess is won, and either the villains are ruefully contrite or their battered bodies satisfactorily litter the landscape" (1989: 29).

Such melodramatic conflict resolution, and the happy endings that typically result, can be problematic. Because melodrama is based to some extent on reality, which is more frequently filled with protracted crises than with divine bolts of lightning, the sanguine endings of most Tamil movies are achieved at the cost of repression – repression of real-life experiences, knowledge and fears that would contradict the facility of the melodramatic solution (cf. Nowell-Smith 1985: 193). Dyer, speaking of American musicals (whose "utopian sensibility" closely resembles that of Tamil films), emphasizes the problems created by the contradictions arising from the genre's tendency to press toward unrepresentative (i.e. "unrealistic") solutions for problems rooted in reality:

To be effective, the utopian sensibility has to take off from the real experiences of the audience. Yet to do this, to draw attention to the gap between what is and what could be, is, ideologically speaking, playing with fire. What musicals have to do, then (not through any conspiratorial intent, but because it is always easier to take the line of least resistance, i.e., to fit in with prevailing norms), is to work through these contradictions at all levels in such a way as to 'manage' them, to make them seem to disappear. They don't always succeed. (1985: 228)

Because of the conflict between the "what is" in the viewer's experience and the "what could be" outcomes in movies, Tamil melodrama – as always incorporating both the reality and the fantasy – is internally contradictory. Melodrama can do its "work" by successfully glossing over the contradiction, making life appear happy and life's problems easily soluble; it can also create a less soothing cover-up by allowing the contradiction to rupture the smooth surface of the film, either within the movie itself (leading to a tragic ending), or within the eyes of viewers when the attempted reconciliation is so transparent that the conflicts remain viable. While Tamil cinema embodies these contradictory aspects within each filmic text, most Tamil movies are structured such that chance, coincidence or villainy makes a conscious resolution unnecessary, masking the contradiction so that it need not be noted by the viewer. Rather, this type of melodrama offers viewers the delusion that the exposed problem is not a problem at all, or at least that it can be solved happily and its unpleasant ramifications avoided. Because filmmakers have crafted their films carefully to avoid creating social and psychological discontent (and, I believe, because they enjoy some viewer collusion in this), Tamil films almost always avoid the potential problems inherent in the mix of somewhat realistic problems with fantastic solutions.

One of the reasons that viewers accept the sugar-coating of real-life problems is that, as will be discussed below, the primary conscious motivation for watching movies is to escape from those very problems. Because of its gripping, absorbing nature, melodrama is particularly suited to offering this escape into another world. Elsaesser suggests that

archetypal melodramatic situations activate very strongly an audience's participation, for there is a desire to make up for the emotional deficiency, to impart the different awareness, which in other genres is systematically frustrated to produce suspense: the primitive desire to warn the heroine of the perils looming visibly over her in the shape of the villain's shadow. (1985: 187)

The identification necessary to enhance escape is also facilitated by melodrama's focus on the point of view of the victim (Elsaesser 1985: 185), a perspective that most viewers have no difficulty empathizing with.

The problems portrayed in Tamil films derive from the real difficulties experienced by many poor urban viewers, as we will see, but are depicted in the very personal terms of individual film characters. This individualizing strategy ignores the social and political aspects and causes of the problems and thus reinforces the tendency of cinematic resolutions to disguise the nature and severity of the crises portrayed. Furthermore, even in individual circumstances the solutions shown to these problems are often coincidental, taking their resolution out of the hands of the individual, let alone society. Thus, in this sense Tamil cinema typifies not only the "blind" for dominant ideology that numerous earlier analysts have identified in popular culture, but more specifically typifies the genre of spectacle as Debord defines it. Debord portrays the language of spectacle as *"signs* of the ruling production" that unilaterally communicate the separation of classes (creators and spectators) (1983: §4, 24, 29). Indeed, Tamil cinema carries and communicates the ideology of its upper and middle class creators; and escape, of course, is not generally conceded as a revolutionary act. Examination of spectatorship reveals that the process of dialogue is more complex than this, however. I will return to questions of communicators and audiences later in this chapter, and thereafter to the other process of separation that Debord identifies in spectacle: the substitution of the appearance or image for reality. It is through this illusion that melodrama attracts viewers and provides escape.

Movie themes and crisis resolution
Critics and analysts of melodrama often speak as if we must approach its viewers' motivation in one of two ways. As Filon phrased this dichotomy in 1897, audiences either "go to the theatre to see a representation of life, or to forget life and seek relief from it" (quoted in Elsaesser 1985: 188n). Are Tamil viewers, then, attracted to cinema because they see in it reflections of their own life circumstances, or because they see lives that are fantastically different from their own? In fact, as the preceding discussion suggests, neither realistic representation nor pure fantasy dominates melodrama's appeal; rather, it is based on a resolution of the two – a psychological resolution, that is, of crises deriving from real life that are resolved in exotic settings through unusual and unrealistic events.

To illustrate the appeal of the different facets of movie form and content, I have chosen three films that are representative of Tamil cinema.

Their representativity lies primarily in that, taken together, they contain those themes of Tamil cinema that recur most frequently and carry the greatest emotional force for viewers. These three films have also been selected for their popularity; all had exceptionally long runs in Madurai theaters, indicating that they are successful combinations of the elements that viewers appreciate in a movie.

Each of the following three films combines elements of the realistic and the fantastic in settings, plots, and themes. Much of the setting is straight out of Tamils' daily lives – so familiar, in fact, as to be unremarkable to the typical viewer. Other elements of the set, however, are pointedly more luxurious or "modern" than most viewers are personally acquainted with. Many film characters have cars, fancy furniture, and western-style clothing, and the locales they move through are often exotic. (Even those movies with supposedly realistic settings, such as recent films shot in villages, are "hyper-real" – as one older English-speaking viewer put it – to the extent that their portrayals are actually romanticized or nostalgic stereotypes rather than accurate representations of most rural or urban environments. Bharatiraja's recent film *En Uyir Toozhan* ["My Intimate Friend," 1990], the only Tamil commercial film to depict slum life faithfully, failed financially.)[7] Plots and themes also mix realism and fantasy, thereby extending the surface departure from everyday life through melodramatic stories excessively dependent upon coincidence.

Many of the film's events are sparked, and its characters motivated, however, by such familiar concerns as young women yearning for children or parents wishing for their children's respect. Thus what we find is a blend of the familiar and the fantastic: while enough of the movies' content comes from the known world to make their scenarios identifiable, there is also sufficient dreamlike luxury and emotional passion for the film to function as an escape from the more oppressive features of that world. Both of these aspects aid in what I see as film's major psychological function – and one of its most appealing, albeit unconscious, attractions: the comforting easy dissolution of familiar psychological stresses.

The movies' central themes deal largely with social relationships and their psychological implications. Most concern one of two types of relationships: first, between men and women; and second, among family members. A third and smaller set deals with class identity and class relations. All of these are areas about which the urban poor experience some anxiety during their daily lives. Such anxieties contribute to a pervasive sense that life is insecure – an insecurity that most people feel is increasing, especially in matters related to these three areas. Madurai residents frequently complained that life was becoming more difficult and less certain, citing these issues, among others, as contributing factors. While there may actually have been little or no change in the security of such areas as family and class relations in the relevant past, it is the *perception* that social and economic circumstances have become insecure and continue to deteriorate that is most salient to this analysis.

The insecurity that poor residents feel is not limited to economic realms; it is also social and psychological. Thus not all the concerns in poor filmgoers' daily lives, including those reflected in films, derive from economic hardships, and these concerns may be shared with members of other classes. Parallel (though not necessarily identical) changes in relationships between men and women and among family members, for example, have occurred in the middle and upper classes. I suggest, however, that the fundamental economic uncertainties of urban poor existence pervade life in such a way as to make the uncertainties of the *expectations* associated with social relationships more pressing and poignant than they would otherwise be. That is, when the physical aspects of life are difficult at best, the reliability of social relationships, and the psychological comfort found in their steadiness, may be more crucial than when basic physical conditions are secure. This argument is suggested both by differences in the reactions of poor and wealthy people to similar social and psychological changes, reflected in conversations and interviews, and in the shifts in attitudes expressed by poor people who had once been financially secure. As an example of the latter case, the woman mentioned earlier whose husband, a doctor, had died and left her alone with five young children and no financial support described at length the differences between her past and present circumstances; one of the most pressing changes was her new fear that her children would leave her alone in her old age (possibly because they have so few resources themselves), something that had never concerned her in the past because she did not expect to rely so completely upon them. Another woman told me that her husband had begun to beat her whenever she spoke up at home or left the house for any length of time since losing his position in an office due to an injury; his inability to work had forced them to live on his small pension and move to much more modest surroundings. Cases such as these are anecdotal and can involve a number of factors besides decreased economic security, but in the aggregate they support the argument that while many of the movie themes discussed in this chapter address issues of concern to all classes, these issues may raise more piercing anxieties for the poor than for those who are economically better off.

Not all typical film themes reflect viewer concerns. Some impose issues that filmmakers merely think should be important to viewers. Conversely, some of the issues central to the lives of the urban poor are strictly avoided by filmmakers. These categories of "imposed" and "avoided" themes can also be characterized respectively as "directors'" and "viewers'" themes, and will be scrutinized for what they reveal about the relationship between producers and consumers of film.

My division of the film themes is not the only classification that could be made, and other observers might well divide them differently, shifting emphasis in various ways. My impressions were corroborated, however, by my informants' comments, which emphasized the same themes that stood out in my mind. These impressions were drawn from films in 1985–87, and some changes have taken place in Tamil films since then (although most of them technical rather than narrative), but the bulk of films still reflects the same emphases.

Finally, in addition to these major sets of themes, each of the following films also includes many individual themes that are deserving of detailed examination and could profitably be investigated in a more purely textual analysis. The purposes of this work, however, restrict us to an overview of the thickest threads and their more general and persistent connections with viewers' lives. To this end, I present below three representative movie stories, introducing each by indicating the key themes it represents in order to give the reader some guidance in reviewing the story. Following the film accounts I turn to detailed consideration of how the major themes of Tamil cinema are portrayed, and their associated problems resolved, in these films. Examples from other movies are also used in the analysis where they help to expand a theme or provide an interesting variation.

The three films recounted below are *Amman Koovil Kizhakkaalee* ("The East Side of Amman Temple"), *Paṭikkaatavan* ("Illiterate Fellow"), and *Sindhu Bairavi* ("Sindhu and Bairavi"). All opened in Madurai in late 1985 or early 1986 and were very popular. Two of them follow the typical song-and-dance formulation of Tamil movies. The third, *Sindhu Bairavi*, strays somewhat from this formula; it includes no dance scenes, and its songs come almost entirely from the classical South Indian Carnatic music tradition (though some nonetheless became popular hits). Its major themes, however, are typical of Tamil movies, and Madurai viewers accepted it as a mainstream film albeit of better-than-average quality.

Following are the stories of these three movies. Because these are my own descriptions of the stories, geared for a western audience, they include points and explanations that Tamils would not think necessary to mention. On the other hand, they also include the points that Tamils noted most forcefully in their own accounts of these films.

Three movie stories
    Sindhu Bairavi ("Sindhu and Bairavi"), 1985
    PRODUCER: Kavithalaiya Productions
    DIRECTOR: Balachandar
    STARRING: Sivakumar, Suhasini, Sulakshana

This film is significant for its powerful portrayal of one of the major gender-relations themes in Tamil cinema, that of the woman who sacrifices her own immediate interests for those of a man. It also addresses issues that fall under the theme of family concerns, particularly adultery.

Sindhu and Bairavi are the names of two ragas in Carnatic music, a classical South Indian style of music. They are also the names of the lover and wife of the movie's hero. The hero, JKB, is a famous Carnatic singer, a man who lives for music and cannot stand for it to be insulted or defiled. As the movie opens, he has just won the Padma Shree, India's highest award for the arts.

At that evening's concert JKB publicly dismisses his mridangam (drum) player, a man named Gurumurthy, who has arrived drunk. JKB promises to the audience that even without the help of the man's drum he will be able to maintain the rhythm; he does, and the concert is a success. Afterward his childless wife, who had gone that evening to a temple, tells him, "Since you were pleased with the applause, we will have a baby." But before they can become too intimate they are interrupted by Gurumurthy drumming madly in their courtyard. The sympathetic Bairavi, JKB's wife, aproaches the drummer, and extracts a promise that he will never drink again.

JKB feels strongly about his music. He calls his wife a "corpse" because she cannot properly appreciate music. At the house of an acquaintance, he refuses the whiskey that is offered and shrinks from the immoral woman who begs him to sing. He proclaims, "You all defile this music with alcohol and a she-devil. I will never bow down to any such thing!"

A young woman attends one of JKB's concerts. She watches much of the audience acting disrespectfully, talking or sleeping through the music. Finally, she rises after a song and asks the singer if she can make a statement. The audience is shocked, but JKB tells her to speak, and she suggests to JKB that he sing in Tamil as well as Telugu and Sanskrit (the languages of most Carnatic songs). He asks sarcastically if he should sing folk songs, saying he will not turn his music into "sewage." But his questioner responds that there are many Tamil songs about beautiful subjects. JKB challenges her to prove this to him – and she does, ascending the platform and singing beautifully. As she stands, poised and sophisticated, she sings, "I am uneducated, a simple person – music is everything." The audience cheers as she finishes, and even JKB gives grudging applause.

In the next few days this young woman, Sindhu, tracks down the singing star and asks him to be her teacher. He refuses repeatedly, but she follows him around undaunted. Finally he appears at her apartment, where she lives alone, and they discuss Tamil songs. He agrees to try singing some of the poet Bharatiar's works.[8] When JKB leaves her apartment, Sindhu gives him a book of Bharatiar's poetry. She writes her address in it, but tells him that her initial has no address. JKB realizes from this that Sindhu has no parents (since the first part of a Tamil's name is usually the person's father's initial).

JKB goes to a rocky beach to practice singing Bharatiar. When he finishes, an old fisherman approaches and hands him a shell garland in appreciation. At home, the singer offers it to his wife, but she refuses it in disgust because it is not made of gold. Sindhu, however, says (in English), "It's exquisite," telling JKB that it is a better award than the Padma Shree. She also gently urges him not to be upset with Bairavi, because not everyone can appreciate music; such a thing depends on one's education and background, she says.

Sindhu and JKB begin to spend much time together. He takes her home and introduces his student to Bairavi. Sindhu approaches Bairavi like a younger sister, but Bairavi is jealous. One day JKB and Sindhu spend an entire evening together, walking and talking. Sindhu tells him about her life, how she is of a high caste but was born out of wedlock and left in an orphanage. She recounts how as a young girl she was able to find some information about her now-married mother, and went to her mother's home one day and watched her through a hedge, but did not speak to her.

JKB deceives his wife about how he spent the evening. But another of JKB's instrumentalists, an inveterate liar who has sworn to JKB that he will never lie again, hears about JKB's deception and cannot avoid telling Bairavi the truth. Bairavi accuses her husband of lying, and he admits that he was with Sindhu. "Music is either in your blood or not," he says to his distraught wife, "and it is not in yours."

One day JKB takes Sindhu to meet his neighbors, a judge and his wife and daughter. Sindhu recognizes the judge's wife as her own mother, but says nothing. They ask her to sing for them. As she fantasizes about a happy family life with sister and mother, she sings, " I am a Sindhu [a raga of tragedy]. What is the name of a relationship that does not exist? Who is the mother of a folk song?"

One evening JKB and Sindhu are walking side by side. She sings, and soon their hands brush and clasp. JKB confesses that he has become a slave to her music, and asks her to wear his ring (a religious ring decorated with the holy mantra "om"). Sindhu accepts it, and they part.

Meanwhile, Bairavi has decided that she must try to learn to sing. After visiting a doctor and discovering that she cannot get a blood transfusion to put "music in your blood," she asks the drummer Gurumurthy to teach her. In the middle of the lesson she begins to cry and tells Gurumurthy that she is afraid of losing her husband. Gurumurthy is very fond of Bairavi, and soon after the lesson, pretending to be drunk, he approaches JKB and warns him that he must stop seeing Sindhu.

That night Bairavi tries to make love to her husband, but JKB keeps seeing Sindhu and springs from their bed to play his vina (a large stringed instrument), which he plays madly until a string snaps and his finger bleeds. As Bairavi bandages his finger, she sees that his ring is missing and asks him about it. JKB lies again. The next day Bairavi convinces JKB to tie a second thali for her, saying that this ceremony will make a baby come immediately.

One day JKB calls Sindhu and says nothing, but smacks her a kiss over the phone. Sindhu is angered by this anonymous affront. When she finds out the next day that the "rascal" was JKB himself, she accuses him of exploiting her pure devotion (*bhakti*) to his music, and leaves. For a week she refuses to see or talk to him. Then, unable to hold out any longer, she arranges a meeting, where she confesses,

If I truly thought you had made a mistake, I should have forgotten you completely within this last week, but I could not. I criticized you on the surface, but I felt differently inside ... I want to lock you into my heart ... My devotion to you is only an outer cover. I think that I love you.

Sindhu and JKB make love, as the screen shows fireworks, flowers, a vina, and buxom deities.

Meanwhile, a famous singer comes to visit the absent JKB at home, but Bairavi does not know where to find her husband. The newly truthful vina player has seen JKB's car in front of Sindhu's apartment, and tells Bairavi where her husband is. She goes there to get JKB, demanding angrily that he come home. As she leaves, she catches sight of the "om" ring on Sindhu's finger.

Once again Gurumurthy pretends to be drunk, but this time he visits Sindhu on the beach. He tells her as he stumbles that she should never see her lover again. "If you do anything against my brother's wife,"[9] he adds, "you will never be prosperous. Do not think that these are merely the words of a drunken man – I am a mridangam player!"

That night JKB has a concert. Sindhu does not appear, and in the middle of a song JKB receives news that his wife has tried to kill herself. He continues to sing. After the concert he goes to the neighbors' house where his wife is recuperating. From her bed, Bairavi tells him that he must see to it that no one comes between them. JKB promises to do so. The next day he tells Sindhu of his vow: "I love Bairavi too. I don't want to lose her, so I expect your cooperation with my promise." Sindhu asks if she should leave town. "You shouldn't run away because of my promise," he answers. "You introduced me to Tamil music and I am grateful to you for that. It is in my blood now." "I am thankful too," says Sindhu. "Our relationship lasted only a short while, but I will never forget it as long as I live."

Later Sindhu returns to her mother's house to give a book to the judge. Her mother meets her outside and tells her coldly never to come back because she wishes to save her husband from Sindhu's seductive grasp.

Although he has parted from her, JKB cannot forget Sindhu. Everywhere he goes, he hears her song. His heart aches, and one day as he wanders forlornly he is picked up by the wealthy acquaintance who had earlier offered him whiskey. He takes his first drink at this man's house, and that night arrives drunk at his own concert, where he begs Gurumurthy not to expose him as he once had exposed Gurumurthy.

Meanwhile, Sindhu has realized that she is pregnant from their affair and goes to the hospital for an abortion. While waiting in an examining room, she hears a doctor in another room say that she has just examined Bairavi, who also seems to be pregnant. But it is a false alarm, says the doctor, and in fact Bairavi is sterile ("has a defect") and will never be able to have a baby. Sindhu rises and leaves the hospital without having her operation.

JKB has become an alcoholic. His concerts are cancelled. His wife lets some of the servants go. One day Sindhu picks the drunken man up from a rainy street and takes him home. She and Bairavi carry him through the door, but there Bairavi says that further help is not needed.

One day soon after, Sindhu sees her mother's other (legitimate) daughter, Gayatri, in the bushes with a young man. She calls Gayatri out and reprimands her. But the girl says, "The whole town laughs at you [for your immorality]! Who are you to tell me what to do?!" Sindhu slaps her. Sindhu walks off, but her mother soon drives up, jumps out of the car and yells that Sindhu should have been ridden out of town. Bitterly, the older woman reproaches, "You have many holes in your house, and yet you are trying to settle everyone else's houses. Who are you? Gayatri's sister?" "And if she were my sister?" Sindhu asks. "Disgusting. Wash out your mouth. [Sindhu laughs.] Have you bought my husband too, the way you lured JKB?" To this Sindhu answers calmly, "You shouldn't cross such limits when you speak. If you do, so will I, and you will not be able to bear it." Then, after some consideration, Sindhu continues, "My story and your story are one – I wonder if you know that. The first half of my story is your story. The first half is your sin, the second half is mine. Do you remember the day you achieved independence from your sin?" Suddenly her mother's eyes open in disbelief and then fill with tears of understanding, and mother and daughter embrace and at last are reconciled. As they part fondly, Sindhu asks her mother not to tell anyone of their true relationship.

JKB has fallen so low that he steals household money to buy his alcohol. One day he returns home from the liquor store to find that his grandfather has died from a heart attack at seeing that an apparent thief had opened the household money box.

None of his friends will give him money any longer, so he goes to the whiskey-drinking acquaintance's home and begs for a drink. The man and the woman laugh, and make him sing pop songs (the "sewage" he had always despised) for his liquor. That night he performs for them at a party, singing drinking songs and making a fool of himself and his ideals. The woman he had called a she-devil phones his wife to come and witness the spectacle. Bairavi arrives to find her husband degraded, dancing and stripping his clothes on the front lawn. Distraught, she goes to Sindhu's apartment and states that only one life in the world can save her husband. She begs Sindhu to come to their house, and Sindhu agrees – for the sake of the man she loves. The next day JKB hears Sindhu playing the vina in his house. He walks to her and falls, and the two women lift him together.

Now Sindhu tackles the job of making JKB sober again. When he sits down with a bottle of liquor, she appears and places another beside it. She announces that if he opens his bottle she will open hers – containing kerosene – and pour it over herself and light it. Later, sober, he half-jokes to Sindhu that she is a cruel teacher.

Bairavi is wrestling with the question of whether to keep Sindhu there for her husband's sake. Finally she consults a deity, who tells her through signs that Sindhu should stay and marry JKB. Her heart settled, Bairavi tells her skeptical maid, "He should be happy. He must have prosperity and fame. That is all that is important to me now."

Gurumurthy overhears Bairavi talking about this, and he and others of JKB's friends approach Sindhu and garland her as if she is about to leave town. She is confused by the gesture, but they explain that she must carry out one more act for JKB: she must leave for a distant place. Convinced that this is necessary for JKB's marriage, Sindhu agrees and leaves for Madras. But the next day JKB, who has learned of his friends' act, gathers them and Bairavi together and accuses them of destroying a woman. He cries that without Sindhu there is no music, and smashes his vina to pieces.

Suddenly recognizing that JKB too will disintegrate without Sindhu, his friends place an advertisement in a newspaper. Sindhu sees it at her office in Madras and reads, "Our foolish act has sown serious consequences. Contact us immediately." Sindhu quickly writes a letter to her former lover, and explains that for the moment she must continue to bear certain responsibilities, but will return afterward. JKB is to be given a musical honor in six months, and Sindhu writes that she will return to sit in the front row at the ceremony.

Six months later, at the concert at which he is to be honored, JKB sings the Sindhu raga. As he sings, preparations are taking place at his home for his marriage to Sindhu. Sindhu appears at the concert and takes her seat in the front row, two seats down from her mother. Her mother's husband smiles at her, but her mother does not. Instead her mother starts to cry, as does Sindhu, thinking that she has been rejected in the end; but then her mother reaches behind their seats and touches her, and Sindhu hands her mother a signed photograph of herself.

Afterward everyone gathers at JKB and Bairavi's home for the expected wedding. But Sindhu stops the proceedings before they begin by claiming that it is her duty to refuse to be married. Sindhu tells Bairavi that she should never share her husband, that behind every successful man stands only one woman. Moreover, she says, it is illegal to have two wives – "just ask the judge," she adds, pointing to him. To clinch her argument, she reminds the surprised group that if the revered JKB has two wives, everyone else will think they can follow his example.

Bairavi demands, "Will you truthfully say that you have never loved him?" Sindhu responds, in English, "I still love him," continuing in Tamil: "JKB is loved by many people; can he marry all of them? So why, do you think, have I returned all this way? I have one gift to give you. But do you suppose I've wrapped it and put a ribbon around it? No – I bore it and wrapped it in a towel." Sindhu retrieves a bundle from another room, and carries in a baby – her offering, as she calls it. "This is JKB's baby," she says, and explains how she had learned of Bairavi's infertility while waiting to have an abortion. "I have to fill the emptiness of this house. Bairavi, my sister, if this child is in your arms, it will grow up in respectable circumstances; in mine it will have a pitiable life. Take this child for yourself." Bairavi takes the baby and holds it to herself as Sindhu looks on. Sindhu tells JKB that the work she came for is now over, and asks permission to leave. Bairavi suddenly puts down the child and yells, "Stop! I cannot ask you to leave. If you go you must take your baby, because unless you agree to stay with us I won't touch this child." Suddenly the baby screams. Sindhu watches, Bairavi watches, and Sindhu's own mother starts towards the baby but stops – as Bairavi recalls all her efforts to produce a child, and finally runs and cradles the baby. All the women smile a bit. Sindhu, turning toward the door, hands JKB back his ring, telling him in English, "Returned, with thanks."

> *Amman Koovil Kizhakkaalee* ("The East Side of Amman Temple"), 1985
> PRODUCERS: Selvakumar, S. P. Palaniappan (VNS Productions)
> DIRECTOR: R. Sundarrajan
> STARRING: Vijaykanth, Radha

This film contains examples of all three sets of film themes. Under the rubric of gender relations, it presents the theme, found frequently in Tamil cinema, of a spoiled modern "girl" who becomes transformed through marriage into a properly demure wife. After marriage, she also provides another example of a woman who subjugates her own needs to those of her husband. Issues of family relations also arise, centering on the responsibilities of natal and marital family members to one another, as do those of class identity and relations, particularly characterological distinctions between rich and poor and their treatment of one another.

The movie opens with the heroine's release from prison. As the young woman Kanmani prepares to leave the jail, she is given a large bag containing all the letters she has written to her husband during her four years of imprisonment. The letters have been returned unopened, and the woman is heartbroken. When the warden tries to pay her for her work in the prison, she replies ominously that she won't be needing more than the Rs. 5 for the train.

As Kanmani rides toward home in the train, she thinks of the events that led to her imprisonment. Her thoughts begin with the time she met the hero, Chinnamani, whom her father had engaged to sing at her birthday celebration in the village temple. In her memory, Kanmani, dressed in western clothes, is an impudent and arrogant young woman. As the guests file into the temple grounds, they all greet her respectfully – all, that is, but the singer Chinnamani. He refuses, saying, "I came to sing, not to worship her." Kanmani tells her father that she will not allow Chinnamani to sing for her because he is so arrogant. The singer calmly accepts her decree, but adds, "I'll watch out for you, Kanmani."

Later we see the heroine driving her sporty red car outside of the village. She stops when she hears Chinnamani singing about her. The hero appears and courts her, teasing. In another scene, after the car has run out of gas, the hero appears again. This time the teasing involves much pushing and pulling of the heroine, who is both attracted and annoyed by the hassling. Afterward she complains to her father, who sends his thugs to beat up the singer. But Chinnamani, in a proper film-hero style, defeats them all.

The next day a newly conciliatory Kanmani appears at Chinnamani's house and asks the hero's stepfather to forgive her. She asks the same of his stepsister, saying, "A woman knows a woman's heart." Then she sees Chinnamani and suggests that, after all that has happened, he must not like her. But he explains to her, "I didn't mean to say I don't like you." She asks, "Then what are you saying?" "Half of the wealth in this town is yours. You have studied all through college, while I only made it to third grade." "As far as I'm concerned, music is the very best education. It is there *naturally*. No other man in this town is like you." As they part, Kanmani adds, "When I come to your house tomorrow, I'll see how much you care for me."

When Kanmani arrives the next day, Chinnamani has rented a gold chain and watch – neither of which he knows how to wear. He seats his visitor on a silk cloth, and she hands him a song she has written. It is a song about wedding preparations. They sing it together, happily, and she tells him to come to her house and ask her father to allow them to marry.

But when Chinnamani and all his relatives come to call, her father yells, in English, "What nonsense!" Chinnamani calls Kanmani, who now laughs at the idea of marrying him. She says to his relatives, "I am a grown-up woman. If I had told him to come here and ask for a wife, I wouldn't make him stand out here like this, would I?" Then she asks Chinnamani's stepfather, "How much have I studied?" He answers: "Through college." "And he?" "Through the third grade." "Is there any equity in our being together? ... He is poor ... He is an orphan. Is there any logic in all of you standing here?"

When the distraught Chinnamani and his relatives have gone, Kanmani's mother asks why the young man had lied. Kanmani replies that she herself was the liar – "I wanted to dishonor him in front of those people, so I told him a lie to get him to come here." Outraged, her mother slaps her. In order to avenge herself for this, Kanmani vows that Chinnamani will never sing again, and runs over his harmonium with her car. In return, he smashes her red car and its windows with a club. Kanmani catches him and grabs the club, but Chinnamani strikes her.

Chinnamani is summoned to appear before the village panchayat for hitting a grown woman. He swears to a friend that he will never ask forgiveness for striking a woman who was at fault. Standing proudly before the panchayat, he says to its leaders, including Kanmani's father, "Do whatever you want to me." Kanmani's father exclaims, "You smashed my car, slapped my daughter, and now you dare to speak arrogantly!" He sentences Chinnamani to be whipped – by Kanmani.

Kanmani, dressed in a tight western-style blouse and skirt, savors the unwrapping of the whip. She lashes his bare back again and again; the strikes are interspersed with scenes of breaking waves. Finally finished, she lowers the whip in disgust. Chinnamani glares at her and, saying, "I'll do what I have to do. You have dishonored me; now look what you get!" throws a thali cord around her neck and ties it. [The audience cheers wildly.] "Now get out of here!" he yells at his new wife.

Kanmani tries to rip the cord off, but her mother rushes forward and grabs her arm, saying, "A woman can receive the thali around her neck only once in her life. For you, it has been done." She drags her daughter home, where Kanmani cries that no one can make her keep the thali. But her mother replies, "I can't watch you forever. Listen to me patiently now. After you have listened, you can keep it or not as you like." And her mother tells the story of her own marriage and of Chinnamani's and Kanmani's births. She begins by asking Kanmani, "Do you know who the real owner of this car and bungalow and everything else is? It's Chinnamani – the man who just tied the thali around your neck. Your father is far from the hereditary rich man you have always thought him to be."

Kanmani's mother's brother had been a rich man in another village. While living with her brother, Kanmani's mother fell in love with a newcomer who worked for her brother, and she persuaded her brother to let her marry the man. A month after the wedding her new husband demanded that she convince her brother to give them all the family property and money, or he would throw her out of the house. She left her husband and returned to her brother's home in order to avoid the husband's demands, but her brother discovered the reason for her return and gave the husband all of the family property so that his sister could return to her proper household. The husband accepted all, claiming he had wanted it only for his wife's happiness and not for his own. The wife's brother and his young son – Chinnamani – left home. Soon after, the brother died from diabetes. His sister then overheard her husband plotting to kill Chinnamani, so she spirited the boy into a boat, gave him one of her gold chains, and sent him off down the river.

Years later, she and her husband moved to a new town where they had built a sugar mill. There a man came to ask for money to save his mute daughter from smallpox. In exchange he gave her a chain – the same chain she had once put around her nephew's neck. Questioned, the man explained that he had taken the boy in twenty years ago and raised him as his son.

The woman's husband fell in love with one of their servants. The servant became pregnant, and died after childbirth, but first extracted a promise from the wife to look after the baby. "That baby," says Kanmani's mother to her daughter,

was you. I accepted you because the mistake made was your father's. I didn't want you to know about this, so I have never had any children myself. You have shamed this young man in front of everyone because he is an orphan – now think of yourself. I am telling you all of this now because of the respect I hold for the thali. Today your father expects to arrange your betrothal [to another man]. Whether you now give respect to this yellow thread is in your own hands!

Later that day, Kanmani's father does hold the betrothal ceremony. While Kanmani is being introduced to her prospective in-laws, her mother collapses. She has poisoned herself, giving her life to stop the wedding. Kanmani rushes to her side. Her mother whispers, "I have made my decision. Now let your decision be good." (The word she uses here for "decision," *muṭivu*, also means "end" or "ending.")

In the next scene, Kanmani arrives at Chinnamani's house, dressed in a nice but demure sari with her hair tied in a bun, the picture of the chaste and proper Tamil wife. At the gate she pulls out her thali and kneels to make a *kolam*.[10] Then she goes inside and starts cutting vegetables and cooking dinner. Chinnamani enters to find her there, and asks what she is doing in his kitchen. She extends her thali and says, "You yourself tied it.

Since that very moment, I have every right to be in this house." "Oh ho? Is that so? I didn't tie it so that we could live together, but to squash your arrogance," he says, and pushes her to the ground. His stepfather defends Kanmani, but Chinnamani is adamant. He leaves and goes to an arrack (palm liquor) shop, where he gets drunk and sings a song about three knots (of the thali). Returning home, he refuses to allow Kanmani into their decorated nuptial bed and pushes her out of the house into the pouring rain.

As Kanmani bravely shivers outside, the police arrive. Her father also drives up. She refuses the police inspector's help, saying that this is a family matter. The inspector points out that it was her father who called the police. Kanmani refutes this, saying in English, "I have no father, no mother, only my husband. [She holds up her thali.] Satisfied?"

After this incident, Kanmani's father hires a huge thug to maul Chinnamani. In the fight, Chinnamani puts up a very brave defense, but eventually is beaten severely. At home, Kanmani cares for his wounds tenderly (unlike the menfolk, who hurt Chinnamani as they dress his wounds) and sings to him. Finally, he grudgingly allows her to stay.

Chinnamani's mute stepsister, Valli, marries a young man she loves, a labor union leader. Like Chinnamani, her husband walks out of the bedroom on their wedding night. But he is not rejecting his wife; he tells her father that he will not sleep with Valli until she can speak because he does not wish to take advantage of her muteness. Moreover, he says, he hopes that the power of his love will help bring back her speech.

Kanmani takes Valli to the Amman temple to consult the priest about Valli's muteness. The priest says that if it was the goddess who took the girl's speech,[11] she will give it back. Kanmani performs numerous acts of worship and sacrifice to the goddess. She rolls prostrate around the goddess's image, pulls a temple car with hooks in her back, and eats off the temple stair in devotion to Amman. Chinnamani sees all of this, and is moved. When Kanmani begins to faint one night as she sings at the Amman temple, Chinnamani jumps up to the stage and catches her, and they continue the song together.

Valli's speech is restored by the goddess, but Valli leaves a note at home saying that it must be her husband who hears her first words. Her husband, meanwhile, meets with Kanmani's father, who attempts to bribe the young union leader into signing a labor agreement. The young man righteously refuses the large bundle of proffered cash, and leaves. The mill owner sends someone after him to kill him. Luckily, however, Chinnamani happens upon the attempted murder in the forest, and saves the young man. Then Valli catches up with her husband, and shows him that she can speak. Kanmani approaches them, giving motherly words of comfort and advice, saying that it is good and proper to give priority to one's husband as Valli has done. Suddenly, Kanmani's father himself is shooting at them, trying to kill the young man but mindless of hitting even his daughter. The young people scatter. Kanmani goes after her father and grabs his rifle, but he pushes her away. She turns to a tiny Amman shrine in the trees behind her, and wrenches away one of the pointed iron stakes surrounding it. Raising the stake to strike her father, she turns to see her husband stabbing him. Chinnamani kills Kanmani's father.

Kanmani and Chinnamani face each other in the woods, standing beside the bloody corpse, and Chinnamani says, "Until now I have had no desire to touch you. Now that I want to touch you, I must go away." But Kanmani convinces her husband to send his family off to safety first. While Chinnamani sends his family members away in a boat, Kanmani walks into the police station and announces herself as the murderer of her father. As she is driven off in the police van, Chinnamani returns to turn himself in; but he finds that his wife has already confessed to the crime, and runs after the van screaming her name, unable to catch up.

Now we return to Kanmani on the train, after she has served her prison sentence. She disembarks at her home town, and, dejected, scans the station. No one is there to greet her. She tilts her head back to swallow some poison, but suddenly hears her name being yelled. She stops, then races wildly towards the sound. Running into the temple, she finds one of Chinnamani's friends and demands to know what has happened to her husband. The man points behind her – to a Chinnamani who has gone mad, whipping himself in his rags. He cries out her name as he lashes. She runs up to him. "Your Kanmani has returned! I am Kanmani!" she cries, but he will not recognize or believe her. "No!" he says. "You are not my Kanmani. My Kanmani was such a good person! Such a good person, and I failed to protect her. I could not protect her!" He begins whipping furiously, and Kanmani turns her eyes to the goddess for help. There, under the goddess's image, she sees a harmonium, which she seizes and begins to play as she sings their old song – the one she had first written about marriage. Slowly, as her words fill the temple, Chinnamani stops, facing her, and begins to recognize his wife. Tearfully, they draw together, and Kanmani rests her head on her husband's chest.

Paṭikkaatavan ("Illiterate Fellow"), 1985
PRODUCERS: N. Veeraswamy, V. Ravichandran
DIRECTOR: Rajashekar
STARRING: Shivaji Ganesan, Rajnikanth, Ambika

Here we have a film that focusses on themes of class identity and relations and family relationships. It makes strong comments both on the strength of natal family ties and on the inherent superiority of the poor over the rich.

Rajashekar is the caretaker of his two young brothers. He loves them greatly, and the three form a close-knit and happy group. Then Rajashekar marries, and his new wife's first view of the young boys comes when she and Rajashekar find them asleep on their nuptial bed. Her husband smiles at the sight and says that they should not disturb the tired children.

Rajashekar leaves to study law in Madras. His brothers stay with his wife. She is cruel and neglectful, and soon the older of the two boys takes on the care of the younger one. He massages his little brother's bad leg, and finds food when their sister-in-law refuses to feed them. He comforts the boy by telling him, "Don't worry, little brother. I will work and take care of you for as long as I live." One day, unable to bear the harsh treatment in their own home, the two boys run away to Madras. There they are abducted and forced to beg on the street, but are saved by a kind Muslim who takes them into his home. When Rajashekar returns home from Madras he is heartbroken to learn that his brothers have run away, but he can do nothing to find them.

Next we see the two boys grown. They have taken on the nicknames of Raja and Ramu. Raja, the elder, is a taxi driver and Ramu a college student. Our first glimpse of Ramu is at a disco-style dance, where he is dressed in western clothes – part of his college lifestyle. Afterward he sits on a couch with two women friends, discussing their upcoming college drama production. Ramu talks about what a big man his brother is – Raja lives all over the world, he says, and travels in his own airplane, and would never come to the small "function" that they are putting on. Ramu's friends find Raja's address, however, and send him an invitation to the play.

Raja has a fancy jacket made for the play and attempts to put on an urbane appearance. But Raja is a hick from the beginning. He cannot walk in his new high-heeled boots, and he misunderstands fellow playgoers' English, hoots at the wrong times, turns the show into a brawl, and then jumps onstage in order to protect his brother during a swordfight.

After the show, as he and Ramu walk to the bus station, he is still the solicitous caretaker, giving Ramu lots of money and admonishing his brother to take care of himself.

Raja has a great hatred of drugs. His taxi, which he has named "Lakshmi," will not start if passengers are carrying drugs. Raja even busts one of his adoptive father's sons for selling opium.

One day he sees a pregnant woman walking down the street and offers her a ride. When Lakshmi will not start, Raja ignores the hint. The next time he sees the woman she is not pregnant, but a few days later she is again heavy with child. Raja is puzzled by this, but he is also a bit naive about such matters and cannot quite figure out what is going on. Then one day the woman moves into a house two doors down from Raja's stepfather's place, and that night Raja watches her and her male cronies distill illicit alcohol, which she smuggles by hiding it in an inflatable bag under her dress. Raja jumps in to break up the act, and beats up all of the accomplices by himself. Then he starts to hit the now-pregnant woman, but suddenly finds himself surrounded by neighbors who prevent him from hurting her and refuse to believe his story about the illicit hooch ring. The woman is livid, and swears to him, "Tomorrow I will get you."

The next day she asks her boss, Johnny, for help, and he sends his goons after Raja. But Raja fights them off singlehandedly and returns to save the woman from Johnny, who has reminded her that "I don't do anything for free." Mary, the smuggler, thanks Raja for saving her "honor." But Raja claims that, considering the work she has been doing, she has no right to speak of honor. To have honor, he says, she must work as a laborer. The next day he sees Mary, now dressed in a simple sari with a cross around her neck, coming from her new job as a coolie. Mary hands Raja the money she has made that day; their hands touch, and they are in love.

A wealthy man named Chakravarthy is the head of another smuggling ring. He uses lorries from his elder brother's legitimate trucking business to smuggle his goods. He has been accused of wrongdoing by the authorities, and one day he hires Raja's taxi in order to visit a lawyer friend of his. The lawyer happens to be Rajashekar – Raja's elder brother. Raja waits outside the office while Chakravarthy attempts to engage the lawyer's help in dismissing the charges against him. Rajashekar refuses outright, saying, "I am here to protect the law, not to sell it," and assures his friend that there will be an acquittal if he has done nothing wrong. Suddenly Raja enters to return the smuggler's expensive watch, which had fallen off in the taxi. Raja refuses to take a tip for this, saying he is an honest man. Rajashekar calls to him, and the taxi driver recognizes his brother immediately. "Younger brother,[12] what is your name?" asks the lawyer. "Raja." "Your parents named you correctly – you are indeed a king," praises Rajashekar, but he does not recognize his younger brother (whom he has not seen for nearly twenty years).

After this incident, Raja decides to meet with his older brother and introduce himself. He goes to Rajashekar's house and is met by his brother's wife. She accuses Raja of coming to ask for money, and of planning to leave his taxi job and settle in the bungalow. He replies that no, he had only come to honor his brother, but the woman tells Raja that if he really cares for his brother he will leave and never return. Rajashekar is hoping to become a judge, she says, but Raja is a nobody, "a common taxi driver," and if people knew that Rajashekar had such a brother it would hurt the lawyer's standing.

Back at home, Raja's adoptive father asks him why he had not told Rajashekar that he was his younger brother. Raja answers that while his brother would have been happy at this, his brother's wife would not. He swears grimly, "Those who have nothing receive no respect no matter where they go, Father. I will educate my little brother, and then I can place him before our brother Rajashekar. That day is not far off."

Ramu leads his brother to believe that he has passed his final college exams. Soon after, a wealthy man comes to Raja's house to ask if his daughter may marry Ramu (who is in love with the woman, a fellow student). The man is Venkatachalan, elder brother of the smuggler Chakravarthy and unknowing owner of the trucking company that Chakravarthy uses as a cover. He suggests that Ramu move into his own house after the wedding and take over the family business. But Raja refuses to let his brother move into another house, and tells the man to get out.

When Ramu hears this news he scolds Raja, telling him that he (Ramu) should have been allowed to take this chance to become a rich man. "Without money I will become an orphan," Ramu says, "but since you are only an uneducated fellow you cannot understand." Hearing his brother's words, Raja gives in and arranges the wedding. Their brother Rajashekar attends the wedding as a friend of Chakravarthy, and speaks kindly to both Raja and Ramu, but still fails to recognize them.

Raja has had to pawn his beloved car due to the wedding expenses, and cannot redeem the loan. One day when he comes home, he finds that his adoptive father has bought it back for him.

Ramu goes to work for Chakravarthy. Raja finds out that his younger brother has lied to him about the college exams, and actually failed them.

Furious, he breaks in on a nightclub-style dancing scene and confronts Ramu with the damning evidence. Ramu answers scornfully, "So you know everything. But you are just a taxi driver. I can earn a great amount of money; if you can earn money, then you go and earn it." Raja tries to leave home in his taxi, but Lakshmi won't start, so he jumps out and breaks all her windows. He heads to a liquor shop and starts to drink as fast as he can.

Suddenly, Mary comes to his rescue in a white sari. She grabs his arms and stops Raja from drinking; he keeps repeating to her, "Everything is play-acting [*ellaamee naatakam*]." Mary tells him to speak what is in his heart, and he starts to sing of his troubles.

One of the trucks belonging to Venkatachalan, Ramu's father-in-law, is involved in an accident. Chakravarthy fears that his brother will find smuggled goods hidden in it, so has his goons kidnap the badly injured driver. The driver is one of Raja's adoptive brothers, and during the fight to abduct the young man the Muslim father is killed. Raja rescues the son, but he dies anyway. At his father's funeral, Raja vows that he will have vengeance for every drop of his father's blood.

Chakravarthy proclaims that Raja must be gotten rid of. When Ramu objects, Chakravarthy says that all of the smuggling has been done in Ramu's name, and that Ramu will be implicated if the business is discovered. Venkatachalan does discover his brother's operation, but believes that Ramu was behind it and, accusing his son-in-law of spoiling the family name and business, orders him out of the house. Ramu approaches Raja and asks him for forgiveness, but the bitter Raja refuses to grant it.

To get rid of Raja, Chakravarthy and company attempt to frame him with a crime. Raja is tricked into going to Venkatachalan's house, where he finds his brother's father-in-law dead. The police arrive and accuse Raja of the murder.

Raja is taken to court, where the judge is none other than his brother Rajashekar, presiding at his first trial. Again and again, the honest taxi driver is falsely accused. Finally he says to the prosecuting attorney, "You may wear your fancy robes, and you are well educated, but you are the one who should be sworn in before you speak." During the testimony, the facts of Raja's and Ramu's true names and birthplace are exposed, and Rajashekar suddenly realizes that they are his long-lost brothers. With tears in his eyes he immediately adjourns the court. Later, visiting Raja in his cell, Rajashekar reveals to his brother that he has decided to step down as judge and act as Raja's defense attorney. He notes how different the fate (*viti*) of the three brothers has been, and swears that if there is a God (*aaṇṭavan*) Raja will go free, but if not he will be hanged.

Through hard work, Rajashekar brings the true events to light. He shows that it was in fact Chakravarthy who killed the murdered man, then arranged it to appear that Raja was the guilty one. At this exposure of his crime, Chakravarthy tries to shoot Rajashekar and then attempts to escape, but Raja leaps from the witness box and apprehends him. After the trial is over, Rajashekar's wife admits to Raja that she has caused him great suffering, and asks for his forgiveness. Then, reunited at last, Rajashekar tells his honest younger brother, "Even though you haven't studied, you are a great wise man."

Each of these three films contains the narrative and dramatic elements discussed at the beginning of this chapter, and employs the typical processes of melodramatic resolution. The ways in which their themes allow for the resolution of crises is examined in the following chapter.

6

Film themes

Taken together, the films recounted in the previous chapter illustrate the typical themes of Tamil movies. They focus on relationships between women and men or among family members, or on issues of class identity and class relations. Movies frequently revolve around a crisis or difficulty in one or more of these areas, thereby raising issues about which many Tamils feel substantial anxiety. Instead of exacerbating this anxiety, however, films mitigate it by subsequently portraying solutions. But these resolutions are not realistic answers that could be applied in everyday life; rather, they are almost always dependent on a coincidence that magically wipes out the difficulty, making it appear that the crisis is not really a problem at all – and certainly not a problem worthy of concern.

Relationships between women and men[1]
Each of these films presents one or more of the images of women and men, and of their relationships with each other, that are typical of Tamil movies. In film portrayals of these relationships, it is frequently the woman's behavior that stands out as worthy of comment. Male behavior appears taken for granted in that it is portrayed as a justifiable reaction to a woman's actions. This is not always the case, but it was both my general perception and the implicit assumption of viewers as they related movie stories to me. By and large it seems that male roles are implied by female roles, and thus it is the images of women that we must look to first in order to also understand those of men. The most frequent images of women in Tamil films are the sacrificing, persevering wife; the self-centered and erotic woman who is transformed into a proper Tamil woman; and the in-marrying woman who breaks up the happy family of men or, by extension, the traditional joint family.[2]

The most frequent of these images – that of the long-suffering woman who sacrifices her own desires and immediate interests for those of a man – predominates in *Sindhu Bairavi*. K. Balachandar, the film's director, has a reputation for making movies that deal with realistic problems and contravene many standard movie conventions. Despite critics' recent claims that Balachandar's movies have become like other commercial cinema, audiences still think of his productions as "good" movies (i.e. worthwhile – "with a message"). The story is in fact very unusual in its emphasis on and sympathetic depiction of the "other woman," as we will see below. However, its main theme of the sacrificing woman is a typical one in Tamil cinema.

The theme also has ancient roots in religious epics and other popular cultural media. Models for this ideal woman abound in Tamil and Indian culture. Those cited most frequently come from the Indian epics *Mahabharata* and *Ramayana*. In the *Mahabharata*, the young woman Savitri argues with Yama, god of death, when he comes to claim her husband. Yama had never before relinquished anyone from death, but Savitri's chastity and righteousness persuade him to return her husband to life. In the *Ramayana*, Sita is rescued from a demon king by her husband Rama, who subsequently refuses to believe that Sita had remained chaste in captivity. When Sita willingly and devotedly submits to tests by fire to prove her innocence, her exemplary chastity permits her to survive unscathed and win back the love of her husband. In the Tamil epic *Cilappatikaaram*, written in the second or third century AD, the fierce power of Kannagi's chastity razes Madurai after the king unjustly kills her husband.[3]

This image continues in current Tamil films. In the movie *Cinna Viitu* ("Little House" – a euphemism for mistress – made in 1985), for example, a husband who had thought his wife fat and ugly and had begun sleeping with another woman is eventually overwhelmed by his wife's continued devotion (contrasting with the mistress's deceit), and, converted by her patient suffering, lovingly returns to his wife and her bed.

In *Sindhu Bairavi*, both the mistress Sindhu and the wife Bairavi portray this common figure. Bairavi brings the hated mistress into her own house in order to save her husband's life and career. She is even willing to allow him Sindhu as a second wife: "He should be happy," Bairavi says. "That is all that is important to me now." As for Sindhu, her religious devotion to the singer and to music are initially overwhelmed by passion, but her passion is quickly overcome by cool reasoning. Sindhu gives up not only her own desires but even her own child for the sake of her love and his marriage. Their devotion to a common man even allows the opposed women to join forces in an effort to save that man.

This portrayal coincides with an image frequently met with in everyday life, one that provides a constantly reinforced ideal for women. Girls are told the stories of Savitri and Sita from a young age; religious tracts urge women to follow the models of these and other legendary figures by cheerfully and steadfastly forgiving their husband his shortcomings; popular short stories (like movies) tell of young wives whose alcoholic, violent or unloving husbands are converted by their wives' persevering devotion into caring and productive men; and women whose husbands mistreat them are encouraged by other women to endure their trials by following the example of Sita.

This image, adhered to in the extreme by both Sindhu and Bairavi, is radically different from the woman that Kanmani represents in the first half of *Amman Koovil Kizhakkaalee*. Kanmani is arrogant, willful, and completely self-centered. She forbids the hero from singing when he refuses to honor her properly, smashes his harmonium in a fit of self-pity, manipulates his affections through deceit and disgraces him before the community. But marriage accomplishes a complete transformation in Kanmani so that she too becomes the ideal Tamil woman, a woman like Bairavi (or Sindhu) who is willing to put up with any hardship and make any sacrifice to gain her husband's love and to improve his life.

This second theme – that of a spoiled rich woman being tamed (or "domesticated") by a poor man – is common in Tamil movies. Two issues related to concerns with the binding of women's power seem to be addressed by such themes: concern over the social power and independence of women, and ambivalence toward female sexuality.

The first of these issues stems from perceptions that women have gained power both within and outside of the family and are less subject to the authority of men. In religious ideology and in most folk models of gender relations (see chapter 2), men hold power; in reality, both men and women do, especially within the family. Any recognition of women's actual power challenges the dominant model of behavior. This conflict between model and reality creates anxiety for both sexes but especially for men, to whom it is most threatening. I suggest that this issue is made palatable in most films by the avoidance of any real-life situations in which men and women might actually confront the conflict in daily life – such as in an office, at school, at gatherings of relatives, or in any other situation in which the concerned man and woman would interact on a relatively equal social level.

Instead, the situation is frequently exaggerated to provide the woman with a reason for her arrogance that is psychologically acceptable to the audience – in *Amman Koovil Kizhakkaalee*, for example, it stems from her wealth and class standing – and thus lessen the scorned man's sense of emasculation. Here the issue is largely resolved when a chance revelation by Kanmani's mother regarding Kanmani's and Chinnamani's true backgrounds (and the fact that, neatly enough, the wealth rightfully belongs to the man and not to the woman!), forces the heroine to see the hero's worthiness and accept him as her husband. The two have switched to a socially and psychologically acceptable relationship: he has become her master. The issue is not totally resolved, however, until the woman proves her own worthiness to hold this position after a period of punishment and rejection by her husband.

At no other time have I seen a Tamil audience react with such wild approval as they did when Chinnamani dramatically tied the thali around the shocked Kanmani's throat. Viewers felt that this was sweet and irreversible revenge for the wealthy woman's extreme scorning of the poor man, and a proper subjugation of her mightiness – proper because a wife must be subject to her husband, and women in general subject to men. The change accomplished through the thali tying, in which a woman's wild sexuality is bound and brought under control, is one of transition to proper Tamil womanhood.

This new position is desirable because it is through her husband that a woman receives the opportunity to achieve the most socially acclaimed status to which she has access – that of auspicious wifehood and motherhood (although in Kanmani's case it does not necessarily bring her additional economic security). In becoming a wife, Kanmani trades in economic power and freedom for the socially delegated powers that accrue to her newly respectable status.

The urgency of this transformation to proper womanhood highlights the second and related issue involved in this theme, that of concern over female sexuality. The new "modern" woman – seen in movies, advertising, magazine articles, and occasionally on city streets – is fashionably dressed and sexy. (This supposedly new and desirable antithesis to the traditional proper woman also has her antecedents in the erotic goddesses and female demons of ancient mythology. Both form ideals that differ from normal human reality.) Men desire this woman, but also fear her; moreover, such desire conflicts with the simultaneous wish for a devoted and subservient wife.[4] Here men get them both. The desired but feared erotic woman that the early Kanmani represents, right through the moment of the whipping, is tamed, first by the surprise tying of the thali and then by her mother's confirming revelation. She has become a proper – and unthreatening – Tamil wife. Kanmani now devotes herself to her rejecting husband, and even goes to jail in final payment for her former sins; and as if this were not enough, her complete transformation to "good woman" is made unequivocal when we find that Chinnamani has gone mad without her after his realization that she is a good person and that he has failed to provide her with husbandly protection.[5]

Thus the desired object has been acquired, although initially rejected for some time, and transformed into a safe possession. This theme of transformation is recognized by other observers of Indian film. Bahadur sees the reconciliation of the traditional image of the devoted wife with that of the modern, free-loving, and liberated woman as one of the major psychological functions of movies.[6] The "new" woman, he says, is portrayed in films as well educated, free from parental restraint in love relationships, intimate with her lover, fashionably dressed and having "extreme sexual desirability in physique," but she suddenly sheds these attributes at a "crucial point" and reverts to the traditional male-worshipping image. The purpose of this image, Bahadur claims, is to resolve a "basic sexual anxiety": the heroine is a "dream bride," combining "the security of the traditional wife and the excitement of the modern woman" (1976: 95).

In Tamil film, the symbol of this transformation is the wedding emblem, the thali. The shocking and climactic knotting of the thali around Kanmani's neck is the central moment of *Amman Koovil Kizhakkaalee*. The tying of the thali is also the central moment of a Tamil (or Christian) woman's life. Here the change accomplished through the thali is absolute, final and complete. The tying is like magic – not just in Kanmani's complete change of character, but in that once the cord is knotted, the woman is bound to the man, no matter how the binding happened – regardless of whether the marriage was desired, proper or equitable.[7]

The finality of the transition derives from what Kanmani's mother calls the "respect for the thali." Kanmani's transformation is complete. She changes from the arrogance and immodesty of her western clothes, untied hair, and brash manners to demureness in every way: her sari, tied hair, respectful behavior, and general composure all reflect her metamorphosis into a proper Tamil wife.

The tying of the thali represents the binding of a woman's dangerous sexual power, which can now be controlled by her husband for the good of the family and community. Before her marriage, a girl's parents, especially her father, have been responsible for restricting her movements to a greater or lesser extent in order to prevent inappropriate behavior, and neighbors' suspicion of the same. This explains why women who are not subject to these external restrictions – such as orphans, or even girls with a mother but no father – are seen as immoral. Sindhu is a prime example of this. She is scorned by society because of her insecure position. (Similarly, the young heroine of *Reevati* [1986] is taunted as a *devadasi* – in this case, a temple prostitute – because she and her mother live alone without her father.) In fact, her liaison with JKB substantiates fears about young women in her unrestricted position. The difficulty of her situation is confirmed when she hands her own baby to Bairavi, claiming that if she keeps the illegitimate child herself "it will have a pitiable life."

In *Paṭikkaatavan* we have an example of a third type of male–female relationship, one frequently portrayed in Tamil literature and cinema: the in-marrying woman who breaks up the happy family of men.[8] This theme seems to reflect specifically a fear of women coming between men, who are united by patrilineal bonds, and more broadly a fear of the break-up of the extended family or a loosening of family bonds altogether. The patrilineal bonds that hold men of the family together are often weakened by conflicts arising from economic or social ambitions. These ambitions are thought to be encouraged by wives, who in Tamils' minds are "naturally" more concerned with the specific welfare of their marital unit than with the general welfare of the extended family.[9]

In *Paṭikkaatavan* it is the wife of the eldest brother Rajashekar who separates the brothers and prevents them from reuniting, accomplishing her misdeed through neglect and deceit. She sees the younger brothers as her competitors. Her hatred contrasts with Rajashekar's devotion to them; her neglect contrasts with Raja's vow to care for Ramu all his life. Her self-interest in refusing to welcome the adult Raja appears in radical opposition to Raja's determination to unite the family again, to the recognition that Rajashekar would undoubtedly have welcomed Raja, and to Rajashekar's later selfless aid to his brother. In the very end, the wife who created the split recognizes and admits her guilt, and apologizes to Raja (and by implication to the other brothers) for the suffering that she has caused. Having admitted her fault, she becomes meek and unthreatening and is now firmly put into her proper place.

Relationships among family members

This theme of the woman who sparks disintegration of the male household is clearly related to concerns not only about relationships between women and men but also about the viability of the family. It is developed somewhat differently in the movie *Camsaaram Atu Minsaaram* ("A Wife is Electricity," 1986), in which the sons of a joint family shift their loyalties to their own wives and children and eventually break off from the natal family. In this case it is the senior and beloved daughter-in-law who recognizes the folly of the family members' competition and tries to reconcile them; in the end, however, she is unable to overcome the deep schisms. Here, it is because of their wives that the sons themselves want to break up the family, but the erstwhile peacemaker comes from these wives. This film differs significantly from *Paṭikkaatavan* – and from most other films with a similar focus – in that it does not offer any hope for the maintenance or reunification of the joint family.

In fact, most of the urban families with whom I was familiar did not reside in common extended households, although other members of the husband's or wife's family might live nearby. Thus few poor urban residents have current concerns about their own extended family's physical dissolution. However, people *are* troubled by apparent changes in the responsibilities family members feel for one another. The elderly especially complain that adult children do not provide their parents with the support that they should – and once would have – and people sometimes complain that siblings to whom they have given help refuse to return the favor. These concerns may be echoed in certain movie characters' transgressions of the bounds of familial roles – such as JKB's extramarital alliance, Ramu's ridicule and rejection of the elder brother who had financed his education, and Kanmani's father's indifference to shooting his own daughter. Kanmani's intention to kill her father also violates the norms of the father–daughter relationship, but this is mitigated by the fact that her father has already shown disregard for her life and therefore does not act as a "father" (as well as by her prior renunciation of their relationship). In fact, because of this and others of his actions that do not qualify as proper human behavior, Kanmani's wish to kill this non-father becomes an understandable, even laudable, desire.

The concern over transgressions of familial responsibilities makes sense of the recurring and otherwise perplexing emphasis on the kindness of adoptive families that appears in Tamil movies. While it might be argued that the child who has been separated from its family and taken in by strangers is simply a narrative convention that supplies the impetus for any number of later melodramatic coincidences, the magnanimity with which the adoptive family frequently takes in the unknown child is nonetheless remarkable. The most striking case in these three movies is the Muslim father in *Paṭikkaatavan*, who rescues the young Raja and

Ramu from their captor, takes them into his household (notably raising them as Hindus), and is so kind and caring as to retrieve Raja's taxi from the pawn shop. The welcoming adoptive father contrasts directly with the sister-in-law who drove the boys out through neglect, just as, in *Amman Koovil Kizhakkaalee*, the man who took in Chinnamani is structurally opposed to the uncle (by marriage) who twice tries to kill his own nephew.[10]

Other issues related to the family appear in these movies. These include the relative importance of the natal versus the marital family for women and for men; adultery; and "love marriages."

Two of the movies described indicate some tension between the demands of families of birth and families of marriage. For women, for whom the tying of the thali almost always means relocation to the husband's household, the marital unit is expected to have primacy over the natal one. Women become a part of their husband's patriline after marriage. However, the relative importance is reversed for men, who retain membership in the patrilineage of their natal family. The wife's proper orientation is illustrated in *Amman Koovil Kizhakkaalee*, the husband's in *Paṭikkaatavan*. The primacy of a woman's relationship with her husband over her family of birth is expressed in several ways in *Amman Koovil Kizhakkaalee*. Kanmani renounces her father in front of the inspector when she allies herself with her husband. Later she even tries to kill her father (very unusual in a Tamil movie; here the action is mitigated by Kanmani's mother's revelation of Kanmani's father's character, and, as mentioned above, by the father's unfatherly behavior). Kanmani's mother was made to stay with her husband despite the resulting ruination of her brother. Valli saves her first words for her husband, rather than sharing them with her natal family, and Kanmani praises this act of giving the husband priority.[11]

For men, in contrast, the natal family retains its importance even after the creation of a new marital one. In *Paṭikkaatavan*, Raja displays the typical reluctance toward uxorilocal marriage, a less preferred marriage pattern. Raja's resistance is overcome by Ramu's insistence on the move, fueled by his desire for wealth and prestige; but eventually even Ramu, recognizing the advisibility of aligning himself with his natal family, chooses his brother over his in-laws (and, in so doing, morality over wealth).

One of these movies, *Sindhu Bairavi*, deals directly with adultery, a frequent real-life occurrence but one that is rarely broached at all, let alone as a central theme, in movies. Wiebe claims that "many of the tenement and hutment people of Madras have mistresses," and notes a social worker's observation that many regularly employed workers were unable to save money because "a major chunk of the earnings were used in maintaining mistresses or more than one family" (1981: 110). Husbands' adultery is so threatening to women – most of whom receive no wages for their labor or are paid very poorly, and who rarely have the education or training to take up a job with wages sufficient to support an entire family – that, unlike the other issues discussed here that relate to real-life anxieties, it may be (or filmmakers may expect it to be) a distressing subject for them to watch even when the crisis has a happy ending. But, as previous examples would lead us to expect, those films that do venture to tackle the subject avoid exacerbating women's fears. In the two other movies I saw dealing with adultery, it was the wife of the philandering husband who triumphed.

Likewise, in *Sindhu Bairavi* the wife "wins" in the end, with her husband returned and the mistress comfortingly removed from the scene; she even gains possession of the adulteress's child. Nonetheless, the general tone of *Sindhu Bairavi* does not condemn the "other woman." Sindhu is not depicted as an evil, immoral woman; rather, she is shown to be a likeable, even good person. Her own problems and her involvement with JKB are portrayed sympathetically and made understandable. And – a point in her favor – she succeeds at something that the wife fails to do (a lack that seriously lessens the wife's social worth): she bears a child. It is the mistress who transforms the wife, at least in appearance, into a *cumankali* (an "auspicious woman"). The affair *itself* is condemned, however, through the portrayal of its negative effects on the players' lives. It makes Bairavi miserable; Sindhu is put in the uncomfortable and scandalous position of the single mother; and most important, JKB's unfaithfulness leads to alcoholism and consequently to his ruin.

A final issue related to families has to do with "love marriages," the indigenous term for those that are not arranged by parents or other guardians. Most close relationships between unrelated men and women shown in Tamil movies are of this type – i.e. resulting from the woman's and the man's mutual attraction – and many result in marriage. Most of these marriages are depicted positively.

This appears to be radically different from the situation prevailing a decade or so ago, when, according to both Tamil and foreign informants who had seen earlier Tamil movies, films usually depicted love marriages as having harmful consequences. Indeed, a few films still portray love relationships in this way. In *Punnakai Mannan* ("Lord of Smiles," 1986, another K. Balachandar movie), the hero is involved in two such relationships that end tragically. (Both affairs also cut across class lines, and one across religious and ethnic affiliations; this kind of "mixing" is often characteristic of real-life love marriages, but not of arranged ones.) The lower class hero and his upper class girlfriend, thwarted by her parents' opposition to the poor man's background, make a suicide pact and jump off a cliff together. She dies but he survives. Later the hero falls in love with a wealthy Sinhalese woman, whose parents are also opposed but eventually relent and agree to the engagement. After the engagement party, hero and heroine drive off together, but their happiness is cut short by a bomb that explodes in their car (engineered by the first girlfriend's father) and kills them both.

Most present-day films portray love relationships more positively. Many films, especially some recent works of the popular director Bharatiraja, are optimistic in the hope they offer that such relationships can both succeed and be accepted by the community. In Bharatiraja's *Kaṭaḷoora Kavitaikaḷ* ("Poems of the Seashore," 1986), for example, a middle class Christian schoolteacher and a lower class, low caste Hindu man are drawn together, but both have already been promised to marry someone else of their own background. They are separated, but the young woman returns to the hero's bedside when she hears he is seriously injured, and they are reunited for good; their union is even condoned by the woman whom the hero should have married. Occasionally, the *prevention* of a love marriage will have tragic consequences. The modern heroine of *Puukkaḷai Parikkaatiirkaḷ* ("Don't Pick the Flowers," 1986) wishes to marry her school sweetheart but is prevented by her father, who arranges her marriage with a corrupt and wealthy older man; in the end, she kills herself to escape the arranged marriage, and the blame rests on her father.

In two of the present movies, *Amman Koovil Kizhakkaalee* and *Paṭikkaatavan*, love marriages are generally portrayed positively. (Sindhu's and JKB's affair in *Sindhu Bairavi*, although based on mutual attraction, would not fall into Madurai viewers' normal category of "love relationships" because it is adulterous.) In *Paṭikkaatavan*, Ramu's relationship with his wealthy wife's family does not work out (what happens to his marriage in the end is unclear), although the cause of this seems to be the young man's insistence on moving in with his wife's family. On the other hand, Raja's and Mary's friendship, which receives much greater attention in the film, seems to have a hopeful future despite the fact that she is a Christian and he a Hindu. In *Amman Koovil Kizhakkaalee*, the consequences of the love marriages vary. While Kanmani's mother's marriage has a tragic history, Kanmani's own non-arranged marriage is a triumph, and Valli's love marriage is represented as a good one.

My own observations of love relationships in older movies were contrary to what other viewers had told me. However, I saw relatively few films that were more than ten years old, and most of these were MGR movies in which the love element was a necessary but peripheral part of the plot. My conjecture is that there has indeed been a significant shift in the overall portrayal of love marriages in "social" or family films, in which the relationship's outcome forms a central theme. One possible explanation for this shift would be an increased tolerance for the idea of love marriages in Tamil society, but I saw no behavioral evidence to support this hypothesis. Virtually all marriages among the urban poor are still arranged, and there seems to have been little historical change in this. Instead, it seems more likely that viewers now feel a greater attraction to romance – an attraction that has been fanned by popular media such as short stories and films.

This is not to suggest that the idea of romance and its expressions are unusual among Tamils. Young people sometimes have crushes on members of the opposite sex known from school or family gatherings. They fantasize and tease each other about their future spouses, much as Roy has reported for upper class Bengalis (1975), and comment on the beauty of brides and grooms at weddings. Women sing romantic songs to girls about their future husbands. There seems to be a great, if often unfulfilled, desire for romance. Movies, which frequently idealize romance and always heighten the expression of the emotions that accompany it, have probably encouraged this desire. It appears that viewers have become more willing to watch fantasy relationships that are sparked by romance as opposed to relationships that merely grow into it.

How does the movies' emphasis on romance contribute to a reduction of anxiety? I suggest two ways. One is that, as viewers' desires for romantic involvement grow without any increased fulfillment of these desires in actual relationships, stories about lovers who overcome great social barriers to achieve their love suggest that surely love can be found among people of the same backgrounds who have no such barriers to cross. On the other hand, love relationships may also represent youth's rebellion against parental restraints, even rebellion against constraining social strictures or "society" itself. Arranging their children's marriages is one of the most important things that parents do for them; going against their parents' wishes with regard to marriage partners is one of the greatest transgressions children can commit. This conjectured link between romance and rebellion is supported by one of older people's most vehement criticisms of the cinema, i.e. that it "turns young people's heads" because it gives them ideas about romance and encourages rebellion against parental authority in general.[12]

Class identity and class relations

All three movies reflect concerns with an identity that derives from class and with relations between classes. Class identities emerge from comparisons between the "nature" of the rich and the poor, the relative sophistication of each, and the value of their different types of education. Issues of class relations emerge in the interaction of the poor and the rich, and receive briefer elaboration in these films than does class identity.

Film portrayals of the rich and the poor often emphasize differences in their appearance, behavior, and personal character. Lower class viewers are aware of these differences, and know that their own characteristics – as generally perceived by members of other classes – are frequently judged negatively by others. Sometimes they wish to change certain of these attributes, such as a style of speech or dress, in order to blend better individually with members of higher classes. Occasionally similar attempts are made to raise the standing of a group, such as a caste group, as a whole. However, there is also a strong sense of pride in lower class "culture" among the poor of Madurai. Patricia Caplan has noted a similar feeling among Madras slum dwellers who, when confronted by upper class volunteer social workers, "would often tell them to go away and mind their own business, or else would ask them how they came to be handing out advice when they could know nothing of the sort of problems faced in the slums" (1985: 211). Varadachar has also observed that most of the slum residents he worked with "do not view themselves as text books and outsiders describe them. They see themselves as poor but not disorganized; illiterate but not unwise or unintelligent; and clean, moral and god-fearing, despite the odds they perceive against themselves" (1979: 135).

This identity is a central theme in *Paṭikkaatavan*, and the characterization that emerges is one of the ultimate worthiness of the poor and uneducated. We see the inner greatness of the downtrodden, and their ultimate victory over oppressive circumstances and the rich. Rajashekar tells Raja, "You are a king," "You are a great wise man." The illiterate and unsophisticated Raja is also honest, righteous, and devoted to his younger brother. But he is spurned for his lack of education, insulted as a "common taxi driver"; in the most telling scene, he states, "Those who have nothing receive no respect no matter where they go." He is disdained and rejected by those with money and education, including his own younger brother Ramu, whom Raja has educated at his own expense. Later, he hopes to use Ramu's education as a means of reuniting the three brothers; but Ramu fails his exams and rejects the sacred gift of education. Raja's commonness forcibly separates him from both his brothers. Driven to despair, he says "everything is play-acting" – all is an illusion (as was the college play that he had taken too seriously, in which his brother was a king). Eventually, however, his inherent honesty wins out over the evil and deceit of the rich and educated, and reunites the brothers.

Raja is a heroic representative of the lower class. Not every underprivileged individual in this movie meets the behavioral ideals he portrays, but this does not lessen the impact of his character; Raja stands as the *epitome* of the subordinate class, the idealized representative of all members. He is honest, hardworking, devoted; a crusader against crime; a converter of strayed fellows; a poor man pitted against the big men who wins against all odds. He unveils the dishonesty of the wealthy. As MGR once did, Raja articulates the hopes and frustrations that most of the audience feel about themselves and the rest of society.

In *Amman Koovil Kizhakkaalee*, the comparison of the self-serving attitude of the rich with the righteousness of the poor is represented in the film's structural oppositions between hero and heroine and between the hero and the heroine's father. Kanmani, the arrogant, spoiled rich woman, is cut down to size by the upright young man whom she has scorned because of his poverty and lack of sophistication – and because of his refusal to worship the rich. After Chinnamani has in turn humiliated her, he says, "I did this [married you] to squash your pride," and still does not consider her worthy of him. The integrity of the poor comes out even more strikingly in the contrast with the heroine's father, who has unfairly deprived Chinnamani of his inheritance, and twice tries to kill him.[13]

Kanmani's evil industrialist father also stands in contrast to the honest labor union leader who refuses a bribe. The moral character of the laborer is also highlighted in *Paṭikkaatavan*, in which Raja exhorts Mary, the former smuggler, to atone for her sins by becoming a laborer. In so doing he makes a favorable comparison between the honor of the worker and the honor even of chastity.

These films also express a more explicit concern with the actual relations among members of different classes, a concern revealed particularly in the interactions of rich and poor. Raja is ridiculed for his hilarious appearance among the sophisticated playgoers in *Paṭikkaatavan*. Chinnamani, who refuses to pay special respects to the rich, is derided by Kanmani for his lack of money and education. These attitudes mirror an occasional concern by the poor that higher classes will disdain them as uncouth or ignorant. As I have mentioned, however, many poor people also feel strongly that their own customs of speech, appearance, and behavior have inherent value, and sometimes scorn those patronizing members of the upper class who try to train the poor in the "superior" ways of the rich.

One of the major differences between the lower and upper classes believed by both rich and poor to affect behavior, values, and even appearance is level of education. Poor parents see formal education as the best chance for improving their children's future; few, however, can afford to provide it. A concern with differences in types and levels of education appears in both *Amman Koovil Kizhakkaalee* and *Sindhu Bairavi*. In the former, this is first voiced when Kanmani attempts her early rapprochement with Chinnamani, saying, "Your education [i.e. music] is the best education; it is there naturally." It appears again when the singer and his family arrive at Kanmani's house to ask for her hand and are laughed off because of the absurdity of a marriage between a poor uneducated man and a rich educated woman.

Similarly, *Sindhu Bairavi* implies that the education and knowledge of the poor, gained outside of schools, is superior to that of the rich. Once again, the point is made by emphasizing the value of musical knowledge over formal education. Sindhu sings, "I am uneducated, a simple person; music is everything." A distinction is maintained between those who "have music in their blood" – JKB, Gurumurthy, Sindhu – and those who do not, including the disrespectful audience, Bairavi, and the she-devil and her companion.

The formal education that so many parents desire for their children is very difficult to obtain. Few films show poor people improving their status through long, arduous years of schooling. Instead, they remove this troubling source and feature of class differences by demonstrating that the poor are by nature superior to the rich, and that a "natural" education (i.e. non-academic and possibly non-formal) is equal – or superior – to a formal academic one.

The working of plots toward the victories of heroes and heroines also serves a wider sense of justice, a theme that runs through many movies. The revenge of Chinnamani on Kanmani's father in *Amman Koovil Kizhakkaalee*; Bairavi's acquisition of the baby and Sindhu's subsequent departure in *Sindhu Bairavi*; and the vindication of Raja against sister-in-law, younger brother, and accusing smuggler all provide a sense of justice, of due victory for those who have been wronged. In Rajashekar's prediction to Raja that "if there is a God, you will go free," we also have a hint that this justice may be divinely inspired, or at least divinely sanctioned: God is on the side of the poor, and so Raja is proven innocent.

Imposed themes and avoided concerns: directors vs. viewers
The themes discussed above address some of the basic psychological concerns in viewers' lives. They make up the majority of the underlying issues portrayed in film content. In addition to these, there are also a few recurring themes in Tamil cinema that do not appear to be of crucial interest to viewers; rather, they are "imposed" by filmmakers for various reasons. This category includes primarily the depiction of the consumption of drugs and alcohol and the portrayal of religious minorities. Moreover, there are also issues important to poor, urban Tamils that do not receive representation in the movies; primary among these "avoided" concerns are caste and inter-caste relations.

By far the most frequent occurrence of an imposed theme or issue is the standard portrayal of drugs and alcohol and the consequences of their consumption.[14] Indian films have emphasized the negative aspects of drinking since before Independence. (The censor code forbids showing the consumption of alcohol or drugs in a positive light; see Appendix.) The depiction of drinking in *Sindhu Bairavi* reflects this traditional stance. Anyone shown drinking liquor in a film is automatically presumed to be a disreputable character (witness JKB's whiskey-drinking acquaintance and the "she-devil," whose loose morality stands in direct contrast with the high ideals and purity of JKB) or, like JKB, on the path to ruin. Alcohol is shown to have disastrous consequences. In *Sindhu Bairavi*, it ruins JKB and kills his grandfather. In *Paṭikkaatavan*, everyone involved with drugs comes to a bad end – the opium-dealing stepbrother, Johnny, Chakravarthy – as do some of the innocent people close to them, including the lorry driver, Raja's stepfather, and Venkatachalan. The only exception is Mary, the distiller who repents.

Movies like these contradict critics' claims that present-day films, unlike older ones, glorify drugs and alcohol. In depicting the supposed perils of alcohol, however, there lies the slightly different danger of glorifying and encouraging it through sensationalization – and the opportunity to spice up films with illicit events included under the guise of condemnation. While this does not occur in any of the three main films discussed in this chapter, it is not unusual. In *Avantaan Manitan* ("*He* is a Man," a film made in the 1970s with Shivaji Ganesan and Jayalalitha), for example, an upstanding man is persuaded to take his first drink at a celebration for his company's recent success. Soon he is drunken and wild. His young daughter runs up to him, but he pushes her away; she hits her head on a pillar and dies. This sort of moralizing is typical of "party" scenes. However, in the course of establishing this moral, the filmmakers have also included scenes of a cabaret dancer and orgiastic crowds – elements decried by some critics but justified by filmmakers as essential to establishing the dangers inherent in such excess.[15]

In considering themes that seem to have greater import for films' creators than for their viewers, it is also interesting to note the images of religious minorities in films. Most characters in Tamil movies either are portrayed as Hindus (caste unclear), or their religion is not made evident. When characters are clearly Muslims or Christians (marked by clothing, religious accoutrements, and/or names), they are shown either as minor villains or as strongly positive characters. Johnny of *Paṭikkaatavan* is an example of a minor villain, a stock character that may be portrayed as Hindu, Muslim or Christian. I was told by viewers and filmmakers that no community objects to such portrayals. I know of no *sustained* negative portrayal of a religious minority, however.[16] Thus, all the more striking are the notably good-hearted characters, since these are not stock figures and have much larger roles to play in the films. Examples, again from *Paṭikkaatavan*, include the ultimately virtuous Mary, who never wore a cross until she started an honest job, and Raja's adoptive Muslim father, who next to the lawyer Rajashekar is the most thoroughly kind-hearted character in the film.[17] Nothing integral to the storyline demands that these characters' community be marked, making filmmakers' choice to portray these positive figures as members of a particular community notable.

While viewers may mention alcohol abuse or the communal affiliation of kindly characters when reciting a movie story (note that they never mentioned the community of a gangster or villain), they do not focus on them as they do other themes (see chapter 8). Themes such as the evils of alcohol and the good-heartedness of minorities are generally of greater concern to filmmakers than to the audience. Overall, their presence seems to indicate an inserted didactic lesson, especially in the case of prohibitionist themes, rather than act as a mode of psychological resolution. The lesson is not necessarily one that producers and directors themselves believe, but one that they think they should teach – both because they will be criticized by the (middle and upper class) public if they do not, and because they think that the poor *should* believe it. In the case of the portrayal of non-Hindus, there is also the pragmatic concern that any characterization that offended a community would create strong and even violent protests by members of that community[18] (while the occasional insertion of a good Muslim character, for example, might boost the attendance of Muslim viewers, although viewers never mentioned this as a motivation for choosing a film).

It should be noted that religious communal tolerance and the evils of alcohol are basic Gandhian themes. While Gandhi remains a popular and even heroic figure for many people at all levels of Tamil society, I heard his name and tenets cited much more frequently by members of the middle and upper classes – from whom the majority of Gandhi's active followers, including the Congress party freedom fighters, were originally drawn – than by the poor. Overall, the middle and upper classes identify with Gandhian values (and/or espouse the rhetoric) more than do other Tamils, and may see these principles as proper lessons for the poor.

Finally, an example of an issue that is of great concern to viewers but ignored by filmmakers is that of caste, specifically inter-caste relations. Dialect, occupation or dress may give clues to a character's caste in a Tamil movie, and a few caricatured or stereotyped figures, such as Brahman priests, may even be clearly identifiable. Generally, however, since a character's caste affiliation is almost never mentioned or implied, the interaction of characters cannot serve as commentary on caste relations. One of the rare mentions of caste occurs in *Sindhu Bairavi*, in which Sindhu tells JKB that she is of a high caste. The significance of this was unclear to me and to other viewers; it may simply have been to point out to JKB that she does not come from a socially and morally disdained *devadasi* background. It may also make her union with JKB (who, we can gather, is also of high caste) somewhat less of an aberration than if she had been of low caste.

I have seen only two films that deal explicitly with caste. One is *Mutal Mariyaatai* ("Honor of the First Order," 1985), the other *Veetam Putitu* ("A New Veda," 1987). Both were directed by Bharatiraja, but the treatment caste receives in each is quite distinct, and the difference in viewers' reactions to the two films is instructive.

Mutal Mariyaatai won India's National Award for Best Film in 1986. The movie depicts the growing affection between a middle-aged high caste man and a young scheduled caste woman. Their relationship never becomes a physical union, but their mutual fondness is presented much more favorably than the relationship between the man and his uncaring wife. In order to provide something of the flavor of this unusual film, I recount it here in some detail.

Malaicami, the main landowner in his village, is married to a vulgar and mean-spirited woman who constantly criticizes her uncomplaining husband. Malaicami is loved by the villagers, unlike his wife, who even demands that the laborers return grain that Malaicami has given them as a gift from surplus stock. One day an old fisherman and his daughter come to live in the village, and Malaicami allows them to live on his land. A friendship grows between Kuyil, the spunky daughter, and the landowner. Kuyil is attracted to him, but hides this, and tries to make Malaicami happy by cooking for him. Once she dares him to lift a boulder in front of her hut, joking that she will marry him if he succeeds. Malaicami occasionally tries to raise the stone when he passes by, and one day he manages it. Although he says nothing about his feat, Kuyil witnesses it, and from that moment her heart settles on him alone.

Malaicami's nephew is in love with a shoemaker's daughter, a scheduled caste girl. They meet secretly, and one day try to elope with Kuyil's help. Malaicami learns of their attempted escape and apprehends them at the river, but Kuyil pacifies him and persuades him to allow the couple to marry. The two young lovers live idyllically for a short time, but one day someone murders the girl by drowning her in the river. Shortly thereafter, the haunted boy follows her into the water and drowns himself.

Now Ponnatta, Malaicami's wife, becomes irritated by her husband's friendly relationship with Kuyil, and spreads rumors about the two of them. The stingy woman even holds a feast for the villagers in order to wheedle them into accusing her husband of an affair at the next village council meeting. Malaicami appears unexpectedly at the feast and, finally losing his temper, denies Ponnatta's long-reiterated claims that he had married her for money, revealing that in fact he had married her out of mercy when her father had begged him to save the family honor by taking the woman, who was pregnant by another man. Malaicami has kept this secret for twenty years.

The village council accuses Malaicami of having an affair with Kuyil. Angry at the injustice, he refuses to deny it. When he visits Kuyil, she admits her feelings for him, but he rejects them. Kuyil decides to leave the village, but on her way she meets a man who thinks she is the river ferry woman and demands a ride in her boat back to the village. During the ride he boasts that he has just been released from prison and is returning to claim Ponnatta, the woman he had made pregnant twenty years ago. Kuyil, horrified, kills the man in order to protect Malaicami's family from disgrace.

Meanwhile, Malaicami has finally realized his true feelings for Kuyil, and goes in search of her. He finds her at the river bank, facing the police. She does not say why she killed the man, but Malaicami visits her in prison and begs her to explain. She confesses the reason to him on the condition that he not try to win her release from prison. He agrees to the condition, but, greatly saddened by the sacrifice she reveals, promises that he will wait for her to return.

Years later, Malaicami is dying, waiting for Kuyil on a cot in her hut. His wife has finally been persuaded to go to the hut, where she continues to rant against him, but he does not acknowledge her. Kuyil, who has been granted a temporary release from prison in order to return for his death, finally arrives at her old hut. Malaicami opens his eyes and smiles and, holding her hand, dies. Shortly thereafter, as she sits in a train compartment on her way back to prison, Kuyil too quietly dies.

I watched this film in unusual circumstances, on a day when I rented a VCR and played three videos in my home. A number of people watched them with me. This was the only time I had done this, and I found that it allowed people to discuss the films among themselves as they watched in a way that was difficult in the cinema hall. Yet even in this situation, which encouraged spontaneous comments, few statements were made that implied any direct judgment of the inter-caste relationships in *Mutal Mariyaatai*. (While it might be argued that this type of inter-caste union would be unremarkable since men of dominant landowning castes frequently exploit scheduled caste women in real life – something even urban viewers should be aware of – in fact the tenderness of this film relationship makes it all the more notable in such a context, marking it as love rather than rape.) The castes of the participants were, however, noted frequently by my companions, especially at the beginning of the film. They pointed out to me and to each other that Malaicami was "high caste" and the shoemaker's daughter and Kuyil were "Harijans." They were pleased in the end when Malaicami's and Kuyil's feelings for each other were finally acknowledged, and it seemed right to them that a man whose wife abused him should find (without actively searching it out) a more appreciative and fulfilling relationship. Others who talked about this movie at other times emphasized the idea that true love and friendship could (and, some said, should) occur across all barriers. However, despite the pointed interest in the film characters' castes and the comments about love and friendship, it is notable that no one made the explicit statement to me at any time (nor to each other during the film) that Malaicami's and Kuyil's relationship had anything positive or negative to do with love between people of different *castes*.

This suggests a point I have already noted, that while there is a great deal of awareness of caste and caste identity in Madurai, nonetheless its expression is consciously muted and submerged. Viewers were fully aware that the relationship in *Mutal Mariyaatai* breached traditional social proscriptions, but did not wish to state so explicitly nor to appear to judge the relationship in that light. It is also worth noting that even this film does not approach the issue of caste in terms of the relations of caste groups, but rather through the melodramatic portrayal of love between two individuals of different castes – i.e. in the personal rather than collective terms typical of melodrama. Moreover, the film does not imply that inter-caste love relationships will work out in the real world, since both of those it depicts end tragically. Rather, in its emotional portrayal of these two couples and their love, it suggests that such relationships *should* be able to succeed in a proper world.

In *Veetam Putitu*, which appeared three years after *Mutal Mariyaatai*, Bharatiraja criticizes both caste distinctions and caste relations directly. The film centers on two families, one Thevar and one Brahman. Caste is criticized in numerous ways: through voiceover narration by the director, through dialogues about caste stereotypes and in the wise voices of the Brahman and Thevar fathers and the young Brahman son, and through the consequences of acts that resist transgressions of caste boundaries. Following is a very brief account of the points most significant to this analysis:

The Thevar son and Brahman daughter fall in love. The Brahman father, an open-minded shastri (priest), tries to prevent their union by arranging his daughter's marriage, but she escapes and stages a false suicide. The man she loves and her father, both thinking her dead, quarrel and then fall off a cliff to their deaths. Her young brother, now without family (his mother had died years ago), is rejected by the village Brahmans because of death pollution restrictions, but is taken in by Balu Thevar, the father of the young man who had loved the Brahman woman. Balu Thevar is the dominant landowner of the village, generous to his fellow villagers and an adamant atheist. He has argued eloquently against caste distinctions and discrimination. Shankara, the boy, makes him realize that he too follows caste rules, in his use of both the Thevar name and the weapons traditional to this caste. Balu throws his weapons into the river and rids himself of his caste name. He adopts Shankara, and allows him to practice Brahman rituals in his home. Vaideki, Shankara's sister, returns to find both her beloved and her father dead, and Balu decides to adopt her as well. But the villagers, thinking her a ghost, are frightened by her reappearance, and angry that a Thevar should adopt Brahman children. They storm Balu's house. No longer a martial Thevar, Balu does not resist, and is killed. Shankara, calling Balu "Father," flings away his holy beads, removes his sacred thread, and as Balu's son he lights the funeral pyre.

This film, which also eventually received a National Award, evoked a far different public response than *Mutal Mariyaatai*. Despite its direct approach to caste conflict, it first passed the censor board without any cuts. Before it could be released, however, Brahman individuals and organizations raised loud protests to both state and national officials, based on what they had heard about the film's insults to Brahman orthodoxy. There was quite an uproar, much of it carried on in the press. Censor officers insisted on reviewing the film again and the release was stalled and debated for some time, but eventually, according to Bharatiraja, only one small cut was made and the film finally released. Brahman community members were reportedly mollified when they saw the film, but the Thevar Association summoned Bharatiraja (himself a Thevar) to complain about Balu's renunciation of caste and denial of caste distinctions (Bharatiraja, interview June 1990). It is significant that, so far as I am aware, no protest was voiced about the union between a high caste woman and a lower caste man – a pattern far more subversive than the hypergamous relationship in *Mutal Mariyaatai* – although it is certain that this element offended many critics. In today's sensitive environment, concerns about caste traditions and identity can be publicized more easily (since they imply no threat to other castes) than can those about inter-caste unions, especially where the latter would reveal differential valuations of castes. The controversy over *Veetam Putitu* demonstrates that although some concerns can be raised more properly than others, caste remains not only a significant topic for viewers but a potentially explosive one.

Bharatiraja frequently deals with the topic of love crossing social boundaries. His emphasis on this is unusual, however, and the general exclusion of caste concerns from the great majority of films exemplifies the control filmmakers can exert in deciding which needs and concerns of viewers are to be considered legitimate. Normally should anyone happen to make a film involving love between individuals of different communities, "word will go round the power centres of the film industry to make sure that it is not effectively released" (Das Gupta 1991: 128). It is striking that communal harmony among castes, and equal valuation of all castes and their occupations, is also a principal theme of Gandhian philosophy. Unlike Gandhi's calls for prohibition and religious tolerance, however, this tenet is one that filmmakers have chosen to follow – if indeed they have done so at all – by ignoring caste. In this case, as Bharatiraja's experience with *Veetam Putitu* shows, filmmakers have little to gain by emphasizing characters' castes, and potentially much to lose should the members of any caste take offense at a film's portrayal of someone identified with their community. It would also be difficult to include frequent identification of characters' castes without touching on existing tensions *between* different communities, which would very likely provoke protests against the film by censors and viewers, and possibly further conflicts between the castes involved – an excessively expensive risk for filmmakers.

A taste of utopia

We have seen that Tamil movies mix elements of fantasy and reality in their sets, plots, and themes. Thematically, they combine representations of familiarly realistic individual and social problems with fantastical resolutions of those problems. Elements of fantasy are also often found in the ways in which familiar problems are portrayed, in that the contexts in which movie crises arise are rarely identical to the actual physical or behavioral environments of poor Tamils' lives.

Dyer suggests that popular entertainment offers its consumers a vision of utopia,

> the image of "something better" to escape into, or something we want deeply that our day-to-day lives don't provide. Alternatives, hopes, wishes – these are the stuff of utopia, the sense that things could be better, that something other than what is can be imagined and maybe realised. (1985: 222)

In order to do this, Dyer maintains, entertainment provides not *models* of utopia but a sense of how utopia would *feel*.

Tamil cinema corroborates this suggestion. It provides viewers with a sense of utopia in two ways: first, through a portrayal of luxury that far exceeds the circumstances of most Tamils' lives; and second, through resolutions of many of viewers' most persistent and deep-seated anxieties, some of which are brought about by the hard physical circumstances of their lives that contrast so thoroughly with movies' spectacular abundance. While on the surface these two routes to utopia may appear distinct, one relying as it does on setting and the other on resolution, it quickly becomes evident that they cannot be split so clearly. Instead, the momentary vision of abundance is a *part* of the message. Films, that is, do not simply provide their audiences with a momentary experience of luxury and ease: they also suggest that wealth and the comforts it buys are within reach. As Enzensberger has put it, "consumption as spectacle contains the promise that want will disappear ... [it] is – in parody form – the anticipation of a utopian situation" (1982: 61). Movies are not just a three-hour relief from poverty; they also feed hopes that a spectacularly easier life is attainable.

While this would suggest that films encourage people to desire or hope for different lives, albeit without offering the means of active change, the deeper mechanisms of the films – the workings of their story themes, which both incorporate and are embedded in spectacular surroundings – act to avoid such encouragement. Most themes, as we have seen, allay anxieties and promote a sense that life, free from many of its conflicts and difficulties, is already "utopian." In order to clarify the mechanisms by which problems stemming from daily life are resolved in Tamil movies, I will review this process in the three films that have been used as examples.

One of the most frequent themes of Tamil cinema is played out in *Sindhu Bairavi*, in which two women sacrifice their own desires for those of a man. This theme often revolves around a woman's attempts to transform her husband's misbehavior (such as drunkenness or neglect of his family) and win his love and attention. Here the tension between the woman's sacrifices and desires and the behavior of her husband is resolved when the husband returns to be fully hers – thanks, in this case, to the sacrifices of *another* woman who subjugates her own desires to the good of the man she loves.

The ideal woman portrayed by Bairavi and Sindhu is an image involved in the resolution of another theme: the transition of a self-centered, arrogant woman into a properly demure Tamil wife. This theme addresses viewers' concerns about the perceived enhancement of women's power relative to that of men, and about issues of female sexuality. In *Amman Koovil Kizhakkaalee*, Kanmani represents the (potential or actual) women that men encounter as a threat to male social and sexual dominance. Here this threat – realized most fully in the whipping, a vicious act of female dominance – is countered by a violent act of male supremacy that is a central cultural symbol of binding women's wild and disruptive power and sexuality: the tying of the thali. In her untamed form, Kanmani may be physically desirable but her behavior is frighteningly unfamiliar to most men. The tying of the thali, and the revelations it sets off, convert her almost instantaneously into the reassuring form of demure Tamil womanhood.

Women may also be objects of anxious concern to both men and other women when they marry into a family. In *Paṭikkaatavan*, this fear is realized in the form of the wife/sister-in-law who instigates the break-up of three happy brothers and then attempts to prevent their reunion. Her power is neutralized by the brothers' efforts and by the forces of justice that reunite them despite her. At the end of the film the ideal situation has been achieved when the disruptive woman, now put in her proper place, apologizes for the suffering she has caused, and the dominant fraternal bonds are reasserted. Such themes offer the hope that other family bonds, which Tamils perceive to be loosening, will regain their preeminence over extrafamilial concerns and cause family members to accept the responsibilities that they should bear.

Other concerns about the family are also salved by movies. *Amman Koovil Kizhakkaalee* reinforces the ideal that a husband will have preeminence in his wife's eyes over the family she has grown up with. In *Paṭikkaatavan*, fears that a young man will transfer his feelings and responsibilities from his natal family to his marital household are assuaged when Ramu's alliance with his wife's household proves disastrous and he returns to his brothers. Concerns about family break-up stemming from another cause, that of a husband's adultery, are relieved in *Sindhu Bairavi* through the termination of Sindhu's and JKB's affair, which leaves the husband and wife together and the mistress removed by self-banishment.

Another issue that links concerns for the family with worries about male–female relationships is the emphasis on love marriages. Unlike most earlier movies, current films usually present positive outcomes for these non-arranged relationships. Examples of couples depicted favorably include Chinnamani and Kanmani, and Chinnamani's sister and the labor union leader in *Amman Koovil Kizhakkaalee*, and Raja and Mary in *Paṭikkaatavan*, as well as countless similar relationships appearing in almost every other current Tamil movie. I have noted that the positive depiction of "love marriages" may reduce anxiety in two ways: first, it supports the hopes many viewers hold for increased romance in their own lives; and second, for younger viewers it may represent the fulfillment of their rebellion against parental restraints, and possibly of more general rebellion against confining social constraints.

Themes portraying issues related to class tend to resolve concerns about discrepancies between rich and poor. They demonstrate the superiority of the inner greatness that characterizes the poor over the "surface" advantages attained through the money of the rich. Thus, *Paṭikkaatavan* implies the ultimate "worthiness" of the poor and uneducated through its portrayal of Raja – the honest, hardworking, devoted, and finally victorious epitome of the lower class. His righteous nature is contrasted with the greed, arrogance, and deceit of the rich. *Amman Koovil Kizhakkaalee* also opposes the self-serving attitudes of the wealthy (Kanmani and her father) with the goodness and righteousness of the poor (Chinnamani and his family). It draws these contrasts between Kanmani and Chinnamani, Chinnamani and Kanmani's father, and Kanmani's father and the labor union leader. Like *Sindhu Bairavi*, *Amman Koovil Kizhakkaalee* also suggests that the "natural" and often non-formal education of the disadvantaged should be compared favorably to the formal academic learning of the wealthy.

Occasionally films also deal specifically with the relations between classes. In *Amman Koovil Kizhakkaalee*, Chinnamani refuses to give Kanmani the respect she thinks due to her standing as a wealthy person. He frequently humiliates her because of her class-based arrogance; she and her father punish him severely for his audacity. In *Paṭikkaatavan*, Raja attempts to imitate the external appearance of a wealthy man, and is ridiculed by sophisticated onlookers. He is rejected and humiliated by his sister-in-law and younger brother for his lack of money and sophistication. Chinnamani and Raja, however, both triumph against the degradations heaped on them by the rich.

The lesson in all these representations of class relations and identity is that despite the apparent advantages of the wealthy, it is the poor who possess true goodness of character. Moreover, wealth may not even be desirable, since its holders are typically short on moral qualities; at the least, the characterological goodness of the poor compensates for their lack of luxury and social graces, making them the "better people." Finally, these films show that the poor *will* eventually receive justice (whatever the viewer may construe this to be) because of their truly good nature.

By offering a view of society in which viewers' hopes are fulfilled and their problems dissolved, most Tamil films suggest either that life will become better without active struggle on the part of the downtrodden, or that the virtues of a life of poverty outweigh its disadvantages. Husbands will reform and children will honor their parents, and riches may appear but are superfluous at any rate because the poor already possess a true wealth of spirit. In the themes of these films, utopia either will arrive on its own or has already been achieved.

Films provide relief from viewers' immediate and long-term worries in several ways. At the very least, a three-hour movie provides physical and emotional separation from the quotidian context of those worries. I have suggested, however, that the relief gained in the cinema hall also persists outside of it, carried into the everyday world. Tamil movies almost always have happy endings. After the villains have been killed or converted, hero and heroine joined in love, and wayward family members reunited in a palatial setting, viewers may leave feeling supported in their hopes for an easier life. Films offer hope that wealth will appear and problems disappear – though there is not *necessarily* a causal link between the two – all without active effort on the viewer's part. Most of all, however, the melodramatic portrayal and resolution of crises in Tamil films allays some of the audience's deepest anxieties – about relationships between men and women or among family members and about the problems of lower class identity – making life at least temporarily less stressful. This process of resolution also suggests that, since these problems are not truly problems after all and the poor have the best of life, life is already good. Both visions, of abundance to come and of present satisfaction, are utopian.

Because the first formulation suggests that the riches the poor desire will shower down while the other urges an inversion of normal status hierarchies to suggest that the poor are better than the rich and thus that wealth is superfluous, these two utopian visions conflict. This paradox is rarely if ever addressed in films, however, which offer both messages within the same text. The implicit assumption appears to be that the greater the number of sources of comfort the better.

Lest it seem that all Tamil movies paint a monolithically rosy picture, however, we should note that films that could be categorized as "progressive" occasionally appear as well, and can be successful. These include two films mentioned in this chapter, *Camsaaram Atu Minsaaram* ("A Wife is Electricity") and *Punnakai Mannan* ("Lord of Smiles"). In the first, a joint family splits up and, although its former members become reconciled, they fail to reestablish a joint household as would happen in a more typical Tamil film. In the second movie, the love relationship established in the course of the film ends in the death of the couple.

Such endings are rare today, however. The decision to give a story a happy or tragic ending rests with the filmmaker, who (as will become evident in the next chapter) is rarely motivated to suggest that viewers' lives are unsatisfactory or lack hope. Yet it should be noted in addition that in doing so filmmakers accommodate viewers' desires. Viewers themselves often reject tragic films, or others whose endings leave them feeling vaguely dissatisfied; they also say that they do not like to watch movies in which problems are shown "realistically," and criticize these films as uninteresting.

Filmmakers are aware of this, and portray crises in settings that are exotically removed from most viewers' daily lives. Thus an independent young woman is more powerful than her suitor because she is much richer; a woman's husband rejects her and takes a mistress who is a beautiful Carnatic singer; a young man is poor because in childhood he ran away from his cruel sister-in-law, and is ridiculed by the younger brother for whom he has nonetheless provided a college education. Each of these difficulties has its frequent correlates in poor urban residents' lives, but virtually never in the glamorized or melodramatic form found in films. Greater realism than this is rejected by most viewers, for whom fantasy is preferred not only at the level of resolution but also in the portrayal of problems in order for the film to work as an escape from those problems. As we will see in a later chapter, escape is the primary conscious motivation for viewers' attendance at the movies.

While most frequent movie themes address issues about which poor Tamils feel anxiety, a few others deal instead with issues of less immediate concern to viewers, while yet other issues of great concern are ignored altogether. Directors' imposed themes, including the negative consequences of drugs and alcohol, and the goodness of religious minorities, act as moralizing lessons to the audience rather than providing psychological resolution. Opposed to these are viewers' themes, such as caste relations, which though of sustained concern in the daily lives of the audience are pointedly avoided by filmmakers.

In including lessons that they think viewers should learn, filmmakers assert their positions as wise patrons fit to teach the unenlightened poor. By excluding such issues as caste from their films, they give weight to Dyer's thesis that while commercial filmmakers must respond to some of the entertainment needs and desires of their audiences, they also exercise power in determining which of those desires are to be considered legitimate. As will become clear in chapter 7, however, the act of bestowing such "legitimacy" on the desires and values of the lower class does not necessarily make them morally "acceptable" in the eyes of the filmmakers who portray and fulfill them.

PART III

7
Filmmakers

The attitudes of a medium's creators toward their creation and their audience are significant for understanding the medium, especially when the creators differ from the main audience in class, gender, or some other fundamental feature. Their values and attitudes shape the content the audience receives, as well as the attitudes with which the audience itself apprehends the material. Exactly who constitutes the "creators" is a complicated matter in the case of commercial film, as it is with many media, because making such a movie is never an individual act. Filmmaking requires numerous technical and often creative assistants. To be successful, it also demands that attention be paid to audience preferences, and thus to some extent involves the audience in the creative process – a point that many filmmakers are reluctant to admit. Nonetheless, it is possible to isolate those who are most directly responsible for the creation of a film. In Tamil Nadu these are the directors, who generally have the strongest hand in determining a film's specific shape. The producers, those who put together the precious financing, may also wield considerable influence. For this reason – and because many producers have worked as directors, and many of the major directors also act as producers – I bracket both directors and producers together under the title of "filmmaker."

The Madras movie industry
Madras has the highest production rate of any film center in India, thanks to its status as home to the Tamil and Telugu and, to a lesser extent, Malayalam and Kannada film industries. (Even without the multiplicity of industries, it would outstrip Bombay; in 1980, more Tamil, Telugu, and Malayalam films were produced than Hindi films – 140, 133, 127, and 114,

respectively [Armes 1987: 120, 121].) Moviemaking in Madras is nonetheless an uncertain business.[1] Finance is difficult to come by, except for the most well-known directors, and can be withdrawn at any moment;[2] actors and actresses work on several movies simultaneously whenever possible, making their schedules unreliable; films once completed may face difficulty with the censor; and even after passing and receiving a "U" (unrestricted) certificate, they may never be released for lack of a distributor. Finally, after passing all these hurdles, most movies do not turn a profit.[3]

Making a movie involves coordinating the work of a large number of people. The director bears most of the responsibility, although the producer, as the person pulling the financial strings, often has final say. In addition to technicians, the major personnel include the writer (who frequently is also the director), musical director, lyricist, choreographer, dance director, fight scene arranger, special effects director, dubbing director, dance team, stunt crew, playback singers, comedians, and actresses and actors. In India, many film artists attempt to make up for a short career by working in several movies at once. Actors and actresses are particularly notorious for this, and commit themselves to films months ahead of time – with the frequent result that a delay in shooting any one film delays the others they are involved in. This can be especially costly for directors who do not work for a major studio and must rent their own equipment.

The first step in making a movie is generally to present a story to a potential producer. Many stories are adaptations or direct copies of previous successful movies. Sometimes, and with growing frequency, movies are simply dubbed from one language to another.[4] Uncertainty about a film's success often causes filmmakers to reach for the "proven element" of a favorite story or acting team. Once the main actors have been chosen and schedules aligned, shooting of at least parts of the film can begin. Most scenes are shot in the studio, but directors try to include at least a few "exotic" location scenes, often filmed for the songs or dances. These are frequently shot in a Tamil Nadu hill resort such as Ooty or Kodaikanal or at a beach resort such as Mahabalipuram. Location shots may also go further afield to Kerala or as far away as the Himalayas.

The music is recorded around the music director's and recording studio's schedules. Music and lyrics can be written, song and dance scenes filmed, and playback singers' songs recorded, before the story is written or even begun. Most movies have at least five or six songs (which actors and actresses sing through their playback voices, as they cavort in fantastic settings), a few dances, and three or four fights.

After all the spoken scenes have been shot, voices are dubbed in the studio. Spoken parts used to be recorded on the acting sets with boom mikes, but this is no longer done. Stars' voices are often dubbed by other actors – completing the frequent phenomenon of the particulate actor, whose body, speaking, and singing voices are all contributed by different individuals. Dubbing is a time-consuming and expensive operation, and once again must be scheduled around the actors' and studio's availability, but it does have some advantages: it frees stars to spend their time more profitably (and to be replaced at lower cost to the director); it also allows filmmakers, as one director noted sardonically, to "choose a beautiful star who can't speak rather than going to the work of finding an actress who can modulate properly."[5] Scenes are usually dubbed with actors individually rather than in groups, in fifteen-second loops of tape, and each loop requires several takes and usually a total of several minutes to dub. The director is present, and a take is not accepted until he or she approves it for dramatic qualities and the dubbing director approves it for lip synchronization.

Once a film is completed it must be submitted to the Central Board of Film Certification to obtain a censor certificate. The film may be passed as is, passed on condition of certain cuts or other changes, or denied a certificate altogether. The institute of censorship in India is significant enough for it to be discussed separately below, along with other official government involvement in the film industry.

With censor certificate in hand, a movie is ready to be released to a distributor, who is responsible for passing it on to exhibitors. Sometimes this process is eased by the fact that major studios own or are associated with distributing companies and/or theaters. At other times, however, a completed film may be stalled for want of a distributor. Of 194 Tamil films receiving censor certificates in 1985, 28 had not been released by the end of the year. Of the 657 films certified in all of South India, 83 were unreleased. At the end of 1985, a total of 117 certified Tamil films were waiting to be released (including those certified in previous years); the total number of South Indian films certified but unreleased was 376 (Anandan 1986).[6]

The distributor must search for the most prestigious possible theater for the film's opening in each city. Releasing a movie also involves advertising, usually through newspaper spreads, wall posters and billboards. In addition the press must be courted with invitations to exclusive pre-release screenings, at which the director and producer will be on hand to pay special attention to reviewers; stars may even give film critics individual gifts (such as a watch or set of dishes) at an annual "function," usually held at New Year. Film reviews come out weekly in many English- and local-language newspapers. They also appear in a number of general periodicals, and of course take up a sizable portion of the movie magazines.

Once a movie is in the theaters, efforts are made to extend its run as long as possible. Posters appear announcing the number of days a film has run. If a film shows signs of lagging shortly before it reaches a crucial point – such as the auspicious 100-day mark (the sign of a successful movie) – fan clubs may buy up extra tickets to keep the show going. After the main run of a popular movie at an important theater is well underway, it will be picked up by "lesser" theaters – those less centrally located or less luxurious. Favorite movies may also be re-released for years down the road. Some theaters show nothing but MGR movies, and others specialize in other old films.

The role of the government in the film industry

There are a number of organizations related to film production in India. Most but not all are official government units. The functions of these organizations include taxation, production and regulation of documentaries, and censorship.

Taxes and other required payments in the cinema industry rose steeply after Independence in 1947, when the new national leaders saw cinema as a rich source of revenue. By 1949 the percentage of box-office receipts being paid to taxes was estimated at 60 percent. "Taxes" on cinema are of various kinds. The entertainment tax is determined by each state. In 1949 the average was about 33 percent of theater receipts. Some cities charge an additional entertainment tax. There are also sales taxes on cinema equipment, import duties on equipment and raw film, and occasionally duties on the transport of films between cities. Other payments include obligatory rentals of documentary films by theaters and per-foot charges for censorship services (Barnouw and Krishnaswamy 1980: 137–39). The Film Federation of India was established in 1951 to represent the cinema industry in its negotiations with the national government, and although one of its major concerns has been taxation, taxes overall have continued to increase.[7] (A notable exception is the abolition since 1975 of the state entertainment tax for films made in Gujarat.)

At the federal level cinema regulation comes under the aegis of the Ministry of Information and Broadcasting. One of the most important units of this ministry is the Films Division, which produces and distributes approved documentaries. In 1947, just one year after abolishing the organization that had produced required war-effort movies and other documentaries under the British, the Indian government decided to make the screening of government-approved films compulsory at all regular showings. The Film Advisory Board was established to review documentaries, and the Films Division then presented all theaters with a block-booking contract under which it would supply the necessary films (almost all of which were produced by the Division itself). Theater owners had to pay for the use of the Division films (Barnouw and Krishnaswamy 1980: 138–39, 194).

In 1960 a different type of film organization, the Film Finance Corporation (FFC), began work under the Ministry. It provides finance for filmmakers whose work falls outside of the mainstream and therefore cannot attract the usual producers' capital. A number of leaders of the "parallel" or "new wave" film movement in India have launched careers with FFC financing, and some FFC projects became commercial successes as well (see Barnouw and Krishnaswamy 1980: 251–59).

The organization with the greatest influence over the shape of commercial cinema is the Central Board of Film Certification. Formerly the Central Board of Film Censors, it was established by the Ministry of Information and Broadcasting in 1951 to bring regional censor boards under a central authority and to make their decisions more uniform. The Board has five regional offices – in Madras, Bangalore (Karnataka), Trivandrum (Kerala), Calcutta, and Bombay – any of which can certify a movie for all of India. Each office reviews the movies produced in its region and determines whether to grant or deny censorship certificates. There are four certificate categories: U ("universal" or "unrestricted" audiences), UA (no children under twelve unless accompanied by parent or guardian), A (adults only), and S (medical and other professionals only) (Ramachandran and Venkatesh 1985: 538–39). There is also a category of "educational" films, which do not received a lettered rating. Unlike in the US, where First Amendment rulings allow most if not all films to play (see Konvitz 1963), censors in India may refuse to certify a film. Where a certificate rating is authorized, its approval is often contingent upon specified cuts or other changes in the film.

Regional censor boards are composed of a presiding officer, who usually has a two-year term, and a varying number of "advisory" panel members, chosen as upright citizens and representatives of various professions, and whose terms vary in length (R. K. Ramachandran, interview September 1986). The evaluating committee is composed of the presiding officer and a rotating selection of three or four advisory panel members. Each of these members has a veto power, and if any one of them refuses to pass the film, it is not given a certificate.

A producer who disagrees with the examining committee's judgment (as many do) can appeal the rating. An eight-member reviewing committee, including only one or two of the original examining members, reviews the movie and decides on its certification by majority vote. If the decision is still not to the producer's liking, the next step is the recently established Film Certification Appellate Tribunal in Delhi. If even this fails, a final appeal can be made to the federal Supreme Court. Overall, the system is weighted in the producer's favor; few cases get through this lengthy appeals process without being granted a certificate (*Indian Express*, 2 March 1986).

Films cannot be released to exhibitors without a certificate. However, once they leave the censor board with certification there are a number of ways to circumvent the censors' regulations. Films that have been cut by the censors may be given to exhibitors with some or all of the cut portions replaced. There is little regulation of videos, and it is said that an uncensored video print is made of most Hindi films before they are handed over to the censor (*Indian Express*, 2 March 1986). Another method is practiced in Kerala – famous for soft pornography – where unrelated blue movies are "interpolated" into commercial films shown in rural areas, where censor officers are rarely able to carry out consistent inspections (*The Hindu*, 14 July 1986; *Indian Express*, 18 September 1986).

Most movies abide by censor regulations after they are released, but almost all involve cat-and-mouse maneuverings between censor and producer before the film is certified. The process is similar to Indian filmmakers' attempts to subvert British war propaganda requirements in movies of the early 1940s, with the difference that censorship in recent decades (except during the Emergency) has focussed on sex and violence much more than on political and other ideologies.[8] Barnouw and Krishnaswamy pinpoint the dilemma caused by the censors' efforts to curb sex and violence, which,

however well intentioned, tended to lead to tricky and fruitless games. Instead of the explicit, one got blatant sexual symbolism or coy suggestiveness, often more vulgar than explicitness. But such problems are inherent in the job of the censor, whose search for "objective" criteria inevitably leads to such traps. (1980: 290)

While many Indians complain that censor standards are too lax, many others, especially film industry members, claim that they are too strict and that left to itself, cinema could be self-censoring. Some producers say that they shoot extensive violent or sexual scenes only in the hope that a small segment will survive the censors' knife. Other critics believe that board members see titillation where it does not exist, that "the common boy or girl does not pay as much attention to the dress or contour of a woman as the censors do" (*Bengal Motion Picture Association Journal*, November 1954, cited in Barnouw and Krishnaswamy 1980: 217). The censors themselves bemoan the distortion that suspicion creates. R. K. Ramachandran, film editor and director and former Regional Officer of the Madras board, has said that

seeing films everyday from the Censor's point of view had a dehumanising effect. Unless they were dull and dry like a documentary film on [a] rural development scheme – all other films looked as if they were produced in defiance of censor rules. It was said that most of the vulgar words and actions to which they raised objection, existed not in the films but in the minds of the Censors. I realised the truth of this statement long after I ceased to be in the Censor Board (R. K. Ramachandran n.d.)

Filmmakers' views on their films and their audiences

I met and spoke at length with fourteen movie directors and producers, most but not all currently successful.[9] Like most other successful

7. An unusual billboard in Madras, where the director Bharatiraja stands on the right. 1991.

filmmakers, they are now members of the upper middle and upper classes but grew up among the urban or rural poor.[10] Most of our meetings were conducted as formal interviews, with questions covering topics such as the process of creating a film, the degree to which audience preferences are taken into consideration in filmmaking, the extent and type of cinema's influence on viewers, recent changes in cinema, and the filmmaker's career in the movie industry. The comments made during these discussions provide an overall picture of directors' and producers' views of filmmaking, of their audiences, and of the reciprocal influences between viewers and films.

Despite the general conception that Tamil films follow a prescribed formula, each of the directors I interviewed emphasized filmmaking as a pursuit of personal aesthetic or creative fulfillment, and most bemoaned the impossibility of predicting a film's success.[11] In the course of the conversations, some directors also eventually noted the role of audience desires in determining the form and content of their movies, but viewers' influence – and the "desires" from which it springs – was generally acknowledged only grudgingly and often with great disparagement. Bharatiraja, director of *Mutal Mariyaatai* ("Honor of the First Order"), *Kaṭaloora Kavitaikaḷ* ("Poems of the Seashore") and *Veetam Putitu* ("A New Veda") among other films, and one of the filmmakers least critical of viewers, noted that he began to "think of the audience" only after one of his films failed. Since then, he explained, he has "compromised" with viewers by providing them with comedy and songs and other elements of "fantasy" while at the same time ensuring that he retains his individuality.[12]

Other directors have a more pointedly negative view of the demands that audiences make on films. These filmmakers, including the majority of those I interviewed, portray the bulk of cinema viewers – the "mass," as they are frequently called – as having narrow, unsophisticated, and even prurient interests in movies. One prominent producer–director, the most articulate holder of this view, divides his potential audience into the "literate population," the "illiterates," and the "ladies." Some films, he noted, could appeal to all three categories,

> but there are certain films which are only intended for the illiterate people. These are all the pictures in which lots of sex, violence, double-meaning dialogues, and baser instincts are met with. These type of pictures can only produce the response from the lower class – that is, what you call the pictures for the mass. There are [also] pictures which are intended for only high class – for [the] literate population – in which the director tries to say something intelligent.

When I asked this director if he has a target audience in mind when making his films, he answered:

I generally make pictures to meet the [viewers] belonging to the intelligent audience, what you call the high class, and also the ladies. By nature, I just cannot involve myself in making films on sex-base or the violence-base – though, I have made a few films on that, on account of the compulsion of the business community.

Later, however, this same director defended the business community's emphasis on such elements because "it is nothing wrong to accommodate that approach. And when I have accommodated those views and approaches, well, the pictures have fared well and collected well."[13]

Other comments about the audience are more muted but nonetheless revealing. L. V. Prasad, head of the leading Prasad Studios, said that after the recent failure of movies that carry a powerful social message, such as his Hindi-language film *Swati*, he and his sons are hesitant to make movies that have a "clean story" and lack the "commercial elements that appeal to the lower classes." K. Balaje, who directed *Reevati*, the Tamil version of *Swati*, also deplored audience response to the film. *Reevati*, he said, is based on the "entirely revolutionary" theme of a daughter who fights against society's criticism of her unmarried mother by finding her a husband. The film was a great success in its Telugu version in the neighboring state of Andhra Pradesh, but was a flop in Tamil Nadu. Balaje said that he had made a movie on this theme "to show the public" that "there *are* women who are suffering ... But today, when we show it in the movie – well, all the hypocrites, they don't want to accept it."

To actor–director–producer Kamalhasan, the filmmaker's goal is to give viewers "what they want, and at the same time try to enjoy yourself." What viewers want, he thinks, is fantasy. They prefer heroic characters – such as "Rambo," he claimed – who support their own personal fantasies. As illustration, Kamalhasan contrasted these agreeably fantastical characters with those played by Shivaji Ganesan, who because he does not attempt to fit the Rambo mold is, in Kamalhasan's view, "less of a star and more of an actor":

Sometimes Shivaji *disturbed* fantasy. He woke the audiences up ... he woke them up from their dreams sometimes, so much reality suddenly creeping in ... It disturbed you because he is not Rambo – he fails, he trips, he falls down, which reminds you of yourself. You are capable of tripping down, you are capable of falling down, and you are capable of hurting yourself, unlike Rambo who dives from heights ... and comes down unharmed.

I asked if people did not want to see this. "Sometimes, no," he answered. "It needs a certain amount of intelligence to accept that kind of representation, where you become more analytical rather than appreciative."

Together, the preceding comments imply a perception of the cinema audience as largely crude and unsophisticated, uneducated, unanalytical, and more interested in fantasy and sexual titillation than in self-understanding. This portrait is borne out by directors' somewhat more sympathetic views on why people attend movies. The directors I spoke with saw their films as providing viewers with escape. Without exception, the directors who were interviewed volunteered the view that people attend movies for escape and relaxation, and specifically not for education. Muktha Srinivasan, director, producer, and prominent member of the South Indian movie industry, said that after a day's routine work and pressures, a person "wants to escape from his daily activity, and so he goes and sees the film. It gives him relief." D. V. S. Raju, producer and chair of the Andhra Pradesh Film Development Corporation, called filmgoing "a daily need, like food and shelter," adding that its importance is enhanced by its position as the cheapest form of entertainment available to the lower classes. Likewise, Bharatiraja emphasized that, in the general absence of sports, drinking, and dating ("'Til the twentieth year," he said, "we don't know what is what"), cinema stands as the only form of entertainment and relaxation for the poor.[14] He too argued that filmgoers attend movies only for relaxation, never for education. Similarly, A. V. Narayanan, General Manager of the South Indian Film Chamber of Commerce, stated that people never go to the theater to learn: "The intellectual doesn't need it, the poor man doesn't want it."

While, like viewers, these filmmakers were in strong agreement that filmgoing is not motivated by a desire to learn, most also believed that their films have some influence on viewers. There was a wide variety of opinions on what those effects are, but most filmmakers implied that cinema's influence is largely a positive one. Bharatiraja said that cinema has a "big effect" on filmgoers, very little of which is negative. On the other hand, he said, cinema has created "no big social revolution so far," although he does not rule out its potential to do so. D. V. S. Raju claimed that cinema can be inspirational to viewers and has had a great impact, one example of which is the creation of political figures drawn from cinematic ranks. He too believes that film's overall influence has been good, with any negative effect remaining "in the background." These sentiments were echoed by K. Balaje, a well established director, producer and former actor, who believes that people apply lessons from film to many everyday acts. Thus he claimed that "films only give the education to people ... Film is a very, very, very powerful media [sic], which educates people, 90 percent, and 10 percent spoils [i.e. corrupts] them." In his eyes, this potent medium is also responsible for the rise of politicians and, through entertainment tax collections, the financial support of governments.

Along with such views of cinema's efficacy, however, there are many implicit or explicit laments that cinema cannot or will not serve a more uplifting role for the lower classes. This complaint was put most sensitively by A. Ramesh, then President of the South Indian Film Chamber of Commerce and, with his father L. V. Prasad, Joint Managing Director of Prasad Studios, who explained that many people lack what they need in their lives, and when they go to the movies, they want to forget about life. But today's movies, he complained, *only* make them forget – unlike older movies, the stories are shallow and do not build character; they are not "moral-building." Thus, along with their sense that lower class viewers attend movies in order to fulfill "base desires" and escapist fantasies, and their belief that films can indeed affect the audience, filmmakers also feel a responsibility to educate the audience (including educating them to want a proper "clean" film) – to improve lives and build character through the enlightenment achieved by providing viewers with what they *should* want in a movie.

This sense of responsibility becomes clear in discussions of cinema audiences. "Producers have a very great responsibility," said Ramesh, but "very rarely do they bear this responsibility." Narayanan, who is a former official of the National Film Development Corporation (NFDC), believes like many other filmmakers that education may come incidentally through movie-watching, and stated that "it *is* important what we show them." People should be given a chance to go to good movies, he said, and then maybe something of the good will sink in. Like Narayanan, Raju advocates greater production of "committed cinema," films that depict and offer viable solutions to social problems. He places much of the responsibility for support of the socially enlightened "new cinema" with the NFDC.

From their remarks about lower class audiences, intentionally critical or not, their assessments of viewers' motivations in attending cinema, and their stated zeal for providing viewers with educational entertainment, it becomes evident that filmmakers see themselves as responsible for furnishing the poor with certain models of behavior that viewers now either cannot – because of cultural (and, it is implied, mental) disadvantages – or will not – because of inherent perversity – accept. Unfortunately, they say, films today do not always offer the enlightening models and morals that they should, and it is clear that these directors place some of the blame for this on filmmakers, including themselves. But the original sin still lies with audiences who, because they refuse to accept clean movies and in fact demand many of the "base" elements that contemporary directors have incorporated into their films, have *forced* many directors to make what are considered shallow, indecent, corrupting films. Thus filmmakers often see themselves and other members of the middle and upper classes as holders of proper cultural and behavioral ideals, which they must try to impart to an unappreciative and perversely stubborn lower class.

Censors' views on film audiences

Filmmakers are not alone in their view that audiences need moral guidance from wiser and more privileged people. This view is shared by censors, and indeed is inherent in the institution of censorship. Censorship implies that those who watch movies cannot be trusted to choose what is best for themselves (or – a different matter – what is best for national stability) and that selected boards of exemplary citizens can.

Some of the strongest criticism of Indian censorship relates to its double standard for indigenous and foreign films. Foreign movies are often allowed to contain much more explicit sexuality and violence than are Indian films. Gaston Roberge, a Calcutta-based critic and analyst of cinema, identifies the understanding of audience that these varying standards imply:

> The assumption at the basis of this double standard seems to be that foreign films are seen by people who are assumed to be mature. The national and regional films are seen by people most of whom are assumed to be like children who must be protected from undergoing experiences which are assumed to be beneficial to enlightened movie-goers and detrimental to the poor, uneducated spectators. This paternalistic, self-righteous attitude legitimizes censorship of films in India. (Roberge 1985: 32)

Roberge's interpretation is supported by the writings of Kobita Sarkar, herself a film critic and former advisory panel member to the Bombay and Calcutta censor boards. Sarkar acknowledges the "double standard," which she defends as necessary in the face of differential audience reactions to what is seen on screen. She claims that audiences of the "more rough and ready type," for example, are "eager to be stimulated and to imitate what they see in their films" (1975: 48). Thus the rough and ready serial type of stunt film, for instance, will necessarily be restricted to the more seedy localities of the urban areas and can therefore hardly be viewed with the same tolerance as the more polished commercial project. (1975: 55)

Audiences for foreign films, on the other hand, are more sophisticated and more prepared, according to Sarkar – and, by implication, less impressionable, thus allowing censors to apply more relaxed standards to foreign movies than to films intended for general audiences (1975: 47, 55–56).

Here again is a view of the lower class audience as unsophisticated and unaware of what is best for it, in combination with the assumption that, because films do affect their viewers, a wiser group must select the elements that are fit for viewing. Left to their own devices, viewers would choose for their films to contain elements that, in the censors' own wiser opinion, would be detrimental to filmgoers' lives and personal characters because audience members are not properly prepared to deal with such contact. Like children, they must be shielded and, hopefully, taught.

The perception of audiences as childlike explicitly informs one of the latest governmental investigations into censorship in India. In the *Report of the Enquiry Committee on Film Censorship*'s consideration of viewer reaction to films, the discussion begins by noting that "the effect upon children and their reaction to the films they see are of paramount importance in the matter of censorship," but concedes that "there is almost universal opposition to censorship of films exhibited to adults, and it is said that an adult must be allowed to choose his or her entertainment" (Government of India 1969: 61). The report then goes on to cite studies of cinema's influence on children and adults in different countries. It concludes that examples in such studies "do show to what extent young and ... impressionable minds may be influenced by films," continuing,

It must be remembered that by far the great majority of [Indian] film viewers are unsophisticated, uneducated persons who are prone to identify themselves with what happens on the screen for the simple reason that they are not familiar with the realities of the type of life depicted in films. Their own life is confined to the village or the suburb, and when they see the glamorous film stars dressed in expensive clothes, living in rich houses and conducting themselves in a manner completely alien to their own, they begin to think that they themselves should behave, as much as possible, like the characters in the film. (Government of India 1969: 73)

The report goes on to make the equation between viewers and children even more explicit:

Many of our adult viewers have minds comparable to the minds of children. They are impressionable, easily led astray and prone to the temptation of identifying themselves with the characters which they see on the screen. That being so, it may almost be said that a large part of the adult viewers are also in need of the sort of protection which can legally be afforded to children. (Government of India 1969: 73, 74)

Because viewers are childlike, and therefore unable to know or act in their own best interests, they are vulnerable and require protection. But in the censors' formulation, viewers are to be patronized and protected not only from the "temptations" of their innate desires, but also from the temptations provided by *filmmakers*, who while members of the upper class are nonetheless errant in their promotion of the values of that class. (Significantly, censors are much more likely to have been born into the middle and upper class than are filmmakers.) Censors decry not only audiences but also directors and producers. The exemplary citizens of their boards are thus portrayed as the true guardians of middle and upper class values and virtue, the true protectors of the lower class against undesirable influences.

Two former censors with whom I spoke questioned the legitimacy of the censors' role. Both had come to their conclusions, however, only after retiring from their posts. One, an author who had served as an advisory member for eleven and a half years, said that she now feels that what the board does is a waste. In part, this is because much of what the censors cut is put back into the film after it is passed; but mainly she questions whether viewers should be prevented from seeing what they want to see and in any case will probably see anyway.

Another former censor, R. K. Ramachandran, who served as Madras Regional Censor Officer from 1973–77, also had doubts about the utility of censorship. He describes one of his own early experiences of watching a film with the board, and his subsequent transition to experienced board member:

A woman in a wet tightly wrapped saree revealing every part of her body in relief encountered a bully. He tried to abduct her ... When the members of the Censor Board wanted me to list the number of scenes to be deleted from the film I told them that I found nothing objectionable in it that deserved to be deleted.

They were quite shocked at my permissive attitude.

... [The scenes] appeared inoffensive and harmless to me ... I realised that I was yet inexperienced to judge the moral standard needed for a film to be cleared by the Censors. I thought that it would be safer to accept the verdict of other members who had years of experience in censoring films.

In due course I trained myself to see films with the eyes of a Censor, when every film began to appear vulgar and offensive. (R. K. Ramachandran n.d.)

Later, after leaving the board, Ramachandran notes he came to realize that the censor's inherently suspicious point of view could create seemingly objectionable material where there was in fact none (R. K. Ramachandran n.d.).

Filmmakers and censors both castigate the audience for their debased desires and see themselves as responsible for educating viewers. Viewers, however, present a much different picture, portraying themselves as moral and intelligent consumers, as we see in the following chapter.

# 8

Audiences

Tamils hold strong views on cinema, both negative and positive. Movies and actors are frequent topics of conversation among the urban poor. People who were unwilling to discuss the cinema in any formal context, such as with an unknown interviewer or in the presence of their elders, were eager to talk about it in informal conversations with one another and with me.

Much of my information about audience views on cinema comes from these conversations, as well as from more structured interviews (conducted after people came to trust me). I also gathered accounts of movie stories from more than forty viewers, some volunteered during interviews and others told by friends who had just seen a movie. Still other accounts – about half of my sample – were elicited directly by asking people to tell me both their favorite movie story and the story of one of the three films recounted in chapter 5.

Stories volunteered during the general interviews were usually fairly short – about five minutes long – and often ended with a proffered interpretation of the movie's "message" or "moral" (*karuttu*). The stories given in response to a formal request were usually much longer, often taking half an hour to an hour in the telling. I asked for the film's "message" at the end of each of these, and most storytellers responded readily. It was clear that perceiving messages in films was a natural way of thinking for many poor urban residents. They also had strong opinions about the effects of movies and the reasons for watching them. Questions about connections between the movies and their own lives, however, were not answered as readily by some people. Nonetheless, while this did not seem to be a subject that most people had given extensive consideration before, after reflection many of them did suggest some connections.

Messages and morals of movies

All three major sets of film themes – gender, family, and class relations – are echoed in viewers' reports about the central "moral" or "message" of a movie. One young man, a Marathavar,[1] told me that the theme of *Amman Koovil Kizhakkaalee* was "the glory of the thali," the wedding emblem that accomplished Kanmani's transition from spoiled modern girl to modest Tamil wife. Emphasizing a wife's duty to persevere in her sacrifices for her husband, a newly married thirty-year-old woman described the story of *Iruvar Ullam* ("The Hearts of Two People"). In this film, she said, a husband changes his bad character after marriage, but his wife refuses to accept that he could change; when he is later (mistakenly?) arrested, she recognizes her error and admits his good character. The theme of this film, according to the storyteller, was that a patient woman can change her husband's character. This woman's sister, a forty-year-old widow, told me the story of *Mutal Mariyaatai* ("Honor of the First Order"), her favorite movie, which she said teaches that "there is no bar or age limit to love."

A middle-aged Pillai[2] woman described *Kataloora Kavitaikal* ("Poems of the Seashore"), and said that its theme lay in stressing how the educated young woman helps a rough young man even though he is illiterate. After recounting the story – in which the poor Hindu hero and middle class Christian heroine have fallen in love while their unknowing parents arrange for each to marry someone of their own class – she commented,

He is her love. She should not leave him. It is not proper to accept the educated and leave the uneducated. In the end there is this theme: an educated girl has loved a rough fellow. Even though he acts badly, she comes to know that he is really good.

Here we see two issues at work. Like the woman above who described *Mutal Mariyaatai*, this woman claimed the film teaches that love can occur across social boundaries such as caste and education; moreover, she asserted, once the bond of love has united the lovers, this bond supersedes the relationships that would normally be socially prescribed. Also noted is the worthiness of the uneducated. She stressed that the uneducated are good *inside* – the true measure of worth – despite a sometimes rough surface or exterior, and that they should be given the same consideration as the educated.

A number of people commented that *Patikkaatavan* had a similar point. One young Harijan man said that "it shows how we poor have good hearts and minds. We are better than the rich people who have cars and fancy clothes." Others emphasized this film's focus on the severing and reconnection of family ties. Another young Harijan man, leader of a Rajnikanth fan club, said,

> When the brothers are young, their elder brother's wife beats them in anger and drives them out. But in Madras they are taken in by another man. Rajnikanth's love for his brother is great. Through his own efforts he gives his brother a respectable position, but the brother doesn't respect [what he is given]. He speaks hurtfully to Rajnikanth, that is, like a child who rejects its mother. In the end, they all unite (*ceerntuvaarkaḷ*).

The majority of statements made by poor viewers about movies' morals and the connections with their own lives had to do with personal relationships, many of them criticizing the moral failings of close relatives. A sizable portion of respondents also made some comment on the injustice of the ways in which the poor are treated and portrayed by the rich, and argued for the moral superiority of the poor over the rich. However, despite deeply felt protests against its effects, few if any viewers suggested that the class system itself is immoral. Viewers hoped to improve their position within the hierarchy, or to eradicate negative stereotypes of the poor – wishes that are fulfilled, as we have seen, in some movie themes – but never suggested the eradication of class.

Connections between cinema and viewers' lives

When questioned about similarities between their lives and those shown in the movies, some people said that no connections exist because films never show ordinary, mundane lives like their own. One man asked, "How can the luxury we see in films ever come to our lives?" Some pointed out that films about everyday life would not be exciting enough to make any money.

Another set of respondents said that films *are* "like our lives" – "our" referring to family or class, depending on the speaker. Most mentioned similarities between types of problems encountered by poor urban families like theirs and families in the movies. One woman put together a formulation that I had been struggling with for some time in trying to connect viewers' stated preferences and self-images. After telling me that many films are unlike her life because the women in them have fun rather than caring for their families, she continued, "Our family's kind of problems show up in films, too. We like the film if it is a family film, one like us." That is, we like family films as opposed to more risque love stories; good films are like us, true to life; if it is like us, we like it; good equals like us – moral and upstanding. This woman, like a number of others, saw connections between general types of problems encountered in film characters' lives and her own family members'.

Many people, however, in fact the largest group, saw specific similarities between their lives and the movies. These were the respondents who were most reflective, taking the longest time to answer my question. The details of their answers surprised me. That is, since the people in the three neighborhoods I worked in often referred to categories such as "poor people like us" or "people who suffer like us," I had expected them to respond in class-related terms (as some of those above had) – something like, "Movies do not show poor people like us." Instead, most people answered in very personal, often role-related terms, as illustrated by the following cases.

A 31-year-old woman whose family was quite poor said that she had seen one movie that was close to her life. This was *Aariliruntu Arupatu Varai* ("From Six to Sixty"), a film starring the actor Rajnikanth in which the hero loses his parents and must assume care of his younger sister and two younger brothers. He works hard to provide them with an education and make them good marriages, neglecting his own wife and children in the process. When he later becomes poor and is starving, his siblings refuse to care for him. Finally, when he regains his wealth, they ask for his help and he gives it once more, so they ally themselves with him again. The woman telling this story said that the very same thing had happened to her husband, who had gone to extremes to help his sisters and brother but now received nothing from them. He had taken out loans in his own name for his three sisters' dowries and arranged their marriages. He had found work for his brother, and now all of them – the brother and the three sisters and their families – were living in the same small compound with her, but they refused to contribute any money to household expenses or give her husband any assistance in return for the great sacrifices he had made.

Another woman, forty years old, told me the story of the movie *Pantam* ("The Bond"), starring Shivaji Ganesan. In it, she said, Shivaji's daughter loses her husband after bearing a baby girl. The mother becomes a nun, and the baby is taken in by a Muslim police Inspector General, who happens to be a good friend of Shivaji's. As the young girl grows older, she often visits Shivaji's house. Shivaji is very fond of the girl but does not recognize her. One day she sees her mother's photograph in an album and says that the picture is of her mother. Later the girl dies from a bad heart, and Shivaji goes mad. This storyteller said that her own life was similar to this film because her younger brother had disappeared five years ago. He is lost to them as the girl was to her grandfather Shivaji, she said, and they have looked everywhere but cannot find him.

A sixty-year-old woman told me that the film *Vaazhkai* ("Life," 1984), also a Shivaji movie, resembles her life. In it, the children fail to take care of their aging parents. This is just like her sons, she said, whom she and her husband have given everything possible but who now refuse to care for them in return. She explained that her sons both have good jobs, and one had just built a fine new house for himself and his wife, but they lie to her and claim they have no money.

A Harijan man of about forty-five years, a friend's husband who openly met with his mistress, told me that films are sometimes based on real-life incidents. They also portray the real-life relationships of men and women, he added. Films show that husbands and wives rarely cooperate. The husbands go after other women, their wives become upset and stay at home. This creates trouble at home because the husband spends all his money on another woman and there is no money for the children's care. The films show that there are many consequences to such action, he said, and that the husband and wife should live happily together.

These examples illustrate many Tamils' tendency to make comparisons between the movies and their own lives in terms of very specific personal relationships. Rather than identify themselves in this case with a larger unit such as a caste or class, these viewers think in terms of the relationships between themselves and a brother, their children, their in-laws, or a wife. Other informants made comparisons to their relationships with husbands and parents. All of these are close family relations, and the reports reflect difficulties and anxieties about them – the same types of concerns reflected in movie themes that address gender and family relations. If, as I have suggested, such themes do parallel issues in viewers' lives, viewers seem to have some awareness of this connection. However, viewers' relatively slow response to questions about these connections implies that such connections normally remain out of the forefront of consciousness, which may help keep the urgency of conflicts in these relationships from disturbing the pleasure viewers feel in escaping them when watching a film.[3]

Influence of cinema

Viewers see the intended purpose of filmgoing as a means of passing time (*pozhutu pookku*) or of escaping (*tappu*) from the boredom or worries of daily life. As a widowed friend put it,

> When my husband was alive, we were happy, and we went only to good movies. Now I go when I'm bored. Sitting there for a few hours, my worries get a little smaller (*kavalai koncam kuraivu pookum*). That's why I go. When I'm worried and I go, then I get a little bit happier.

Viewers almost never suggest, for example, that they go to the movies to learn something. At the same time most of them believe that cinema can serve a purpose, or have effects, other than the immediate and conscious ones that draw viewers to the movies. Almost everyone can cite an instance where filmgoing has caused or contributed to family tensions. It is said that frequent filmgoing can cause financial problems, and that women's desires to see films may create problems with husbands who want their wives to remain at home. Certain crimes are believed to have been patterned after thefts and murders seen in particular movies; most of these have happened in other parts of the state, but their cinematic models make them notorious.[4] Often people also remark on the positive influence of cinema, but give fewer references to known cases. Family movies are thought to have a beneficial influence. It is said, for example, that a viewer may watch a family movie and decide that her or his own family should live as the film characters do, that they should raise their children in the same way, and that the husband and wife should treat each other well and not fight.

Most viewers insist that cinema's effects can be either positive or negative, depending on the type of movie and the particular viewer's personality. This interaction of the film and the individual was first expressed explicitly during a conversation with a forty-year-old woman whose family was high caste but very poor. I asked if she thought that films had any influence on the people who watched them:

A: Yes. It makes for hardship in the families. When someone sees a film, they may get a great desire to see more. If the family is in difficulty, they do not have any money, but the person will want to go to movies all the time anyway. This creates hardship because of the desire and because of the money it takes from the family. In another family, the husband and wife may fight because of movies. She wants to go to them, but he says she can't, or maybe he says that she can go only once a month or once a week. If she goes anyway, after he has gone to work, and he finds out, then they will fight.

Someone else can see a family film and see how they should live. They come home and decide that that is how their family should be, that is how they should raise their children, that is how the husband and wife should act. They decide not to fight anymore. But someone else sees a very bad picture, and because of it they act badly. They go bad. They treat their family badly, and their family members won't act well.

Q: How is this?

A: If they see someone [in the movie] with another man's wife, or drinking illicit liquor, or with other bad habits.

Q: Everyone?

A: No – usually good families won't see bad movies. Ninety percent of people see movies and improve. Ten percent see them and go bad. If a good person sees a bad movie, they won't go bad.

I repeatedly heard similar statements suggesting that the potential influence of cinema depended on the nature of the person watching it. One of them came from a 29-year-old Thevar[5] man, who told me that most movies have a message for one or two people in each family. (This was in contrast, he said, to the film *Camsaaram Atu Minsaaram* ["A Wife is Electricity"], which held a moral for everyone – mother, father, sister, brother, wife, and husband.) When I asked him if this meant that these messages or morals would have any influence on filmgoers, he said that they would have some effect on reflective people but none on bad people, who either would not recognize the message or would reject it.

Thus most people saw cinema as having a variable influence dependent on each viewer's innate propensity for good or bad and, perhaps, for self-reflection. A few people, however, rejected the idea of "mixed" effects. While almost no poor city residents ascribed invariably negative effects to films, some saw cinema as having a profoundly positive influence on society. One older Chakkiliyar man, for example, claimed that cinema keeps people out of trouble by giving them something to do with their free time. Without cinema, he said, "everyone will be in jail. That's the effect of film. Without cinema, there would be no country (*naaṭu*), no people (*makkaḷ*)."

Others argued that it was impossible to determine what cinema's influence was, since the audience had as much effect on films as films had on the audience. A Chettiar woman who had once danced in films made this point elegantly, explaining: "Directors take from real life and society, then we see the movies and learn from them. It's like adding water to milk – you can't tell which is which." Still others denied that cinema had any influence at all. One of these, a young Marathavar man who claimed to see fifteen films a month, told me that "we cannot say that they [viewers] become bad just by seeing the films. We go bad on our own. Nor can we say that movies improve people . . . The filmmakers create their films from watching *us*. We are not going bad from seeing the films."

Viewers actively evaluate what they see on screen, and reject films or film elements that seem either too realistic or too remote from real life interests. They seek out movies as entertainment and as an escape from the difficulties of their lives. This desire for escape does not suggest, however, that they view what goes on in the movies as completely disconnected from their lives. Rather, they see very personal connections between themselves and their relationships, on the one hand, and the characters and relationships shown on the screen on the other, and occasionally see more general class-level connections as well. In reporting movie stories they focus on themes that address these relationships and issues of class identity. These poignant issues are central to poor Tamils' lives: they involve among other things the effects of marriage on individuals and families, possibilities for romantic love, the responsibilities of children or siblings, and the disregarded inner virtues of the poor. Films create utopian resolutions of these issues. Escape and reality are intimately connected.

Viewers also believe that watching the movies and seeing situations that speak to their own circumstances can have effects on behavior. Many of these effects will be positive, but the nature and occurrence of cinema's behavioral influence depends in the last instance on each viewer's preexisting character. Good people will probably improve; bad people may become worse. Viewers' own statements thus contradict critics' claims that filmgoing has pervasively pernicious effects. Some even point out that cinema-going is a more personally and socially beneficial activity than most of the other time-filling options available to the urban poor. In many filmgoers' eyes, participation in cinema can have lasting and positive effects. They often added comments to the effect, however, that viewers need to choose carefully among films, since it is difficult nowadays to find good, clean, moral storylines. In 1990, when several viewers I spoke with continued to bemoan what they considered an increase in bad, indecent films, they attributed the success of two popular films – *Karakaaṭṭakkaaran* ("Karagattam Dancer," 1989), a phenomenally successful village love story, and *Putu Vacantam* ("New Spring," 1990), an urban story of a woman's friendship with four men – to their lack of sexual explicitness.

The attitudes that viewers express in private conversations differ not only from some critics' and filmmakers' opinions but also from general public opinion, which holds cinema to be at best distasteful and at worst depraving. The "public" who hold this opinion include all classes. Half of the lower class respondents to a questionnaire administered by my lower class assistant reported that cinema "makes people go bad." This is the respectable view, even among those of the poor who watch movies most frequently, and is the only one that can be expressed outside of the company of close friends without risk of being accused (with varying degrees of derision) of "cinema madness." As the previous discussion indicates, individual conversations produced this idea only rarely; thus there is a discrepancy between what is admitted "off the record" to represent viewers' personal feelings and what is recognized to constitute the "proper" attitude toward cinema. The implications of this discrepancy will be discussed in chapter 10.

Presentation and reception of class-based values in Tamil cinema
Despite some similarities of opinion, viewers and filmmakers have notably divergent impressions of the medium in which they both participate. They agree that audiences attend cinema for escape. Directors and producers, however, emphasize that this desire for escape implies a rejection of intellectual activity or a disinterest in enlightened depictions of social problems, while viewers stress the difficulties in their everyday lives that fuel the interest in what they admit to be a temporary release. The filmgoers I spoke with could also recognize very personal connections between the movies they saw and their own lives. They were analytical enough to distill morals from the films they saw, and, some insisted, to apply them to their lives. Like the similarities they noted between their lives and films, these morals address relationships between men and women and among family members, as well as class-related concerns of identity, oppression, dominance, and privilege – the same issues dealt with by most movie themes. Significantly, however, viewers never made similar statements about the issues addressed by what I have called "imposed" or "directors'" themes, such as the evils of alcohol and drugs.

While the intention of filmgoing was often stated to be escape rather than education, both groups felt that audiences could nonetheless learn from the movies. There was also a general impression – especially among directors – that the learning that takes place can be constructive, in contrast to the general public opinion that filmgoing has a detrimental effect on viewers' morals and behavior. Filmwatchers, too, contradicted the "proper" view on cinema when they suggested that it could have salutary effects. They linked the potential positive or negative character of film's influence to the corresponding personal nature of the viewer.

Filmmakers (who had a much stronger tendency to depict viewers as an undifferentiated category) complained that current films should be more uplifting than they generally are. While they criticized fellow directors and producers for making increasingly "cheap" movies, they ultimately placed the blame for this on the audiences whose rejection of "clean" films makes the switch necessary. Since filmmakers wish to see their films as personal aesthetic creations rather than as formulaic responses to the entertainment desires of audiences, it is not surprising that they bemoan the necessity of incorporating "base elements" in their films.

The disappointment that they expressed derives from a responsibility felt to teach respectable – i.e. middle and upper class – values to "the mass" (as well as from a need to be *seen* by their peers as doing so, as I discuss below). They are outdone in this respect by film censors, who not only claim that general audiences are unable or unwilling to choose what they ought to see, but also criticize unscrupulous filmmakers for providing audiences with what they ought not to see. While the directors I spoke with portrayed themselves as responsible for teaching proper values to their audiences, censors on the whole disparaged directors for failing in this duty, thus seeing themselves, untainted by concerns for financial returns from the movies they judge, as the real arbiters of virtue and protectors of the audience.

Meanwhile, viewers contradict filmmakers' and censors' images of them by complaining about the lack of good wholesome movies and about what they perceive as increasing amounts of violence and sexual explicitness. Moreover, they identify the types of characters found in "good" movies with themselves – moral and upstanding. Rather than depicting themselves as demanding sensational material, most viewers emphasize their attraction to family films and their ability to learn and apply behavioral lessons from these films. Sometimes they also cite bad films as the cause of degenerating values, especially among younger people, but very few of them believe that this happens in their own households. Thus, while audiences' preferences for clean entertainment may not be communicated to filmmakers through filmgoing patterns, at the level of ideology – the same level at which filmmakers deny their own interests in sensationalism – viewers do not fit the filmmakers' image.

What are filmmakers and viewers saying to each other, how clearly do their expressions enter films, and what significance does the dialogue have for film's meaning to its viewers? To what extent do they, as representatives of different broadly based classes, influence the shape of film? Filmmakers avoid themes that they do not want audiences to see. Censors guard against elements of violence and sexuality that will undermine viewers' morals. Both groups hope to guide audiences to better values and a better way of life by educating them in higher values and ideals. Their comments make it clear that filmmakers and censors wish to impart something of their middle and upper class values to filmgoers. But, just as clearly, filmgoers have had at least a limiting effect on the extent to which those values are expressed in films, and appear to influence filmmakers to include expressions of sentiments important to the poor.

All of this suggests that films do not embody a direct, unadulterated representation of either group, its values or ideology. Some analysts have shared Althusser's conception of the mass media as "ideological apparatuses" that enable the "reproduction of submission to the ruling ideology for the workers" (Althusser 1971: 132–33). This is a view expressed, for example, by members of the Frankfurt School and many of their intellectual descendants. Filmmakers' and censors' concern with imparting "respectable" or "decent" values – i.e. the ideal values of their own classes – suggests that those who shape films most directly do shape them at least partially in accord with class-based values. On the other hand – as studies of contestation and counter-valuation of dominant values in expressive media have demonstrated in other contexts (see Lombardi-Satriani 1974; Limón 1989; Radway 1984) – certain values of the urban poor also find their way into Tamil films. These are most obvious in class-related themes, which rebut upper class stereotypes of the poor as lazy and feckless, and glorify the productive lives and praiseworthy inner nature of lower class people. These themes reverse the normal status hierarchy. The poor are now good, i.e. honest, trustworthy, kind, strong, and noble; and the rich are bad, i.e. dishonest, unjust, cruel, weak, cowardly, and arrogant. There is, thus, some limited contestation of the beliefs and values of the wealthy in Tamil cinema, which *may* aid viewers in resisting or subverting those elements of upper class judgments that they find oppressive.

Thus the extent to which films include consistent portrayal of either upper or lower class values, and especially their significance when present, is difficult to determine unequivocally. Reflections of upper class morals are found, but those that are most distinctively upper class are ignored by viewers. Images and values supported by the poor are represented, especially in depictions of upright and responsible poor characters who are explicitly contrasted with immoral wealthy characters. These portrayals contradict the degraded images that filmmakers construct (outside of films) of their lower class audience; indeed, the film images are ironic considering filmmakers' self-stying as moral arbiters for the poor. Nor can images of a debauched upper class fit into a dominant ideology in any straightforward way, at least not when communicated to subordinates.

Tamil films include convoluted incorporations of both sets of class-based values and beliefs, and rejections of certain elements by both sets of participants. Films are not straightforward representations of either a dominant or a subordinate ideology, nor are their communicated elements absorbed without question. Why, then, are these values included in films – why are they allowed and what purpose do they serve, from both viewers' and filmmakers' points of view?

The answers to the first part of this question have already been suggested. Viewers, I have argued, tolerate the inclusion of values and images that upper class directors insert as moral lessons, although they are not as enamored of them as they are of other story elements. Thus while the inclusion of some strictly upper class values is not likely to sell a movie, it is also unlikely to hurt a film, as long as the values are not directly offensive to viewers. As to why the relatively wealthy individuals who make and finance films introduce and tolerate characterizations that are at the least unflattering to the upper class, such ritualized status reversal is unlikely to threaten as long as it attracts viewers without prompting a social revolution (cf. Gluckman 1959: 125, 132; Bailey 1977: 177–78, 180). The sources of the non-revolutionary nature of Tamil films lie, of course, in the individualizing elements and avoidance of collective comment that are typical of melodrama, and in the mechanisms of utopian themes.

The more interesting question, it seems to me, is what purpose these elements of rudimentary ideologies serve. The role that the inclusion of lower class values plays in providing escape has been examined above, and will be explored further in chapter 10. What remains is to examine the purpose served by the imposition of upper class values. Many traditional Marxist analyses of dominant ideologies assume that the primary function of ideology is to inure the lower classes to oppressive conditions, thereby preventing revolution and ensuring the continuation of the current means and relations of production. It seems likely, however, that those elements of Tamil films that are most notably connected with upper class values are not aimed solely at viewers but in fact are intended, in whole or in part, for filmmakers' socioeconomic peers. I would argue that they function, as Abercrombie and Turner (1978) and Abercrombie, Hill and Turner (1980) have suggested, more as a means of solidifying the upper class than of indoctrinating a subordinate class.

Filmmakers' remarks support this contention. While ambivalence toward cinema can make filmgoing a problematic act for audiences – as is apparent in individuals' statements disowning their own desires and interest in movies – similar conflicts can also make filmmaking problematic for directors and producers. Filmmakers' comments imply a dual system of valuation. On the one hand, most of their movies implicitly promote desires that the filmmakers ascribe to the poor, including desires for sexual titillation, violence, and fantasy. In portraying these elements, filmmakers must have a sufficient understanding of and commitment to them to be able to portray them well, that is, in a way that viewers will appreciate. Cinema personnel gain prestige from their association with an industry that promotes these elements, and of these personnel, filmmakers – those who most directly shape the portrayal – gain the greatest prestige. On the other hand, filmmakers despise the more sensational values that they promote (at the same time as they may gain fame and wealth from portraying them) and must dissociate themselves from these values in order to maintain a respectable position in their own class. They must prove to society (that is, to their middle and upper class peers) that while cinema itself may be lurid and smutty, they themselves are not. (The urgency may be compounded by most filmmakers' origins in the urban and rural poor.) To accomplish this, filmmakers must maintain a strong outward affiliation with the values of the class to which they now belong.

This derision of and dissociation from elements associated with cinema is evident in some of filmmakers' comments. The director who divided audiences into "literates," "illiterates," and "ladies," for example, made it clear that he did not see himself as the type to become involved in making films on a "sex-base" or "violence-base." His ambivalence quickly surfaced, however, in his justification of "those views and approaches." Others who lamented the scarcity of "clean" films, blaming audiences for demanding indecent movies, revealed similar attitudes. It is not that they *want* to include "base elements," they implied, but that they are forced to by the paying audiences.

The need to adhere strongly and publicly to upper class values also emerged from these conversations. The most telling statements came from directors' comments about allowing their own daughters to enter the cinema. Such information is instructive because control over women's behavior tends to be highly resistant to change, and therefore an important area in which to mark adherence to perceived tradition. Balaje, for example, explained to me that today's actresses do not deserve their reputation for loose morals. "All are *very* good people," he said. But when asked if he would allow his daughters to become actresses, he hedged by replying that they were not interested; when pressed, he admitted, "Well, if you ask me as a father, I would say no." The reason, he said, is that actors and actresses have no privacy, and actresses develop bad reputations because even when "they're extremely good [people], they [the public] talk nonsense" and gossip. Another director, Kommineni, was shocked when I asked if he would allow his daughter to act. "Madam," he replied, "we are a religious family – we don't allow our daughters – we come from a good family." Later in the interview, he explained his response this way: "Society is such that if a girl from a good family acts, society doesn't like it. When society changes, my feelings may not be like that." Both of these filmmakers justified their feelings with reference to public opinion – that is, to the criticism that their daughters and therefore they themselves would receive were they to violate a middle and upper class code that looks harshly on women who act on stage or screen. While the filmmakers themselves are involved in cinema (and, in both cases, would allow their sons to join), and may argue that women who enter it are as upright as any other women, they are very careful to show that in the case of their own families they adhere strictly to respectable values.

Do filmmakers' values entirely dominate their films and their audiences? It seems not. Filmmakers respond to audience demands, giving the audience a contributing role, presumably in order to attract them into the cinema. Films represent the values of both; the influence from either side, and the purpose of the values expressed, is anything but straightforward.

9

Fan clubs and politics

Many of the issues centered on utopian escape that arise in film themes are echoed in other aspects of cinema, although resolved differently. They appear in various ways in connection with fan clubs, particularly in the verbal images that fans construct of their heroes, the social services carried out in support of the star, and in the political use that stars have made of the cinema.

There are thousands, perhaps tens of thousands, of fan clubs in Madurai.[1] Some are part of a tightly organized statewide or even national network, while others, usually for minor stars, spring up independently and have no connections with other groups. Most of my work took place with members of the three largest fan club organizations in Tamil Nadu – those of the actors MGR, Kamalhasan, and Rajnikanth. I met members of local or "branch" clubs, and officers and members of Madurai ward, city, and district "head" clubs, for all three organizations. Meeting club members was often difficult in the beginning, since virtually all organized fans are young men and therefore not easily approached by a woman, but I worked around this problem by first getting to know club members with whom I had other connections (in two cases, for example, I knew the members' mothers well, and so was able to establish a comfortable informal relationship with the young men). Later these men introduced me to fellow club members and officers, and my contacts spread.[2] City and district leaders were difficult to contact but very willing to discuss their stars' merits once we met, and more knowledgeable about the administrative aspects of their respective organizations than were branch members. On the other hand, they were also far more concerned to give the club's "party line" when it came to sensitive matters such as members' caste makeup.

Fan clubs and politics   149

Almost all fan club members are men, most in their late teens to late twenties. Women rarely join, and when they do they join women's-only clubs (*racikai manrams*). By the time most women reach their late teens, they are being prepared for marriage, and it would be unseemly for them to participate in the public activities of a fan club. This remains true even after marriage, when the majority of women are at any rate too busy with household work to be involved in most outside organized activities. The vaguely licentious reputation of cinema also keeps women away, since they must be careful to keep their own reputations unsullied.[3]

Young men, on the other hand, often have the time, the lack of family responsibilities, and the freedom of movement that permit participation in outside activities such as fan club work. Most fan club members come from lower to middle Hindu castes and the lower or lower middle class, and are not highly educated. The clubs also include Muslims and Christians in what appeared to be rough proportion to their numbers in the general population. Class and communal makeup vary according to the organization, however, and within it according to individual clubs.[4] Hardgrave noted these differences between Shivaji and MGR groups in his research in 1969–70. Shivaji members, he said, were "primarily from

8.   Kamalhasan fan club officers flanking their club's signboard outside of the Tholilpatti neighborhood. 1990.

the lower middle class ... the majority [having] at least some education"; most clubs included some college students (1975: 18, 19). MGR's fans, on the other hand, were "primarily lower class, with education, status, and income a notch below the Shivaji clubs" (1975: 22). These generalizations were still valid in Madurai sixteen years later (see also Pandian 1992: 19–20). Kamalhasan and Rajnikanth club members are demographically fairly similar to those of MGR's organization, although their average age appears to be lower (unlike MGR or Shivaji, these stars' appeal inside and outside of fan clubs is largely limited to people under thirty). There were also a few Kamalhasan and Rajnikanth clubs made up of college students, but students' MGR clubs were almost unknown in Madurai.

Individual clubs are neighborhood based. Their members are drawn from a particular neighborhood, and reflect its distribution of religions, castes, and occupations. Size can vary anywhere from ten to a hundred members, but usually ranges between fifteen and thirty. Most clubs meet weekly or monthly; but some gather daily, while others meet only just prior to their star's new film releases. Occasionally clubs are able to rent a building for their meetings – or will have a generous patron who provides meeting space – but most of them meet in open public spaces, often on a street corner or in front of a member's house.

Much of what goes on at these meetings is simply conversation about the star and his or her current performance, with a dose of neighborhood gossip. Generally there is also some discussion about future activities for a film release, upcoming club celebrations or public meetings, and occasionally the proper strategic response to challenges or attacks from a rival star's organization. Sometimes a couple of members try out the star's latest dance steps, and movie magazines or club newsletters may be passed around. Unless the club is highly organized (as some MGR units are), however, and conducts formal discussions of the larger organizational plans or policies during its meetings, the appearance of these meetings is likely to resemble any relaxed and informal gathering of young men.

Each club that I met with had three to seven club officers. At minimum, this included a president, secretary (in charge of organizing activities), and treasurer. Often these officers would have official assistants. In addition to this internal structure, all major actors' fan clubs are part of a larger organizational structure, the intricacy and significance of which vary greatly. In the most highly organized groups, such as MGR's, there will be "head" (*talaimai*) clubs at the village or city ward[5] level that are responsible for helping and advising new and smaller "branch" (*kiḷai*) clubs. Above these are city, district, state, and even national (or international) level clubs and officials. Kamal's and Rajni's organizations have a similar but somewhat collapsed version of this structure. They have no head clubs at the ward level, and combine the city and district clubs into one. Of the two, Kamalhasan's groups appeared to be the most systematically marshaled in 1986. (Shortly before I returned in 1990, Kamal had officially disbanded his organization, but the club officers I spoke with disregarded this and continued to function as before, including taking regular trips to visit with the actor in Madras.) State offices are all in Madras, where most filming takes place, and the leader of the state-level head club is usually the president of the entire fan club (most organizations' official names include the term "All-India" [*akila intiya*], such as the "All-India Kamalhasan Social Welfare Fans Club"). Fan organizations' hierarchical structures are used to provide aid to local clubs, spread news about upcoming films and release dates, and disseminate information about the star's position on important issues.

I will draw illustrations from three of the clubs I knew best, one from each star's organization, to discuss fans' feelings for the star and their supporting activities. The Rajnikanth and Kamalhasan clubs are both based in Tholilpatti, and the MGR club is in the Lakshmipuram area; each has thirty to forty members. The Rajnikanth club was established in 1984 and the MGR and Kamalhasan clubs in 1985. Examples will also be cited from the Rajnikanth and Kamalhasan district head clubs and the head MGR club of the Madurai tenth ward (the ward in which Lakshmipuram is located). (Rajnikanth, Kamalhasan, and MGR clubs are found in the downtown area also; I worked most intensely with those clubs with whom I had a close connection to a member, for the reasons described above, and these happened to be in the other two neighborhoods.) Rajnikanth's district club began in 1976 and was claimed to be the very first Rajni club in India. Likewise, the Kamalhasan district leaders said theirs was established in 1978 as one of the first clubs for their star, beginning as the main Madurai club north of the Vaigai River (covering approximately half the city) and becoming the head club for the entire city and district two years later. The head MGR club of the tenth ward is the oldest of these six clubs, established in 1972 when MGR left the DMK. In addition to these six clubs, examples will also be taken from other groups when necessary to give a sense of the range of activities and feelings involved in belonging to a fan club.

152 *Cinema and the urban poor in South India*

Feelings for the star
Each major actor has a distinctive image, and the choice to join a particular star's fan club implies a preference for that image since membership in one group bars a person from joining any other star's club. The images of the four stars mentioned most often here – MGR, Shivaji Ganesan, Rajnikanth, and Kamalhasan – merit a brief description.

M. G. Ramachandran began acting in films in the 1930s. Along with Shivaji Ganesan, he has been one of the most popular stars for the last forty years. MGR played swashbuckling heroes and victorious underdogs, and was closely identified with the poor. He was portrayed as the savior of the downtrodden and of the victimized heroine, and is the most renowned of all Tamil stars for his screen fights. MGR was said to be seventy years old when he died in December 1987 (although unofficially estimated to be five years older) and had ardent fans of all ages, both men and women.

Shivaji is about ten years younger than MGR. When young, he was associated with the DMK party and played a number of "revolutionary" roles. He soon switched to the Congress party, however (and later to the Janata Dal), and is identified by fans today as a "family man." His acting is somewhat stylized and overdone by current standards, but less so than MGR's, and Shivaji is generally acknowledged to be the finer actor of the two. He too appeals to people of all ages, but this appeal tends to be stronger among the middle class than the poor. Nonetheless, he had many fans among the people I knew, especially women.

Rajnikanth is from the southern state of Karnataka, but has been starring in Tamil films since the mid-1970s. He has also worked as a producer and director. His characters are usually forceful men, and, like Raja in *Paṭikkaatavan*, sometimes experience the degradations suffered by the downtrodden. In his middle thirties in 1986, he is famous for his talents in dancing and fighting, and his appeal has been strongest among young men.

Kamalhasan's image is in many ways comparable to Rajnikanth's. Both men are about the same age. Like Rajnikanth, Kamal is celebrated among fans for his dancing and fighting abilities – although he is seen as a slightly more romantic hero than Rajni – and is also very popular among young men. He too is a director and producer. Kamalhasan is considered to be more of an "artist" than most Tamil actors because he acts in non-stereotypical roles. In 1986, he and Rajnikanth were comparably popular (and commanded the same amount of money per movie), but by 1990 Rajnikanth was a more popular hero, though fans admitted his characters rarely varied; meanwhile Kamalhasan had lost some of his following but was widely praised as a highly talented, sensitive, and resourceful artist.

Fans of these heroes rarely describe their emotional attachment to the star in explicit terms, but their feelings can be inferred from actions and from statements about him. Fan club members were eager to talk about their star's personal character (*guṇam*), and often went on at length about his goodness. Their descriptions focussed on the help he gave to the poor, good-naturedness, humility, and strength. They might also include praise for his unique acting ability. All of these actors' public images emphasized each of these ingredients, but in varying proportions.

Rajnikanth's fans often pointed out that the actor was a bus conductor before he got his film break. The president of the Tholilpatti Rajnikanth club reported that his club's main function was to promote Rajni by explaining to people, "Rajni is a good actor. He is a great man. He suffered when he was young. He was a conductor and lived like an ordinary man, but now he has come up." A fellow club member stated,

If you ask any actor or actress in the cinema industry about Rajni, they say that he is a good man. That's what we've heard. He has the heart of a child. If you go to any other actor's house you'll see a sign saying "Beware of Dogs." But if anyone goes to Rajni's house to get help from him at any time of the day or night, there will be people there to greet them. At any other actor's house there is the sign, "Beware of Dogs," but in Rajni's house there are people who will let us in.

The head of the Rajnikanth district club spent most of an hour's interview telling me how Rajni had risen from "poverty" and was still hardworking and concerned with the problems of "the people" despite his current fame. Rajni is "like a machine (*macciin maatiri*)," he said. "He shoots Tamil films 200 days a year, Hindi films 165 days a year. And anyone who needs help, he helps." Perhaps defending against recent charges of discontent in the Rajnikanth fan organization, he continued, "As long as we believe in him, the organization will function well. Rajni is our god and elder brother. As long as we are alive, we must believe in Rajni."

Kamalhasan was portrayed as good-natured, talented, and concerned about his fans. He has a reputation for an even temper. One ardent fan, a club officer who had been to meet Kamal in Madras, explained, "He is good. He treats people with love, and makes them laugh. He does not yell angrily at them. I have never seen him talking to people in an angry mood; I've only seen him with a smiling face. He is happy, and makes others happy."

A number of fans lauded Kamalhasan's acting and dancing ability.

Some called him their *guru*, a respected teacher, especially in dancing. Fans seemed to like the fact that Kamalhasan sometimes plays vulnerable and tragic characters, and praised these roles most often. (On the other hand, the film that most young fans mentioned watching more than once was *Vikram*, in which Kamal plays a tough, cool secret agent.) For example, a club leader in Tholilpatti who had visited Kamalhasan in Madras described his acting and his role in *Cippikkuḷ Muttu* – in which he plays a young simple-minded man who marries a widow by grabbing a thali from a temple offering plate and tying it around her neck – in this way:

In that film, he gives life to a widow. By giving life to a widow he acts as an innocent, immature person. It is very difficult to play that kind of role. Disco dancing or glamorous roles – those anyone can do. But not everyone can act like an innocent child. His acting is terrific.[6]

The theme of the ingenuous child appears again in a description of Kamalhasan given by the district club secretary, who had made several trips to meet with the actor. This man said that Kamal has "the heart of a two-and-a-half year old child." When I asked him to explain what it is like to have the heart of a child, he answered,

If some director is with him asking for his call sheets and a family friend or the fans come and want to meet him, he stops everything and comes out to meet them. He keeps the influential people waiting in order to meet the fans ... He does not gossip. He does not interfere in matters that are not his concern. If we ask about his personal problems, he says, "It is my personal matter and if you interfere, we will lose our friendship." If anyone says something that he doesn't like – well, that is, if you give a two-and-a-half year old child something that it doesn't want, then the child throws it down and starts to cry. But if you give the child something it needs then it stops crying and grows quiet. In the same way, if anyone says something he doesn't like – for example, when we tell him that Rajnikanth has just visited Madurai and that he should come too, he answers, "I do not need fans who clap and whistle when they see me. They can function without me there. I need fans who feel that Kamalhasan is in their hearts." That is Kamalhasan the two-and-a-half year old child.

Some of these qualities were also found in MGR's image, which included characteristics of compassion and unsparing generosity, but also gave equal emphasis to physical strength. In 1985–87, MGR's generosity and his power both received the most persistently glowing praise of any star. Fans frequently pointed out that MGR had grown up poor, and therefore understood and wished to alleviate the problems of the poor. They claimed repeatedly that MGR welcomed all his fans who visited him into his home. He was both greatly loved and greatly respected; one of the titles he was known by was *vaattiyaar*, "teacher," a position of great reverence among Tamils.

Unlike other stars, MGR had the advantage of added publicity as the head of the state government. Thus his fans frequently cited the government welfare programs MGR had established (or in some cases merely expanded) as examples of his commitment to the poor. I asked the president of the tenth ward head club, a man in his forties, what MGR's nature was like. He answered, "He has a thoroughly good character. This is important. He helps the poor people, and gives liberally to them, without reserve. He has been like this from the beginning. That is why we like him." When I asked this man what he thought of Shivaji, he compared him with MGR:

When Shivaji gives things away, he is "economical" about it. But MGR has always been liberal and uncalculating about giving – that is why there is a difference in their behavior. When MGR gives Rs. 10,000, Shivaji gives Rs. 5,000. MGR runs a school for poor children in Madras in his own name. Some 2,000 students study at his expense – it is a free private school. He gives them clothing and books. There are two or three places like this. At Madurai Meenakshi Women's College, he supports two students. He has helped people like that from the beginning. Not just now – even in his early film days. [He has] a mother's heart (*oru taay uḷḷam*) – that's what we say.

Such claims about MGR's generosity and compassion were heard from all of MGR's fans and followers, not just those who belonged to fan clubs. But unlike most other fans, the club members also stressed their hero's political and physical potency. One MGR member stated that MGR was the most significant figure of the Dravidian movement, and "of all actors today, the only one who cares about the Tamils." The treasurer of the Lakshmipuram branch club, who volunteered a detailed (if somewhat erroneous) history of MGR's political rise, told me in 1986 that "MGR is the center of the Dravidian parties: Jayalalitha, Karunanidhi, even Annadurai achieved success only by MGR."[7]

But it was the actor–politician's physical prowess that received the greatest tribute. The fight scenes in MGR's films (which his detractors claimed were filmed with stunt doubles) figured heavily in such praise. The young Lakshmipuram officer gave me an extended description of the different types of fights MGR waged in his films (based on the weapons used) and claimed that no current actors display the grace and skill of MGR in their fights. He continued: "No one has his majesty. Even a coward would become brave after seeing our leader like that in the movies." This young man vehemently denied that his hero, then seventy years old, lost physical or mental strength as he grew older. "We expect him to live not to 100 years of age but higher, and for every year he grows older he becomes that much more vigorous. He will be just like a twenty year old man."

Hardgrave has reported fans' statements about Shivaji Ganesan, which, while not specifically attributed to fan club members, indicate that he shares some similar appeal. In particular, generosity is again a primary element of the image. According to Hardgrave,

> his contribution of 1 lakh [one hundred thousand] rupees to the mid-day meal program for children was repeatedly mentioned by survey respondents, as was [sic] his contributions of food and money for the relief of Madras flood victims in 1962. Although most of his contributions have been through government agencies, one fan, echoing the words of a Shivaji publicity release, said, "He has never refused to give money to anyone who asks him for it." Another fan was sure that Shivaji had donated at least 85 lakhs to the public cause. (1975: 5)

Most fans have very strong feelings about their heroes, as shown by their statements about the stars and the vehemence with which they pronounce them. These feelings may originate even before they have seen one of the star's movies, when as children they listen to older fans praising different actors and arguing about their talents. Many little boys I knew could dance on cue in the style of Rajnikanth or Kamalhasan, and had already made up their minds about which of the two they liked best. Passions grow even stronger once the children are old enough to watch movies regularly, and fans can be passionately devoted to the movie stars without ever seeing them in person.

Fan's descriptions of the stars suggest the qualities that they find attractive in film heroes. All of these share a connection with either the attributes or the desires of the urban poor. The predominant attribute of the heroes is a spirit of generosity: a willingness to help anyone without reservation, and especially to aid the poor. The star is believed to feel concern for his (lower class) fans, who depict themselves as the deserving but less influential and thus lower status persons who are welcomed into the star's own home – an act connoting roughly equivalent status between host and guest – perhaps even in preference to prestigious individuals such as film producers.[8] Fans also recount the romanticized poverty that the stars were subjected to "before," either in childhood (MGR) or into adulthood (Rajnikanth), and the hard labor they continue to endure; these accounts buttress claims of solidarity between the poor and the star (as well as providing exemplary instances of individuals who have "come up" to social and financial success). Thus these fans emphasize their hero's abiding interest in the poor as a group (a category that includes the fans) and in the fans themselves as individuals. MGR's emphasis on physical power rather than words identified him with the lower class, who perceive their chances of besting wealthier and better educated people to lie in, if anything, their ability to fight rather than to debate.

There is another side to these heroes that is best captured in the fans' phrase, "a heart like that of a child." Along with unguarded generosity, such a description suggests a loving rather than a guileful or calculating nature, spontaneity, openness – all portrayed as a refreshing ingenuousness. All of these heroes are described (with pride) as humble: they want their fan clubs to act as instruments of service to the poor rather than as mouthpieces of praise. Generosity and ingenuousness imply a personality and an approach to the poor that are starkly in contrast to those of most powerful people known to urban lower class residents.

The stars' supposed childlike natures do not preclude respect from their fans. Kamalhasan and MGR are addressed as teachers, as "*guru*" or "*vaattiyaar*." But the emphasis on the ingenuous, especially among Kamalhasan's fans, becomes striking when we consider the primary element of MGR's image that is lacking in the others: extreme physical (and political) potency. MGR is seen as compassionate and giving, but exceedingly powerful and forceful. The fight scenes in Rajnikanth's and Kamalhasan's films are renowned, and yet physical prowess never entered a fan club member's description of the *personal* nature of either actor. While MGR's image is like that of traditional South Indian folk heroes – usually portrayed in oral and written accounts (Srinivasan 1964; Kulkarni 1965) as strong and valiant in battle as well as wise, generous, compassionate, and revered – these younger actors represent a departure from the traditional image.

All of the attributes cited serve to associate the stars with the poor and dissociate them from the wealthy people with whom the poor are most familiar. Much like film themes that invert the social hierarchy, fans' descriptions of the stars imply respect for the lower class despite their poverty, chide the rich for their scornful and miserly attitudes, and portray the poor as ultimately more moral and (therefore) more worthy than the rich.

"Devotion" best characterizes the club members' feelings for the stars. Their praises suggest a mix of passionate affection and respect. The ways in which the three heroes are referred to in the descriptions above – as elder brothers, teachers, gods or, indulgently, as children – all imply devotion in Tamil culture. Fans' commitment to the stars grows out of their devotion; actions are intended to demonstrate such feelings. Sacrifices of time, money, physical comfort, and safety made in order to see an important film showing or the star himself indicate a fan's love and loyalty; there is even a sense that individual sacrifices are appreciated by the star and will eventually be rewarded by him, in an undefined manner, as acts of merit.[9]

Fan club activities

Fan clubs employ a variety of means for promoting and glorifying these objects of their devotion. Different clubs' activities vary widely, both from organization to organization and within a single organization. Some are recreational, others more purely service-oriented. Recreational activities include attending films, promoting them by pasting posters or buying up tickets to bolster a film's lagging run. At the theater, especially during the first week or two of a movie, fans throw confetti, cheer, and recite dialogues (memorized beforehand from scripts distributed by the head clubs) whenever their hero or heroine appears on the screen. Rival fan clubs fight inside the theater when a film stars two major actors. (Such films appear infrequently, however, and rivalry erupts more often outside the theater, when one star's club attacks another's during a meeting or when rival clubs deface one another's posters.)[10]

Whenever possible, fans attend a film on its opening day. Tickets are expensive (ranging in 1986 from Rs. 5 to Rs. 25 for a II class seat that usually cost Rs. 2.50, for example), and difficult to obtain even at high prices. (Members have greater access to them than most viewers, since club officials buy large blocks of tickets from theater managers in advance and then sell them to their members, generally making a small profit for the club.)[11] Opening days of popular films draw huge crowds to the theaters – where hopeful viewers suffer a long wait, crushing throngs of people, and even police clubs in attempting to obtain one of the remaining tickets – and enduring the difficulties of such crowds adds to the extent of the devotion that club members (and other fans) demonstrate in attending the first day show (cf. Hardgrave 1975: 16).

Other recreational events include club "functions" (for which the English term is used). Most are celebrations. In general, fan clubs have at least two of these a year: one for the club's anniversary and another for the star's birthday.[12] Some clubs, however – most of them MGR groups, including the head club in the Lakshmipuram area – put on up to six or eight large events during the year, staging public meetings (*kuuṭṭam*s) in addition to the regular celebrations.[13] The clubs make an effort to ingratiate themselves to neighbors at these times, and to strengthen their star's reputation for generosity, by distributing food, clothing or other articles to area residents. These items most often include sweets, books, and saris, and are distributed to neighborhood children and/or elderly residents.[14]

In large and small organizations alike, club functions serve several purposes. Group-centered activities such as anniversary and birthday celebrations strengthen members' solidarity and renew their commitment to the group. They give the clubs public exposure, and sometimes – particularly when gifts are distributed to neighbors – promote a positive image within the neighborhood. Positive images of both club and star become of greater focus in social service activities, however, than in celebrations.

While most club activities are recreational, almost all clubs profess an interest in carrying out "good deeds" or "social services" (*narpaṇi, nalla kaariyam*) and members represent service activities as their club's most significant work. The label "social services" subsumes a wide range of deeds, varying from civic services, such as notifying authorities of fires or policing the neighborhoods, to disaster relief, to donations of food, clothing, and other items to the poor. It is the latter that club members refer to most frequently. Even these donations vary widely. At one end of the continuum are the distribution of goods or awards of sports prizes at the "functions" described above, and at the other are charitable donations of costly tools to area laborers or the establishment of blood banks. Clearly these cover different levels of "service," and members may have any or all of them in mind when referring to their clubs' philanthropic deeds.

Public opinion about fan clubs is ambivalent, sometimes portraying them as groups of "rowdies" who gather together simply to waste time and boast about their star[15] and other times complimenting the groups' service projects (thus recognizing the dual purposes of the clubs). All the club officers I met, however, claimed that the main purpose of their organization was to do good works in aid of the poor. (MGR's officers also stressed the importance of their clubs' political work, which for them is often inseparable from social welfare projects.) Some of them even stated that their members were not supposed to have "fun," only to do good works in the star's name. The president of the Rajnikanth club in Tholilpatti, for example, told me,

We have opened this club to do good and to work hard. We don't like to play around. We must do services for the public – we must help people – that is what our purpose is. We don't enjoy putting up stages and dancing, either. As for

Rajnikanth, we cannot spoil his name. If we visit him, he will receive us warmly and solicitously and [say], "You should do only good works. Do not put up stages and dance or sing. You should help the poor. This is the way you must run the organization – if not, there is no reason to have the clubs."

Similarly, the secretary of the neighborhood's Kamalhasan club said that when he and his companions went to register their new club, they were told by district leaders how a club should be run:

We must not just have a club. It must not be started for the purpose of whistling, singing, disco dancing, and performing. If we start the club, we should work continuously to do good. We must not spoil Kamalhasan's name. Kamalhasan's own goal is for the club [to work] this way.

Unlike the president of the Rajnikanth club, the Kamalhasan club leaders told me that, in addition to attempting to carry out good works, their members could also put on dance performances. It is clear from both statements, however, that these club officers wish their activities to strengthen the reputation of their star, and believe that a failure to do laudable deeds or an involvement in disorderly acts might hurt his reputation instead.

Like the branch club officers, the leaders of both organizations' district-level clubs stress the importance of social welfare activities and the star's own mandate to carry out such activities. The secretary of the Kamalhasan district club reported that when he and a few others approached Kamalhasan to start one of the first clubs in Madurai, the film hero told them that clubs could be established on the condition that they "not be like normal fan clubs." According to the secretary, Kamal admonished, "The clubs established in my name must not be for the mere passing of time. They must aid the people; it must be a social service organization."

In this case, the impetus for an ethos of social service does indeed start at the top. When I interviewed Kamalhasan (September 1986), he too told me that he had allowed his clubs to be formed only because they would be "unusual":

We are trying to do things different from what existing fan clubs do. So it becomes very difficult because they [members] cite examples [of other clubs' more leisurely activities], and they feel that we're making life more difficult for them, because instead of just being fans they are given hard work, they don't simply whistle ...

Slowly, it's a *very* big task, because either usually they've been trained to become political, or a personal army who'll help them [the star] out in times of stress and need. So these people have not been trained in it [social service] so it becomes more difficult when we're trying to accomplish [something unusual].

The president of the Madurai district Rajnikanth club explained the need for a social service orientation because "our brother Rajni has given us a rich life; in this same way, we must try to enrich the people's lives and satisfy their needs." He recited an ambitious list of services to be provided, including aid to people with physical handicaps; improvement of public hygiene, drinking water availability, and ration shops; road development in rural areas; free schooling by educated members for poor children; provision of eyeglasses and medical "eye camps" for poor people with vision problems; and donations to poor couples on the occasion of their marriages.

Most club members made more modest claims, although almost all stated that such services are one of their major aims. Even those who admitted that they had not *yet* carried out any service project (including the Rajnikanth branch president cited above) held on to the belief that these services were one of their main functions and intended to carry them out as soon as possible. In fact, only a small percentage of any branch club's time and energy is spent on social services. Nonetheless, the ethos of service is very important to members – demonstrated by their insistence on listing service as the club's primary purpose – and the intention to carry out welfare projects and the belief that these remain the clubs' main objective are as important to members as the actual accomplishment of such projects. Members and officers alike appeared to have a genuine desire to carry out aid projects, and their faith that they and fellow club members would give aid whenever possible convinced them that they were helping to change the circumstances of the poor.

Indeed, I saw evidence that various aid projects were accomplished, and heard reports of many more occasions. Fan magazines always carry stories and photographs of service projects, and even local newspapers may report them. (For example, in March 1990, the Madurai edition of *Maalai Muracu* carried a large story with photos of a Vijaykanth club's presentation ceremony.)

Most of the club members reporting activities that fall into the "civic service" category belonged to MGR's organization, and in fact, because of their political interests, MGR's fan clubs tended to be more involved in the daily affairs of their neighborhoods than did other stars' clubs.[16] During my first visit to Madurai in 1985–87, the major prestations of goods were also most likely to be carried out by MGR's clubs, because of the greater political and financial resources available to the MGR fan organization at that time. (Moreover, these acts of charity are an important element of leadership in Tamil Nadu, and thus may have been

162 *Cinema and the urban poor in South India*

somewhat more important to MGR than to the younger stars who have not [yet] entered politics.) They require a substantial presentation ceremony, including lavish stages and distinguished political speakers.

The tenth ward head club staged one of these ceremonies in 1985. According to the club's president, neighborhood residents who make their living by pressing clothing had asked club members to procure "iron boxes" from government welfare programs for which the laborers were qualified. The fan club members then petitioned the Collector (the top government official of the district), who reportedly came to the neighborhood to determine the legitimacy of the request. Once the "donation" was agreed to, arrangements were made for the presentation ceremony. As always at such functions, the occasion involved a great number of speeches praising MGR. The Welfare Minister played a prominent role, eager as political officials always are to make a personal appearance, to be associated with a popular leader, and to gain credit for providing charity. Once the speeches had been made, the chosen recipients came forward as they were called, presented their cards, and received their new irons. Afterward, the club president said, "these forty people each gave us ten

9. Stage erected for an MGR fan club's presentation ceremony, viewed after the performance has ended. The stage is decorated in the ADMK party colors of red, black and white, with pictures of C. N. Annadurai and MGR above and the party's "twin leaves" symbol at the back. 1986.

rupees and said, 'Take these 400 rupees and conduct meetings and do something for the poor.'" (It was explained that this money helped to meet the club's basic operating expenses.)

Like newsreel depictions of MGR's own acts of benevolence, such events have had the effect of spreading their influence beyond the immediate recipients to others who come to learn of them. Presentations such as this one allow the fan clubs, attending political officials, and, most importantly, MGR himself to receive credit for giving – even though the irons actually came from public government programs and money.[17]

Because it takes time to build up the necessary financial and/or political capital, events such as these occur only infrequently. In contrast to these largely one-time activities are the ongoing social service projects operated by one or two organizations. The best example of these is Kamalhasan's campaign to set up blood supplies and eye "banks." Kamalhasan described the projects and explained the need for them in this way:

They [Kamalhasan fan club members] have gone into something which is very different from [what] other people have done. They've gone into a blood donation campaign, they've started donating their eyes. And now slowly from next year, we're trying to reach a mark of 35,000 blood donors, free blood donors, throughout Tamil Nadu, which will take care of the blood shortage in Tamil Nadu according to the census ... Probably it's not a big problem in a country like America, but here you must have come to understand that there are professional blood donors. They are drunk, syphilitic, sometimes; we don't know what they carry. Probably even AIDS, sometimes. So we need healthy people to do that and that's what we're trying to promote. Right now a few of them have gathered somebody appreciative of their work, who has donated a two-acre land near Salem [a city in northern Tamil Nadu]. They're trying to build a hospital ... I go every six months to inaugurate a blood campaign. I think it's a nice way of shedding blood. (interview, September 1986)

All of the varieties of activities I have described and the reports that fan club members had heard and read of them were crucial to creating a conviction among members that their clubs were doing good works for the poor. While most club activities are in fact recreational rather than service-oriented, members were sincere when claiming that their clubs' main purpose was social welfare. And while the opportunity to serve the poor is not the main reason that most fans join clubs – rather, they would say, they join "to promote and support the star" – it is nonetheless what they believe to be the "ultimate" purpose of their clubs, and in fact essential to promoting the star. Moreover, the lack of time actually spent on service activities relative to recreation need not imply that these clubs are less service-oriented than other voluntary welfare organizations, since this relative time apportionment is also characteristic of some other organizations that cite social services as their primary objective (see P. Caplan 1985: 159–61]. I would argue that the service orientation of these clubs is not to be measured by the amount of time spent on service relative to recreation, since the *perception* of making a social contribution is as significant to members as are the acts of service themselves.

An informative comparison can be made between the type of aid that fan clubs provide the poor and that provided by other social welfare groups in South India, most of which are comprised of relatively wealthy people, described in the literature as upper-middle and upper class members (see P. Caplan 1985; Driver and Driver 1987: 106). Lower class aid societies such as the fan clubs emphasize what Thompson calls an "ethos of mutuality," embodying an emphasis on the collective that contrasts with "middle-class ideas of individualism or (at their best) of service" (1963: 423). Although Thompson is speaking of nineteenth-century England, the attitudes he cites are strikingly parallel to those in contemporary South India, where most upper-class social service associations call for remedies of "*uplift, reform, rehabilitation, guidance*, and *enlightenment*" for recipients whom they characterize as "*poor, suffering, helpless, backward*, and *ignorant*" (P. Caplan 1985: 202, emphasis in original). This terminology and depiction are also strikingly similar to those expressed by Tamil film directors. While both these groups would offer "guidance" and "enlightenment" – consonant with a middle and upper class ideology of self-help – fan clubs attempt to provide material aid, addressing what they see as the true cause of hardship in working class lives. Rather than accept an upper class model that insists on moral betterment, lower class fans, who believe themselves to be morally superior to the judgmental and exploitative rich, suggest that what the poor need to escape their problems is financial assistance.

Thus, to the extent that fan clubs stand as *mutual* aid societies, participation strengthens members' identification with the lower class and their intentions to assist that class. While more good is claimed than accomplished, most clubs give at least token assistance by distributing small amounts of food and other goods at their anniversary celebrations. Since the great majority of members of the clubs described in this chapter would depict themselves as well as their beneficiaries as "poor" or "suffering" people, it is clear that they are helping a group of people that they identify themselves as members of. This equation is underscored by the location of most acts of service in the members' own neighborhoods, among the people with whom they reside.

It must also be noted, however, that the "collective" aspect of this aid has its limits.[18] While the identity of class standing between fan club members and the recipients of their charity can be made indirectly, as I have just done ("I am poor" and "I help the poor" suggest "I help people like me"), it is never stated in words by fan club members, and the consistency of this omission is striking. Rather than being expressed, for example, as, "We help ourselves" or, "We help people who are poor like us," statements of aid never associate the speaker with the group to be aided. Instead, beneficiaries are always categorized as "the poor," "the people" or "the laborers." In portraying themselves as helpers and even leaders of the poor, fan club members thereby set themselves apart from the rest of the poor, superior to them; in aiming to improve their lives, they often patronized them. Perhaps the proper characterization of members' relationship with their own "class" is that they are members of the poor but also stand above them.

Cinema and politics
Of all the stars whom viewers applaud and fan clubs support, there is one who stands out in the depth of devotion he received and the skill with which he utilized his clubs. This is MGR. He was the first actor to take full advantage of cinema's features as a political tool – in particular, its potential for broadcasting a carefully crafted and widely appealing image in an area with no comparable mass media,[19] and the accompanying network of fan clubs. Unlike the situation in many other industrialized nations, few people in India can watch the nightly news on television to see politicians and hear their speeches, nor can politicians rely on newspapers for contact with voters, since few people read the paper with any regularity. Even radio is limited as an information medium, since most people listen to radios only to hear movie songs. Film, on the other hand, is widespread and accessible to the majority of viewers. While several South Indian actors have made political use of their film success (including Shivaji Ganesan, Jayalalitha, and N. T. Rama Rao), MGR remains the most successful in translating a movie image into an effective political persona.[20] In the process, he also transformed his network of fan clubs into a powerful political support system.

In forty years of film acting, MGR developed an image as a dashing romantic hero and the protector of the poor, an image that became accepted as a representation of his own personal nature. Born in about 1915 to a Malayali family[21] in Sri Lanka, MGR is supposed to have left school at the age of six when his father died. His impoverished family then

166 *Cinema and the urban poor in South India*

moved to Tamil Nadu, where MGR and his elder brother joined a boys' drama troupe. By 1936 MGR had made his first film, and his first hit came out in 1947. It was several years after this that he joined C. N. Annadurai's DMK party.

As Tamil political consciousness flowered in the 1950s and '60s, MGR

10. A Jayalalitha cutout towering above Mount Road in Madras. 1991.

11. Jayalalitha in a poster advertising a recent showing of an old MGR–Jayalalitha film. 1991.

crafted his film and political image carefully. Called the "Douglas Fairbanks of South India," MGR had often played the swashbuckling hero in his early films. With his growing political involvement he added many roles that reflected the populist ideology of the DMK party, frequently playing the oppressed but victorious underdog. Like other Tamil movies, MGR's films were filled with flowery dialogue, love songs, and dramatic fights. I was told (always by men or by women who disavowed such feelings) that MGR's female fans were greatly swayed by his love scenes. His acrobatic fight sequences, however, were the most acclaimed of all. Handsome MGR fought the dark-skinned villains with swords, sticks, and fists – and always won. Good triumphed over evil as MGR rescued the heroine and brought justice to the poor.

The film *Nadodi Mannan* ("Vagabond King" or "Vagabond and King") was one of his most popular movies and a prime example of the use he made of rhetoric and action to build an image as a hero of the downtrodden.[22] In this film, MGR plays the double role of vagabond revolutionary and aristocratic king. When the two characters first meet, the vagabond tries to convince the king of the need for people's rule. When the king responds that he *is* one of the people, MGR the vagabond argues passionately,

> How is it possible for you, accustomed as you are to seeing your cup filled to the brim with milk, to understand the people who live in the midst of sewage? *You* have to struggle over which of your two thousand garments to wear. The people long to have just one thin garment with which to hide their nakedness and save their honor – how could you possibly understand this? Your courtesans leap to spread a silk carpet before you. The people must break off the thorns that tear into their feet as they go, trudging onward. How is it conceivable that you should be one of them?

Quickly persuaded by such argument, the king agrees to join forces with the revolutionary and together fight the evil agents in the land (whom viewers readily recognized as signifying the Congress party).

Characters and speeches such as these foreshadowed MGR's own political rhetoric. A proclamation delivered at the end of the film – after the vagabond disguised as the king has rescued the real king from his evil ministers and an island princess from the adoptive father who tried to force her into marrying him, and the two MGR characters have returned in triumph – "could easily pass for the DMK election manifesto" (Hardgrave 1975: 14). The president of a Madurai fan club told me in 1986 that *Nadodi Mannan* was his favorite movie because "that film is the fight between the ruling class and the working class … Everything MGR announced in that court, he does now as Chief Minister."

In his many movies, MGR smashed tyrants and replaced them with his own populist rule, worshipped his mother, condemned the use of alcohol, gave food and clothing to the poor. He played rickshaw pullers and revolutionary leaders, charming lovers and dutiful sons. His characterizations identified strongly with the lower class. Combined with a bewitching glamor and charm, it added up to a glittering championship of the poor.

This was an image that voters believed in. Fans knew that MGR *was* what they saw in the movies, and accepted the movie image as the real person. Poor and uneducated voters especially saw MGR as their hero. Unlike most other film stars, MGR was perceived as someone who not only understood and cared about the problems of the disadvantaged and oppressed, but also possessed the necessary power to attack and solve those problems.

The nature of this identification of MGR with his screen roles is interesting. It was not a simple equation of the two. Rather, in conversations about the film star it became clear that people believed that MGR would not have chosen to play the roles he did unless he sincerely believed in the values his characters espoused. For his followers, MGR's roles were an illustration of how he himself would act in real-life circumstances.

Once he achieved state leadership, MGR's immense personal popularity continued despite the fact that he had made no movies in the last ten years. When I was in Madurai his old films still played in numerous theaters to packed houses. As Chief Minister, MGR took care to maintain his film image by associating himself with emotionally charged and easily identifiable issues (including prohibition, subsidized housing, and food and clothing for children) – and with legislation regarding these issues – with the result that voters would cite his government welfare programs to me side-by-side with his actions in movies as evidence that MGR "helps people like us."

One of the measures of his popularity was the personal closeness that many followers felt to the Chief Minister. People talked about MGR as if he were a close relative. Many followers thought of him as a protecting, helping older brother.[23] Some women talked of him as a father, and told me that others fantasized about him as a lover.[24] MGR's critics used to claim that he won elections only because of all the rural women who were in love with him.

The perception of such relationships, at least the platonic ones, implies the assumption of reciprocal feelings from MGR; and in fact there was a regularly expressed belief that MGR was directly interested in each of his followers, as well as in the poor as a whole. A number of popular myths testified to this. For example, it was often stated that the childless MGR gave all his money to the poor, who took the place of his own children. As proof, people would point to their children and say, "See that school uniform? MGR gave that to us last year at the harvest festival." It was also believed that when MGR died, he would leave a little money to his wife and bequeath all the rest to the poor. (When in the event this did not happen, people explained that either his wife had taken the money or intra-party rivalries had consumed it.) For most voters, MGR's honesty and integrity were beyond question: I heard repeatedly that while his ministers might be corrupt and greedy, MGR never was.

Statements such as these demonstrate the compelling strength of MGR's film image in propagating a public perception of the Chief Minister that corresponded to that image. Poor voters believed that the honest MGR, who had nothing but their own best interests at heart, would defend them in real life as he had for years in his films. After all, would he have made such movies if his heart did not agree with them? For his part, MGR demonstrated a reciprocal devotion to the poor through well publicized acts of charity and populist political measures. The strength of his image was such that the actual effects of his economic policies, which were ultimately detrimental to the poor and beneficial to the rich (see Pandian 1992: 21ff for one discussion), went unnoticed by most voters. Nor was he held accountable by followers for aberrations such as the behavior of the ministers he had chosen. Indeed, it was not the ministers who had attracted them to MGR's party; it was MGR, whom they would follow – as was stated repeatedly – to any party he chose to grace.

MGR's cinematically generated image survived many attacks by political rivals, and much evidence of his own corruption. Nonetheless, while the strong personal appeal of someone like MGR is difficult to combat, it is insufficient by itself to keep a leader in power. Hence the importance of his fan clubs. Their political significance derives first from their position as a crucial grass-roots network in the ADMK party, and second from the propaganda value of the social services they perform, which operationalize a star's philanthropic image.

MGR's clubs began organizing in the mid-1950s, the first of any fan organization. When MGR left the DMK he was accompanied by very few high-level DMK officials but took much of the party's mass following with him, including many thousands of fan club members. These groups soon evolved into a tightly organized, intricate network of political support.

They have been involved in politics in a number of ways, maintaining their involvement even after his death. They provide indirect support to the party by advertising the re-release of MGR's important films and cheering him at his movies. Members attend ADMK party gatherings as a group, and help in the preparations for rallies. Clubs campaign for party candidates in important elections, and – although this seems to have declined since MGR's death – often had some say in determining who those candidates would be. During MGR's tenure in office, ward head-club leaders claimed that they were sometimes even allowed to put up slates of candidates drawn from their own ranks. Because members are devoted to promoting MGR in all his capacities, they have been zealous canvassers and fundraisers. Finally, social service projects also provided critical support for MGR. Presentation ceremonies, for example, allowed the fan clubs, attending political officials, and most importantly MGR to receive credit for the important act of giving. There was very little a political rival could say that would sway voters when they had concrete proof of MGR's giving nature.

No other politician or party could claim such a well organized, widespread, and reliable cadre. Campaign and service activities provided the support and promotional adjunct to the heroic image MGR had built through cinema. While fan club members respond to the same cinematic image as other viewers, their accounts of it differ from those of the general public. As mentioned above, these young men emphasize MGR's virility in addition to his generosity and compassion. A substantial portion of their conversations about MGR consists of praises for his fighting ability and political power. The significant difference between these fans and others of MGR's followers seems to be their status as young men – who (much more than women) are allowed to engage in public action but, despite their eagerness to do so, have even less social stature to back their desire than do older men. While many followers fantasized about themselves in MGR's place, fan club members are those who have identified most closely with MGR, and see his values and accomplishments as those they wish for themselves.[25]

For these fans MGR was and, as an image, still is powerful and vital, a leader who stands in stark contrast to their own perceived helplessness. The young male fan club members, disadvantaged and relatively powerless in Tamil society, are (like others of the urban poor) frustrated by the perception that their lives are worsening while the forces of change seem beyond their control. For them MGR represents the strong and potent men they would like to be, someone who could overcome the gigantic forces and change the circumstances that frustrate them and their families.

MGR has been the most successful of all actors in capitalizing on his film popularity. He was the only star whose image assured viewers that he had not only compassion but the potency to put it into action. Many followers saw him as someone who could actually change the circumstances that frustrate them and overcome the forces that make their lives insecure. His fans believed MGR to be an ally in real life just as he was in film. Perhaps the most effective action yet to grow out of cinema was the mass electoral support that pushed MGR and his party into power. Rather than resigning themselves to the present, an overwhelming number of viewers voted for a man who was identified as a hero of the oppressed, a man who had risen through a lower-class entertainment medium, and put him into power. For those who ask what effects the daydreams of cinema can have in real life, the crucial role of films in promoting MGR's ascent to power provides a striking answer.

Fan club and political activities, like films, reveal ambivalence about urban poor identity. Club members protest the subordination of the poor by supporting heroes who, while rich and famous, nonetheless act in great contrast to the wealthy, treating and portraying the poor as the poor would have the wealthy treat and portray them. Heroes respect their fans and help them with money. In return, fans support them and embellish the heroes' reputations by doing good works, works that involve material aid to the poor. They insist that the poor deserve respect and assistance as morally upright people.

On the other hand, there are signs of attempts to escape this lauded identity. While club members seek to aid their deserving fellows, they choose to interpret their own patron and helper roles as indications of higher status. Heroes are loved best when they remember that they too were once poor – when they are both *of* the poor and *above* them. The spectacular "rags to riches" success of these few individuals highlights the chances of those who are still poor to escape their situation. MGR pulled off what Bailey has called the "supreme trick of identification in which the mass see [the leader] not only as an ideal above them but simultaneously as one of them" (Bailey 1988: 119). And voters supported him not only because of his ties to and compassion for the poor, but also because he vowed to ease their distress and remove them from poverty. Like the movie themes that oscillate between promising the poor wealth in the future and telling them they have true (i.e. moral) wealth now, these activities express a tension between the desire of poor people to be other than they are and to be proud of who they are.

10

Conclusions

Critics castigate Tamil film for artificiality, for its distance from reality. The lack of the real is, as Silverman (1988) argues,[1] intrinsic to cinema, but these critics' complaints focus on what is in fact a rather trite artificiality, and miss cinema's connections to the real. Films draw heavily from reality, portraying situations that bear remarkable resemblance to the everyday stresses and aspirations of viewers' lives. Audiences recognize the links. They see connections between their lives and films in both general and specific terms, apply morals to parallel circumstances, and remark on the impact that cinema has on lives not divorced from it.

That they do all this in very personal terms highlights the lack of collective lessons drawn in or from melodrama, a result in part of the genre's emotional structure. Melodrama draws suppressed fears and desires into a public realm, but suggests personal solutions. While giving concrete form to anxieties caused by shared socioeconomic circumstances, it rarely advocates collective solutions. In fact, as we have seen, far from encouraging collective efforts, films may imply that no effort at all is required for the removal of obstacles. Nor do viewers make the connection back to class discrepancies, one of the predominant sources of their problems, the very problems they attend films in order to escape. While they clearly recognize connections between their lives and movies and derive morals that can be applied to their lives, they do all this in thoroughly personal terms. A similar conflict between class roots and personal application emerges in the rhetoric and activities of fan clubs as well. As aid organizations, movie star fan clubs embody some collective effort. Yet both in the individual success stories that they cite for stars, which highlight these actors' individual efforts and escape from poverty, and in their own disassociation from the poor, the clubs encourage a lack of collective action.

Throughout this book, there has emerged the sense that class-based problems are portrayed and interpreted in individualizing and individual terms. The potential for escape from these problems is also stated in such terms. The conflict between class roots and individual desires is visible in many aspects of cinema, and integrally connected to the escape that cinema provides. In the remainder of this conclusion, I return to the question of how escape is constructed in cinema.

Tamil film critics complain about escapism just as they complain about artificiality, depicting it as an improper and even irresponsible indulgence in fantasy (cf. Radway 1984). Thus escapism in their minds is enabled by, and equated with, fantasy. The successful resolution of movie crisis and viewer anxiety is based, however, on a critical balance between both fantasy and reality, and ignoring films' roots in everyday life prevents an understanding of how escape is constructed. In order to allow viewers to escape from the insecurities of real life, the concerns dealt with in movies must draw from those very insecurities so that the problems in movies can stand for the real ones in a recognizable way. That they do so successfully is clear from viewers' comments. Both the portrayal and the resolution of those problems, however, must be clothed with sufficient fantasy to allow an escape from the insecurities they draw on. Hence the ambiguous status of the image, the illusion that Debord sees at the heart of spectacle: here it must both mimic reality and differ crucially from it if it is to provide escape. Escape is constituted by substituting the image for reality.

This process may be more active than Debord believes, and certainly is more *desired* by spectators than in his portrayal. Debord sees spectacle as demanding passive acceptance by its very nature (1983: §12). But modern-day participants in spectacle, including Tamil filmwatchers, want illusion, enjoy playing with the image; urban poor Tamils reject movies that are too realistic, that allow too little play of the imagination. While the resolutions and escape provided by illusion do not encourage viewers to achieve their goals through extra-cinematic effort – corroborating by omission the general belief that effort aimed at removing or modifying the causes of insecurity rarely bears results – and while viewers' comments likewise reflect little challenge to the social order, it is nonetheless clear that, in MacAloon's words, "the image of the passive victim will not now do" (1984b: 271).

Similarly, the communication that takes place between audiences and creators of spectacle is an active negotiation; it is in no sense unidirectional. Analysis of film themes and viewers' responses makes it difficult to agree with Debord's contention that in spectacle, "one part of the world *represents itself* to the world and is superior to it" (Debord 1983: §30). As cultural performance theorists suggest, filmwatchers are presented with images of themselves. These images are filtered, however, by viewers' idealized perceptions of themselves (their insistence on presenting themselves as moral and deserving beings, both individually and as a class, an image projected by fan club members as well); by filmmakers' interpretations and representations of those ideals in a manner that they believe will attract audiences; and by filmmakers' desires to provide moral benefits to audiences, desires that are based on stereotypes of the poor as immoral and the need to present themselves to peers as moral. Thus what we see of Tamil society in cinema is reflected through "magic mirrors" (Turner 1986: 22). Spectators see images of themselves; they see the real problems of their daily lives, and the ideal image of their moral selves. Films objectify (some of) the anxieties of their lives and then dissolve them, in part through the glorification of the character of the poor and in part through promises of a life of luxury. Unlike fan club activities, where there are no upper class filmmakers to mediate the expression of values, none of this addresses the material causes of the anxieties.[2]

Spectacle does objectify, does externalize, does remove the viewer from action. Yet much of what is objectified is not only what the filmmaker urges on the viewer but also what viewers have demanded as a vision of their *own* lives. Moreover, as with any other form of expressive culture, what is portrayed becomes a part of the public sphere, to be discussed, applied, and – as viewers themselves argue – manipulated back into their lives, potentially effecting change. Spectacle works as escape partly because viewers are watching *themselves* – because they can temporarily replace their real selves with the image they see. The question of who speaks to whom cannot be clearcut.[3]

This book has aimed to explore the significance of Tamil cinema for its urban poor viewers. While the significance appears to lie largely in an escape constituted through utopian fantasy, the pleasure of that escape derives from its roots in real-life social and psychological stresses and from the soothing of those stresses through melodramatic crisis resolution. This connection between escape and reality also appears in viewers' ready distillation and application of morals from film stories and in the concrete and very personal connections they see between those stories and their own lives.

The split between image and reality repeats in other aspects of cinema, and indeed appears frequently enough that we may ask whether such a split or contradiction is central to the pleasure that Tamil cinema (and perhaps others) offers. It is found in the contradiction between the privately acknowledged pleasure found in cinema and the publicly espoused disdain for this low-culture entertainment. The disdain is associated with the socioeconomically dominant middle and upper classes, and, regardless of whether originally adopted from that source, reflects a conflict between pride in one's own culture and desire for distance from that culture, a distance achieved by voicing high-culture tastes (cf. Bourdieu 1984). This split, as we can now see, is homologous to that found in the films' utopian formula, divided between glorification of a present that needs no transformation and promises to transform the present into a glorious future.

Other instances of the conflict between identification with and distancing from the lower class include the attributes praised in movie stars, the intentions of fan club service activities, and voting preferences for moviestar politicians. Fans praise heroes who, in their projections, respect the poor and aid them generously; they also laud them for having transcended their lower class roots. Club members work to help their poor fellows through social services; and their tacit separation from those who need to be helped, and the accompanying transformation into the category of "helpers" rather than "helped," allow members to perceive themselves as separate from the difficulties of the poor. By their activity itself they have removed themselves from those who need to be helped, carving an identity that differentiates them from the masses of needy urban residents. They and other voters supported a film hero who was identified with the poor but also stood as their savior, a man once again who was both of and above them.

This split is intrinsic to the pleasure of Tamil cinema.[4] Cinema suggests that life is fine now, in no need of change since the poor already possess the best aspects of life (i.e. morality and strength of character), and *simultaneously* that present difficulties will soon resolve without effort and be replaced by abundance (i.e. material wealth). Thus we might say that the image does not so much replace reality as divide itself into (present) reality and (future) fantasy. Pleasure is intensified by the simultaneous offering of contradictory utopias, by the understanding that even if the everyday world does not turn out to be perfect, the future will, and vice versa. Viewers are not urged by film, either collectively or individually, to create a utopia in the "real" world; rather, in a medium where even the realest reality is somewhat fantastic, the activity and pleasure of the individual viewer consist of seeking out the utopian image of self. Viewers are active participants in the construction of a spectacular image that both represents them and allows them to escape who they are.

Appendix

Regional censor boards follow a uniform code. Following are pertinent sections of the Central Board of Film Certification Guidelines.

1. The objectives of film certification will be to ensure that
    (i) medium of film remains responsible and sensitive to the values and standards of the society;
    (ii) artistic expression and creative freedom are not unduly curbed;
    (iii) censorship is responsive to social change.
2. In pursuance of the above objectives, the Board of Film Certification shall ensure that
    (i) anti-social activities such as violence are not glorified or justified;
    (ii) the modus operandi of criminals or other visuals or words likely to incite the commission of any offence are not depicted;
    (iii) pointless or avoidable scenes of violence, cruelty and horror are not shown;
    (iii-a) scenes which have the effect of justifying or glorifying drinking are not shown;
    (iv) human sensibilities are not offended by vulgarity, obscenity and depravity;
    (iv-a) visuals or words depicting women in ignoble servility to man or glorifying such servility as a praiseworthy quality in women are not presented;
    (v) visuals or words contemptuous of racial, religious or other groups are not presented;

(vi) the sovereignty and integrity of India is not called in question;
(vii) the security of the State is not jeopardised or endangered;
(viii) friendly relations with foreign states are not strained;
(ix) public order is not endangered;
(x) visuals or words involving defamation or contempt of court are not presented.
3. The Board of Film Certification shall also ensure that the film
   (i) is judged in its entirety from the point of view of its overall impact;
   (ii) is examined in the light of contemporary standards of the country and the people to which the film is related.

Adapted from *Indian Express*, 2 March 1986.

Notes

1. Introduction

1. 1,568 of these were permanent theaters and 863 were "touring" cinemas. In 1990 in Andhra Pradesh there were a total of 2,612 theaters; in Karnataka, 1,253; and in Kerala, 1,396 (all 1990 figures posted in the South Indian Film Chamber of Commerce, 14 August 1991).
2. They are, in chronological order, C. N. Annadurai, Mu. Karunanidhi, M. G. Ramachandran, Janaki Ramachandran (followed again by Mu. Karunanidhi), and the present Chief Minister, Jayalalitha Jayaram.
3. This work focusses on the urban poor. Cinema is important in rural areas as well, but access to the countryside is more limited than in the cities. Differences in exposure and in the lives of the rural and urban poor suggest that while many of the meanings derived from cinema would be similar for the poor as a whole, they would not be uniform across this division; a comprehensive comparison, however, is beyond the scope of this work.
4. A few notable exceptions to this are Thomas (1985), Barnouw and Krishnaswamy (1980), Kakar (1981, 1989), and Slingo (1990).
5. Nor are there significant signs of change in this attitude. A recent *New York Times* article describes Indian film as a "bewildering mixture," an "all-purpose dream engine delivering gaudy three-hour extravaganzas" (Steven Weisman, 14 August 1989). Iqbal Masud, a noted Indian journalist and film writer, has recently chided sympathetic analysts such as Thomas for naively favoring popular cinema. In an article titled "The Road to Serfdom" he argues, "Writing from our ancient and comfortless chairs, one is likely to be less enchanted" (*Express Magazine*, 7 September 1986).
6. The perception of this association is long-standing. In 1927, the President of the Corporation of Madras told the Cinematograph Enquiry Committee, "I find the uncultured flock to the cinema. It could be said that 75 percent of cinema patrons are of the lower order" (Baskaran 1981: 89).
7. Heston reports that 34 percent of the urban population in India is at or below the poverty level, which in 1988 was approximately Rs. 90 per person per

month, and in 1986 (during my fieldwork) was slightly lower; in southern India, 30 percent of the urban population lives in poverty according to these standards (1990: 103, 106, 109). Levels of poverty are relative, and Heston points out that over 95 percent of Indians would be considered poor by US standards (1990: 103). It should be noted that the Rs. 90 figure was determined for rural areas, and is even less adequate in urban areas where a higher percentage of commodities must be acquired with cash.

8 Caplan notes the use of similar terms for people located at the bottom of an indigenous socioeconomic model in Madras, including the "poor," *eezhaikal*, and "those who don't have," *illaatappatta vanaka* (L. Caplan 1987: 11). The model his informants constructed was three-part, and most informants placed themselves in the middle category (and are identified by Caplan as middle class). My informants, however, always placed themselves at the bottom.

9 On the other hand, L. Caplan (1987: 6–8) points out that the few anthropological studies of class tend to be urban-based.

2. Lives in Madurai

1 Note that the *perception* of increasing insecurity is of greater concern here than is the actuality. Similar perceptions have been reported among tenement residents in Madras, who state that they are economically worse off than their parents were. They "recall life as being 'easy' in those days" when the cost of living was lower and families were more supportive, and now express discontent with their occupations, levels of education, and economic security (Wiebe 1981: 127–29). Whether insecurity has in fact increased is unclear; it is the perception of this increase that is significant here.

2 *Jati* is related to the four *varna* categories laid out in the ancient texts of the *Rig Veda* and *Laws of Manu*. Of these four categories, the only ones traditionally found in southern India are Brahman (the highest) and Shudra (the lowest), along with scheduled castes (the "Untouchables" whose caste names the British colonial rulers recorded on lists or schedules that determined eligibility for government benefits). Shudras are divided into a great number of *jatis*, units which in South India have much more social salience than do *varna* classifications.

People of scheduled castes are often referred to as Harijans, "People of God," a name bestowed by Mahatma Gandhi. Many educated scheduled caste members reject the name of Harijan because they consider it patronizing, but it was the term most of the scheduled caste people I knew in Madurai used to refer to themselves. They considered it to carry less demeaning connotations than their *jati* names (predominantly Paraiyar, Chakkiliyar or Pallar).

3 See Appadurai (1985) for one discussion of the ideological implications of westerners' focus on caste.

4 It is possible that people expected me as an outsider to disapprove of the caste system, and thus modified their statements accordingly. It seems unlikely, however, that this would account for all or even most of the lack of mention of caste during daily conversations, especially since other potentially sensitive topics were discussed frequently and easily.

5 Those ineligible believe themselves to be more qualified than the recipients. I

received a striking illustration of this resentment from a 29-year-old woman of a "forward" caste who had a master's degree in social work. One day she began talking about the reservations available to scheduled castes in schools and government jobs, and complained that "scheduled castes used to be at the bottom, but now they are at the top because of all the help the government gives them. Now we are at the bottom." She gave me two examples. First, when her elder brother was in medical school, she said, he told her that the "s.c. fellows" could get into the school with entrance exam marks of 40–50 (out of 100) – while others had to have at least 70 – and didn't even know "their ABCs." Next she told me about the time she had applied for a Welfare Officer's post in another city. She had expected to get the position because her uncle, a civil service officer, had promised to speak with the official in charge and recommend her. Four other candidates applied, none of them scheduled caste. This young woman was thus surprised to learn that she was not selected, and sent her uncle to find out why. As it turned out, one of the other applicants (a Brahman, supposedly) was married to a member of a scheduled caste and so had to be given the job "because of the rules." "The government is not fair to us," she complained, saying that all government jobs went automatically to scheduled castes if they applied, then to backward castes, and then only if neither scheduled nor backward castes applied for a position would it go to a forward caste member. This must, of course, be a frustrating system for members of upper castes, but this was the only time I ever heard of the reservation system working so thoroughly and consistently. The fact that these statements came from a professional social worker with first-hand knowledge of the depressed circumstances of most scheduled caste members highlights the resentment that protective discrimination has generated against lower castes.

6 Commensal restrictions are traditionally an important aspect of caste prohibitions. People of higher castes generally refuse water or cooked food from people beneath them in caste status, since a person's substance (which is more or less "polluted" according to that person's position in the caste hierarchy) passes into food during cooking and into water (for a thorough discussion of the transactional nature of hierarchy and the transmissible substance of persons, see Marriott 1968 and Marriott and Inden 1977).

7 A language related to Gujarati.

8 Both religious and linguistic issues have historically sparked violent conflict in India.

9 The members of this movement defined "Dravidians" – technically, speakers of Dravidian languages (including Kannada, Malayalam, Tamil, and Telugu, among others), which are not related to Hindi and the other Indo–Aryan languages spoken in the North – as all non-Brahman South Indians.

10 See Washbrook (1989: 205ff), however, for a cogent critique of the accuracy of these perceptions – and the policies (or lack thereof) issued in response – as well as of the policies of later Dravidian parties.

11 Prime Minister Jawaharlal Nehru found this indicative of a "tribal mentality" (Geertz 1963: 106).

12 One of E. V. Daniel's informants connected women's *cakti* ("inherent power") with the amount of work they do, saying that women need so much more

power than men because they must do so much more work. Daniel quotes the man as asking, "Have you seen any man who has the sheer energy to do a fraction of the work that a woman does?" (1984: 167).
13 Wives ideally should be "of fair complex" (i.e. have light-colored skin), and at least be lighter skinned than their husbands. A betrothed friend of mine who had relatively dark skin was teased painfully at the engagement and wedding gatherings by her relatives, who frequently mentioned her dark complexion and wondered aloud why her handsome fiancé had agreed to marry her.
14 Parents of doctors and engineers, for example, can demand very high dowries, and the bride's own high education cannot serve as compensation; in fact, higher education for women has proved to be a financial liability, since the higher a woman's education the greater her husband's must be, and thus the greater the dowry her parents must give to acquire that husband for her.
15 This essentially realistic assessment of future costs should not be, and is not, interpreted as a lack of affection for daughters. I have seen fathers who are playing with their young daughters curse their fate for having had so many female children, and the daughters laugh in response.
16 The thali is a pendant worn on a saffron-colored thread or gold chain around a married woman's neck. It may also be worn by Christians.
17 Other symbols of binding are also associated with marriage. A married woman must wear her hair knotted or plaited at all times and must wear (in Tamil, "tie") a sari instead of donning the young girl's dress of skirt and blouse. Both of these symbols also appear in the coming of age ceremony – the time when a girl typically wears her first sari – which begins the binding of a woman's *cakti*, released at puberty, which only marriage can fully contain. Finally, the traditional wedding sari has a wide border, recognized as a symbol of containment (see K. David 1980). Reynolds has pointed out that one of the Tamil terms for "wife" is *taaram*, which also means "limit" or "boundary" (1980: 46).
18 The equation of popularity with influence is widespread and virtually unquestioned. It is accepted not only by analysts determined to discover these effects but also by social critics and planners who wish to put cinema to constructive use. The argument of the latter, as Roberge parodies it, runs thus: "because cinema is immensely popular, it must have a power, and that power should be marshalled into the service of specific interests (the common good, of course, as defined by those who have the power to do so)" (1985: 70).
19 I was looking for someone who could speak English, which usually meant a college-educated woman, and someone who had several hours of free time every day, which meant she must be unmarried; but most highly educated women came from upper class and/or upper caste families who were reluctant to allow their unmarried daughters to accompany me to the homes of unknown people, particularly when they learned that most of these people were poor.
20 Most money amounts in this book are given in rupees. One rupee contains 100 paise. The international exchange rate was about twelve and a half rupees (Rs. 12.50) to the US dollar during most of my 1985–87 stay in India. (It was about seventeen to the dollar in 1990, and twenty-five per dollar by 1991.) The rupee's buying power – a more useful equivalent – was much closer to the same

number of dollars, however, for obtaining basic commodities. That is, in 1986 a monthly income of Rs. 500 could be used to acquire roughly the same amount and quality of food, housing and clothing in Madurai as $500 could in a US city.

3. Activities and attitudes

1 66 percent of viewers surveyed reported going to films with family members, and 30 per cent with friends. 42 percent of the men said they sometimes went alone; only 12 percent of the women reported this.

4. History of Tamil cinema

1 This section on the history of Tamil cinema owes much to two works, *Indian Film* by Barnouw and Krishnaswamy (1980) and *The Message Bearers* by Baskaran (1981).
2 The dedication of girls and women to temples as *devadasi*s, which was viewed by the British and later by some Indians as a form of prostitution, was outlawed in most parts of South India by 1947 (Marglin 1985: 5–8, 306).
3 Those who paid only four annas, a quarter of a rupee.
4 In 1923 there were over 150 cinema theaters throughout India (Barnouw and Krishnaswamy 1980: 298n).
5 There has been widespread – if irregular – access to cinema in the South since the industry's first days.
6 This is also true of Hindi cinema, since it has few viewers outside of northern India. While Hindi films are sometimes played in the largest South Indian cities, such as Madras, only a few poor viewers in Madurai had seen even one.
7 As in the rest of the world, the coming of sound was not so beneficial to everyone. The reduction in market size and the costs of shifting to soundproof studios, new lighting techniques and recording equipment put many companies out of business.
8 One early Tamil film had over sixty songs (Guy 1985: 465).
9 Baskaran sees the migration of stage artists as having mixed effects. While he lauds the introduction of politics into cinema, he also perceives the florescence of music and dance as having the "rather disastrous" effect of turning films into mere "photographed dramas," preventing development of a cinema based on "the unique capabilities of the camera" (much as the earlier reliance on well known mythological stories had crippled development of a truly cinematic syntax) (1981: 87–88, 101–102).
10 One of the few exceptions is Bhanumati, an actress and musician who sang her own parts and played often opposite MGR in the 1950s. When I met her in 1986, Bhanumati Ramakrishna had become president of the prestigious Music Academy in Madras.
11 Alternatively, Beeman claims that "for Indian spectators the psychological distance between speech and song is considerably narrower than for Western spectators. The artificial 'break' which is felt in the West when an actor bursts into song is thus less apparent to the Indian viewer" (1981: 83).
12 Armes has argued that the postwar films of Bombay, in contrast, were often marked by somewhat less of an emphasis on spectacle, instead mixing "an

awareness of the requirements of box office success with a clear sympathy for the poor and the oppressed" to create a cinema with a wider appeal, both nationally and internationally (1987: 115).
13 MGR died in December 1987 after ten years as Chief Minister of Tamil Nadu. Shivaji Ganesan's political activity has since increased. He formed his own party in 1988, then merged it with the Janata Dal in 1989 when he was made state president of that organization, a coalition party that had recently gained control of the national government.
14 During the 1960s, the Communists also attempted to use films for propaganda work, but these attempts proved ineffective (Guy 1990).
15 Occasionally politics might take on more subtle forms as well. I once noticed an interesting shot when I paused a video of *Amman Koovil Kizhakkaalee* on a VCR – a view I had never noticed while the film was playing. As the angry heroine began to wipe bird droppings from her car windshield, the letters "DMK" came into focus on the wall behind her. Whether this conjunction was intentional cannot be said, but it is unlikely that the film crew were unaware of the backdrop.

5. Films

1 The director Bhagyaraj was recently said to have shot song and dance sequences for five movies before developing "even a bare storyline" for any of them (*Aside* 10, 11: 46 [1–15 October 1986]).
2 While female fighter–vigilantes were popular in Bombay productions during the late 1980s, this trend was never established in Tamil cinema. A few recent Tamil films, such as *Puu Onru Puyalaanatu* ("A Blossom Became a Gale," 1987) and *Bharata Peṇṇ* ("Woman of India," 1990), have specialized in women who take bloody revenge on political and other gangsters, but the actresses who play these heroines nonetheless have not built images based on fighting prowess.
3 *Masaala* means "spice," and usually refers to a mix of spices.
4 Also see Sarkar's argument above that ancient epics have influenced the form of films. I have some difficulty with any argument such as Derné's that portrays mythological elements or influences as straightforwardly "religious." Rather, works such as the *Mahabharata* or *Ramayana* are one part of the stock of South Asian cultures, and to separate them as religious in such a case is to create a particularly problematic division of religion from the rest of culture.

Nonetheless, there are some intriguing connections between film and worship. I mentioned in chapter 2 that temple visits and filmwatching are Madurai residents' two most frequent leisure activities. The two of them, frequently portrayed as moral opposites, may serve similar needs. The devotion (*bhakti*) to deities and to film stars shares significant characteristics, including the powers ascribed to the object of devotion and the relationship (primarily as family member or lover) conceptualized and enacted in the process of devotion. Such connections are suggestive but cannot be explored thoroughly in this work.
5 *Moocam* has an old meaning of "deceit" or "danger" that stil colors its present-day use. Colloquially the term applies to a wide variety of objects,

including people, food, and fabrics. When applied to humans it carries connotations of immorality as well, and is always said with distaste.
6 This point assumes filmmakers' membership – or aspirations to membership – in the dominant class. The assumption has some merit in Tamil Nadu, as most filmmakers belong to the upper or upper-middle class. It should be pointed out, however, that "dominant" class standing does not necessarily require filmmakers to support their class and its ideology in their films. The 1960s saw sustained and trenchant social criticism in Tamil cinema – although much of it made with an eye to attracting audiences who had become enamored of the DMK party and its populist rhetoric.
7 Roberge has likewise argued that "in conventional [Indian] cinema ... a sham naturalism masquerades as 'realism'" (1985: 34).
8 C. S. Bharatiar, a Tamil, was a famous nationalist poet of the early 1900s.
9 Here, "brother's wife" is a fictive relationship.
10 A *kolam* is the geometric decoration of rice powder mentioned in chapter 2. The powder is sprinkled in front of Hindu homes by women of the household, usually in the early morning. The *kolam* welcomes the goddess into the home.
11 Valli had lost her ability to speak as a result of smallpox – leading her father to approach Kanmani's mother – and in South India, the Amman goddess is commonly thought of as the bringer of smallpox.
12 A common term of address to younger men.

6. Film themes

1 It will become clear that although, for the sake of analytical clarity, I have chosen to discuss these three sets of issues in separate sections, individual movie themes often deal with them simultaneously. The theme of the in-marrying woman who breaks up a household, for example, has to do with anxieties about both male–female relationships and family relations. Concerns about adultery and about "love marriages" also have to do with both issues.
2 Some fans of Tamil cinema would doubtless protest that this list should also include the image of the sacrificing mother. While suffering, devoted mothers do appear in films, unlike sacrificing wives they are rarely the films' central figures.
3 Like some other movie themes and images, this image is not limited in its import to the poor. The image of wives as "self-sacrificing, patient, and totally attentive to their husbands, regardless of the latter's character and behaviour" (Caplan 1985: 192) is an ideal held pervasively throughout Tamil society. In her study of upper-middle and upper class women's organizations in Madras, Caplan cites the following story, taken from the *Mahabharata* and quoted in a "souvenir" booklet produced for an organization's ceremonial event:

Panjali told Satyanha that women should never do things which gave displeasure to their husbands. Sacrificing her own self, she should devote herself to the welfare of her husband. She should not eat before him. After finishing the work in the house, she should spend some pleasant time with him. Women should not waste time standing at the door and roaming about the garden. Controlling her anger and other evil habits, she should act according to his wishes. In his absence, she should not pay much attention to her dress and beauty, and train herself to develop a taste only for what he eats and drinks. She should obey her mother-in-law, and do the duties expected of her to their ancestors. She should take an interest in all her husband's activities and help him in his tasks. She should take charge of the household duties and accounts, and do her duties tirelessly. Women should go to bed only after their husbands and get up before them. Panjali had been practising these things and she was a very good and loyal wife. (ibid.)

4 One young man, for example, the eighteen-year-old son of a friend, looked surprised when I asked him if he would like his future wife to be "modern" like Kanmani. "We [i.e. men] would like that for a while," he said, "but it could never last; she would not want me or take care of me."

5 This situation may supply further evidence for the ambivalent feelings with which men regard the image of the modern woman. It is interesting that Kanmani must be punished before Chinnamani's desire for her can be felt or fulfilled, first by Chinnamani himself and then by the authorities for a crime that he has committed.

6 The two others he lists are the alleviation of fears of the rural joint family's breakdown and the vicarious fulfillment of a new "consumer goods consciousness" (Bahadur 1976: 94–96).

7 A similar act occurs in the film *Cippikkuḷ Muttu* ("Pearl in the Shell," 1986), in which a good-hearted but simple-minded man takes the thali from a goddess's offering plate and ties it around a young widow's neck during a temple festival, having heard his grandmother say that the widow's problems would be solved if only she could be married again. The community is aghast, especially the young widow, but all recognize that the thali cannot be untied.

8 This theme – the intrusion of women into male society – also appears frequently in Hollywood Westerns.

9 This suspicion of daughters-in-law is found throughout South Asia, and can be more extreme outside of Tamil Nadu. In Nepal, for example, Lynn Bennett (1983) documents the particularly strong hostility between mothers-in-law and daughters-in-law among upper caste Hindus. Within India, the suspicion of in-marrying women is greater in the north than in the south, where it is mitigated in part by preferences for cross-cousin matches, and for spouses from families who are known or live nearby; neither of these practices is preferred in North India generally (see Wadley 1980; Kolenda 1984). As is often the case, however, preferred forms are not the norm, and most spouses are not related or, in my observation, even well known to one another's families ahead of time, thus still easily allowing for a daughter-in-law to seem unknown and suspect. Moreover, the existence of a blood relationship to her parents-in-law would not necessarily prevent a woman from wanting to separate from them.

10 It is interesting to note that both relatives who drove out the children are related only by marriage – one of them male, one female. Perhaps the concern with the breakdown of familial rights and responsibilities is so fresh or deep that it must be deflected to someone other than a "real" family member, someone both similar and crucially different.

11 Kanmani's advice to give one's husband priority is also consonant with the ideal image of women discussed above – which is fitting, since Kanmani is now a representative of this ideal womanhood.

12 This is a widespread concern about cinema. See, for example, the study by Hartmann, Patil and Dighe of villages in Kerala and West Bengal, where identical fears are voiced (1989: 203, 233).
13 It should be noted, however, that the home of the poor man looks "poor" only in comparison to that of the wealthy industrialist, and that in fact the poor man is essentially the rightful holder of the wealth. Although Chinnamani is apparently unaware of his wealthy background, this seems to add to his inherent integrity.
14 It is not that prohibition, especially of alcohol, is not of concern to the poor; a number of women worry about household finances because of the money their husbands or sons spend on drinking. (Despite the fact that Tamil Nadu is from time to time a "dry" state, some amount of alcohol can always be procured.) Many also fear the physical abuse they may receive from a man who has been drinking, or the loss of work and income that drunkenness can lead to. However, this type of anxiety is much more limited in the number of people it affects and, in general, the depth of concern it creates than are the relational anxieties discussed above. To posit a world without drugs or alcohol would relieve most viewers much less than would the idea of a world in which, for example, family members always cared for one another as they should.
15 A similar pattern is seen in the recent run of "anti"-rape movies in North India.
16 Note that the types of portrayals that count as negative vary by community. While neither Muslims nor Christians object to the gangster image, filmmakers reported that Muslims will not allow girls or women of their community to be shown falling in love. On the other hand, one Christian woman, a daughter of a filmmaker, told me that directors often portray their heroines as "Christian girls" when the character must engage in risqué behavior, because "Christians never take offense." With Hindus the question of community per se is unlikely to arise because Hindus generally identify with the community of caste more closely than with "religion," and the caste of a character is rarely marked. Where it is – as with the Brahmans or Thevars of *Veetam Putitu* – filmmakers must take care (see below).
17 The kind stepfather who takes care of Chinnamani in *Amman Koovil Kizhakkaalee* also appears to be a Muslim, based on his clothing and fishing occupation. This characterization is a bit equivocal, however, since his daughter Valli has a Hindu name, wears a red *pottu* on her forehead, and is taken to the Amman goddess for treatment.
18 A similar reasoning may be at work in depictions of Tamil language chauvinism, such as Sindhu's advocacy of Tamil lyrics and her demonstration of their beauty to the artist who sings only Sanskrit and Telugu lyrics because he considers Tamil songs to be "sewage." The perceived linguistic and cultural invasion by northern Indians is a politically popular issue but nonetheless of rare immediate concern to viewers, especially when such concern is not being fanned by political leaders.

7. Filmmakers

1 Although this discussion is drawn primarily from observation of the Madras industry, it applies to the major northern film industries as well, except where

the details provided are clearly linked or limited to Tamil Nadu. I am less confident of its applicability to Malayalam film production in Kerala, an industry whose financing, casting, and audiences are in many ways distinct from those in the rest of India.
2 Financing may be even more difficult in Bombay, where budgets are reported to be at least four to twenty times as high per film (Armes 1987: 120).
3 Based on statistics from the 1980 *Report of the Working Group on National Film Policy*, Roberge states that 65 percent of the films produced in India are financial "flops," 25 percent break even, and only 10 percent make any kind of profit (1985: 70). Armes reports that the risks of production in Bombay are also such that most investors lose their money (1987: 120). One minor caveat is that the accuracy of reporting on film finances is dubious, particularly since the financing often involves black money (i.e. funds gained from illegal sources or unreported for tax purposes; also see Armes 1987: 117).
4 227 of the 897 films certified in South India in 1990 had been dubbed (*Journal of the Film Chamber*, South Indian Film Chamber of Commerce, XXXIX, 2: 30 [February 1991]).
5 Most actresses' voices are said to be dubbed (according to directors I knew, almost all female parts in all movies are dubbed by the same woman), but most actors do their own dubbing.
6 Madras Film Labs is said to hold "the largest number of completed but unsold films in the world" (Hariharan 1986: 51).
7 Tax revenues are substantial. In 1986–87, the last year for which all-India figures are available, entertainment taxes resulted in a gross collection estimated at Rs. 6,000,000,000 (South Indian Film Chamber of Commerce 1989). In Tamil Nadu in 1987–88, the figure was Rs. 606,033,573; of this, Rs. 68,786,651 were collected in the Madurai zone (one of eight collection zones in the state) (*Journal of the Film Chamber*, South Indian Film Chamber of Commerce XXXVI, 11:34–36 [November 1989]).
8 See Appendix for regulations of the uniform censor code.
9 This would have been exceedingly difficult – since I was far from alone in wishing to meet with these filmmakers – had I not had the good fortune described above of being escorted and aided by two respected members of the cinema industry, one a journal publisher, editor, and film critic, and the other a film historian and public relations officer.
10 Most filmmakers I asked could identify only one Tamil filmmaker with a privileged background, A. V. M. Chettiar.
11 During one interview, I asked Kamalhasan (a starring actor, director, and producer) how he decided what to include in his films. He offered an interesting and, to me, surprising reply:

> First of all, there has not been a clear research angle as to what we put into it, unlike in the US. I think [the] US and Japan are the only places where they go through computers ... What they do is collect all the hit movies of the past, and find out as to what made them run, combine it together and make a movie with whatever kind of artistry that they could add into it ... Whereas here, we don't have that kind of researched approach as to what we put into film. It becomes like moonshine business: you drink it, you're alive, it's good; you're dead, it's bad stuff ... There's no precise method as to how we arrive at the commercial formula ... But somehow Spielberg and his group of friends have hit on a

"public appeal" kind of situation where they give them this modern circus: all the acts put in together.

My surprise at Kamalhasan's answer came from the formula orientation he ascribes to Hollywood cinema, which I in contrast had been accustomed to associating with Indian film.

12 All information from the directors, producers, and other industry leaders cited in this chapter comes from interviews as follows: K. Balaje, September 1986; Bhanumathi Ramakrishna, December 1986; Bharatiraja, September 1986; Joseph Enok, June 1990; Kamalhasan, September 1986; Kommineni, December 1986; Muktha Srinivasan, September 1986; A. V. Narayanan, September 1986; L. V. Prasad and A. Ramesh, January 1987; D. V. S. Raju, January 1987; and Arun Veerappan, June 1990.
13 A film reviewer also told me that films today appeal to the lower class's "urges and needs," reflected in films' recent incorporation of "double meanings." The middle class, he said, do not go to movies to fulfill these urges.
14 Bharatiraja also allots film a role in helping India's population crisis, since without films to watch in the evening, he says, people would spend their time sleeping at home.

8. Audiences
1 A middle-level caste descended from the Marathas, warriors who migrated from central India several centuries ago and conquered areas north of Madurai.
2 An upper-middle caste.
3 On the other hand, it could be suggested that people were simply reluctant to answer a question that would reveal some of their most personal problems. This explanation seems unlikely, however, since most of the people interviewed had by this point already discussed a host of similar difficulties, past and present, in their lives.
4 During my 1990 visit to Madurai, friends discussed a notorious figure named Auto Shankar, an auto driver who, they reported, copied the plot of a certain film when he began procuring women for government officials and then murdering the women.
5 A lower-middle caste with a reputation for rough behavior.

9. Fan clubs and politics
1 It is difficult to estimate how many fan clubs there are in Madurai, since the only individuals with accurate information are district and state leaders who tend to believe that it is in the interests of their star's reputation to claim as many clubs as possible, and often make contradictory statements. Even they are working with incomplete information, since there is no account of the "unofficial" fan clubs that have not paid to register with the central body. The district Rajnikanth president claimed that there were 1,300 Rajni clubs in Madurai city and 2,600 in the district – a number that, based on my observations, is far too high. The Kamalhasan district club leaders estimated a more likely figure of 350 clubs in the city. A ward leader of the MGR organization

put the figure at almost 1,000 MGR clubs in Madurai. *The Hindu* had reported more than 800 MGR fan clubs in the DMK in 1972, but MGR himself claimed 20,000 when he split from the party that year (see Barnett 1976: 312n), Hardgrave reported claims of four to five thousand for all of South India in 1969 (1975: 18), and Pandian recently cited an unattributed figure of "about 10,000 branches" in Tamil Nadu (1992: 30). Shivaji Productions boasted of more than 3,000 Shivaji clubs in 1969, but one club leader estimated that there were only 700 in the state at that time (Hardgrave 1975: 18). My very own rough estimate in 1986 was 500 or more MGR clubs in the Madurai area, and approximately 300 Rajnikanth and Kamalhasan clubs respectively. Based on the less than definitive evidence of talks with fan club leaders and observations of new club signboards, I suspect that the number of MGR clubs has declined slightly and the others increased somewhat in the subsequent years. I have too little information about Shivaji fan clubs to estimate their numbers.

Unfortunately, these are the most helpful statistics to be found. As far as I know there are no reliable quantitative data about any aspects of fan clubs, and my contacts did not provide a sizable enough sample from which to project such data.

2 It also proved useful to have a male research assistant accompany me on these interviews. This made the men I interviewed more comfortable, since they were not alone with an unknown young woman; bringing a female companion would not have accomplished this.

3 The only women's club that I encountered was an MGR Women's Association (*makila anni*) club, which appeared to be devoted entirely to political service rather than to the more typical fan-oriented activities of most clubs.

4 Leaders of upper-level fan clubs vehemently denied any suggestion of caste or religious distinctions in their organizations. I had only to ask them which castes were most frequently represented to receive the response, "There is no caste in our star's club." Leaders and members of branch clubs, on the other hand, answered the question without hesitation, suggesting that they were less concerned with maintaining the appearance of egalitarianism – and probably not aware that it should be maintained. But their deviance from the official party line did not mean that communal distinctions were important within individual clubs; the diversity of communal groups within clubs, outside activities among members of different castes, and the fact that the leaders of each club almost always came from a variety of castes suggested that communal distinctions were of less significance among fan club members than in most of the rest of Tamil society.

5 In Madurai, at least, the boundaries of these wards correspond closely to those of the city's political wards.

6 Kamalhasan himself described the film and the character in the following way:

> It is about a village boy. You cannot call him a moron, you cannot call him a fool, nor retarded, but he's somewhere in between a retarded man and a maharishi [great sage]. You cannot define him as a fool, nor can you say that he's a maharishi. Those qualities – there's a thin line dividing a prophet and a fool ... He makes them think with simple works. (interview, September 1986)

7 C. N. Annadurai was the extremely popular founder of the DMK party, and

drafted MGR into its ranks. Mu. Karunanidhi succeeded Annadurai as party leader and Tamil Nadu Chief Minister, and ejected MGR from the DMK in 1972. He and Annadurai had written film scripts for MGR in the 1950s and '60s. Jayalalitha Jayaram was MGR's last major co-star and joined his ADMK party in the early 1980s, where she served off and on as Propaganda Minister, and after his death emerged as the leader of the party; in 1991 she became Chief Minister of the state. At the time that the club member made this statement in 1985, she led one of the two main factions in the ADMK.

8 Film stars' reputations for liberal giving are also important because gifts strengthen the leader–follower relationship. Even those who have had no personal contact with the star see him as someone who "gives to people like me/us." The perception of the gift binds the fan more tightly in his commitment to follow and honor the star (see Dickey 1993).

9 The intensity of this devotion resembles that felt toward deities worshipped in *bhakti* relationships (see chapter 5, n.4). It is also interesting to note that the fan organizations themselves bear some resemblance toward religious sects. In addition to devotion for the idolized leader (who may be credited with godlike and miraculous powers), shared features include a promise of proximate salvation for the poor, and a strong social ideology and related behavioral ideal. Of the fan clubs discussed here, MGR's bore these features most strongly.

10 At least three clashes by fans of Tamil film stars were reported in the Madurai English-language newspapers between May and November of 1986. On May 15, the *Indian Express* reported that "two rival groups of fans associations of cine artistes indulged in rioting" in Pondicherry, using stones and "highly explosive crackers." *The Hindu* related the arrest of MGR fans in Bangalore after they "tried to pelt stones on another group but were prevented from doing so by the police" during a procession to mark the release of an MGR film (23 June 1986). Both the *Indian Express* (10 October 1986) and *The Hindu* (11 October 1986) reported an incident in which four policemen were injured after intervening in a clash between "two groups" of film fans arguing over which star's film would be screened as part of a Mariamman Temple festival.

11 Hardgrave reports that "some theatres, particularly in Madurai, will turn over the responsibilities for ticket sales in the first week entirely to the fan clubs. On occasion, the fan clubs have been in charge of advance booking and accounts" (1975: 20).

12 MGR club members celebrate the birthday of C. N. Annadurai, the founder of the DMK party, instead of MGR. This official club policy appeared to be an attempt to demonstrate MGR's humility and – like the name of his party (the Annadurai-DMK) – his abiding connection with Annadurai despite his break from the party that Annadurai founded. An officer in the Lakshmipuram club told me in 1986, "Even MGR celebrates only Annadurai's birthday."

13 These public events require the construction of a decorated stage and canopy, whenever possible, from which club officials and perhaps local politicians make speeches enumerating the film star's good deeds. At Kamalhasan and Rajnikanth club events, the speeches are often supplemented by "disco dance" demonstrations. Whatever other content they may include, these functions

always involve the broadcast of movie music and dialogues at full blast from numerous speakers placed in strategic locations (often from 2 or 3 a.m. one morning until 2 or 3 a.m. the next).

14 Such functions are most typical of clubs that are an official part of an extensive fan organization. Other clubs, in contrast, spring up in isolation and have only the loosest connections with other fan clubs of the same star. Their idols are usually relatively minor actors or actresses. These clubs celebrate their anniversaries and stars' birthdays as larger organizations do, and may well try to engage in neighborhood social services, but in general they rarely engage in activities involving any other club.

15 This impression was widespread among Madurai residents of all income levels. Occasionally complaints would appear in the editorial pages of the area's Tamil and English newspapers. In the "Citizens' Voice" column of the *Indian Express* (18 August 1986), a college professor wrote deploring the conditions of movie theaters and complained that "the various Rasikar Manrams (fans associations) play havoc in the sale of black market tickets and in spoiling the upkeep of the theatres." In another *Indian Express* column of the same day, it was charged that fan clubs with political associations lent their names to "encroachments" (buildings or other structures illegally intruding onto a sidewalk or roadway). According to the writer, the structures associated with fan clubs would be allowed to stand when other encroachments would not, and while the fan clubs would rent them to businesses in the day, the shelters "become veritable 'casinos' with gambling and other unlawful activities when night falls. They also become nerve-centres of anti-social elements causing nuisance to the neighbourhood."

16 The civic activities MGR clubs listed most frequently included notifying authorities of emergencies, such as fires or accidents, and providing emergency aid when possible; arbitrating fights among residents ("or," one member added, "if we can't pacify them, we beat them and tie them up and hand them over at the police station"); and reporting problems with utilities, such as an electricity shortage or a failure in the water supply, and bringing the authorities to the site to investigate.

17 From what I could gather, acquisition of the articles donated by MGR's clubs was financed almost without exception by government funds. (This is not likely to be the case in the infrequent instances of other stars' clubs' donations.) The audiences at these ceremonies and club members themselves often believed that the goods had been provided out of the star's own resources. It should be noted, however, that fan clubs do in fact provide a service in these cases, since it is usually very difficult for the poor to take advantage of the welfare programs directed toward them. See Dickey (1993) for a discussion of the traditional role of charity and patronage in leader–follower relationships in South India and the significance of this for fan club activities.

18 Nor are other collective or mutual aid societies found frequently in urban poor neighborhoods, in my experience. In general, participation in any type of voluntary association appeared to be infrequent (although I did not ask about such participation directly). A few people belonged to religious *manrams*, sharing *puja* or worship at members' homes on a rotating basis, and

practitioners of certain occupations, such as masons, belonged to unions, but I heard of no other organizational membership aside from political parties.
19 Few people read newspapers or watch television news, and most listen to radio only to hear film songs.
20 These other film star–politicians have nonetheless achieved striking success. Shivaji has been a member of the national parliament and recently became leader of the Janata Dal in Tamil Nadu. Both N. T. Rama Rao and Jayalalitha have become Chief Ministers, NTR of Andhra Pradesh from 1983–90 and Jayalalitha of Tamil Nadu beginning in 1991. Other Indian movie stars who have entered politics include Amitabh Bachchan, Sunil Dutt, and Vyjayanthimala. None, however, has made political capital of the film image as effectively as MGR.
21 Whether or not MGR was truly a Malayali (and thus originally from Kerala) or a Tamil became a political issue when he split from the DMK. One of the stiffest charges the DMK was able to raise against the new party was that it was run by a "Keralite" and "foreigner" – and thus could not co-opt the Tamil nationalist ideology (cf. Barnett 1976: 302–303). Many poor voters in Madurai recognized that MGR's family may have come from Kerala, but considered him a Tamil.
22 *Nadodi Mannan*, based on *Prisoner of Zenda*, appeared in 1958 and was written, directed, and produced by MGR. The first half was shot in black and white and the second half in color. The film, which "assured" MGR's position of strength within the DMK, made clever use of the rising sun, symbol of the DMK (Sivathamby 1981: 39), and closed with a shot of the party's black and red flag.
23 I was once surprised to see even a twelve-year-old girl point to one of the many pictures of MGR in her family's tiny house and refer to him as "*enkaḷ aṇṇan*," "my elder brother."
24 In a novel by the renowned Tamil author Jeyakanthan, *Cinimaavukku Poona Cittaaḷ* ("The Construction Laborer Who Went to the Cinema"), a poor young woman falls in love with MGR, becomes obsessed with him and, despite the efforts of her husband, eventually goes mad (Jeyakanthan 1972).
25 They mark this identification in several ways. Club members often emulate MGR's style of speech and appearance, wearing shirts and scarves with ADMK colors, trying to speak in "chaste" literary Tamil, using speeches from MGR's movies to illustrate points of conversation. Fights with rival fan clubs are copied after MGR's fighting style. Fans may also adopt the ethics MGR promoted in his films and government programs, as when they speak of respecting their mothers and make a show of this in public, or help other poor people in their neighborhoods.

10. Conclusions

1 Silverman locates this lack or loss in the "foreclosed real" and the "concealed site of production" and in the lack of phallus that enters through the female (1988: 2). While most Indian critics and reviewers may not recognize the lack of phallus, the other two points of loss are central to the conscious complaints against and attractions to mainstream Indian cinema, although again such

complaints address these points of artificiality only in their superficial and not essential forms.
2   In those media in which producers are of a different class than the recipients, and have no stake in any of the social changes that would be required to address recipients' problems and insecurities adequately, it is unlikely that the performance will instruct the audience in how to change the situation. Instead, as in Tamil cinema, anxieties will usually be considered in a fashion that allows a temporary escape from them, and at any rate – in those media where producers' success depends on the amount of audience consumption – only to the extent needed to draw an audience. The result can be different in cultural performances in which the "audience" is the same – or at least of the same class – as the "performers" or, even more importantly, the "creators." Where the members of a subordinate class are directly involved both as recipients and creators, the performance can act as a more direct and thorough expression of opposition to domination. Such performances are represented, for example, in the Italian and Mexican–American folkloric expressions discussed by Lombardi-Satriani (1974) and Limón (1982). An example closer in form to Tamil cinema is Javanese *ludruk*, a "proletarian drama" (Peacock 1968). Like Tamil film, *ludruk* deals with issues of change or perceived change that are of immediate concern in the daily lives of the urban poor. Unlike the portrayals found in Tamil cinema, however, the problems created by Javanese modernization are dealt with in their "natural" contexts. That is, rather than being removed from reality in an attempt to provide escape from these very problems, the issues are portrayed realistically, as they occur in the participants' own lives, and offer real solutions to these problems as well as a safe setting in which to test their applications vicariously.
3   In other areas as well of what Appadurai and Breckenridge (1988) call "public culture," such as tourism, consumers may simultaneously become self-spectators, and the line between creator, actor, and spectator blurs.
4   This closely parallels the two processes that Mulvey (1989b) identifies as the source of pleasure in filmwatching. One is scopophilia, the voyeuristic pleasure in looking, closely akin to the escape derived from fantasy. The second is narcissism or ego identification, the identification with a superior image that is enhanced by "the complex process of likeness and difference" (1989b: 18), in which the ordinariness identified in Tamil film stars encourages solid identification while the glamor of the hero allows ego inflation.

References

Abercrombie, Nicholas, Stephen Hill and Bryan S. Turner. 1980. *The Dominant Ideology Thesis*. London: George Allen & Unwin.
Abercrombie, Nicholas and Bryan S. Turner. 1978. "The Dominant Ideology Thesis," *British Journal of Sociology* 29, 2: 149–70.
Adorno, Theodor. 1941. "On Popular Music," *Studies in Philosophy and Social Science* 9, 2: 17–48. (With the assistance of George Simpson.)
Althusser, Louis. 1971. *Lenin and Philosophy and Other Essays*, trans. by Ben Brewster. New York: Monthly Review Press.
Anandan, P. "Filmnews." 1986. "Statistics of South Indian Films." Unpublished ms.
Ang, Ien. 1985. *Watching Dallas*, trans. by Della Couling. London: Methuen.
Ang, Ien and M. Simons. 1982. "Interview with Stuart Hall," *Skrien* 116 (March 1982).
Appadurai, Arjun. 1985. "Is Homo Hierarchicus?" *American Ethnologist* 13, 4: 745–61 (November 1986).
Appadurai, Arjun and Carol A. Breckenridge. 1988. "Why Public Culture?" *Public Culture* 1, 1: 5–9 (Fall 1988).
Aravamudan, Gita. 1992. "The 'Tali' Trap in Tamil Films," *The Hindu*, 8 March 1992.
Armes, Roy. 1987. *Third World Film Making and the West*. Berkeley: University of California Press.
Bahadur, Satish. 1976. "The Context of Indian Film Culture." In D. Bose, *et al.*, eds., *Film Miscellany*, pp. 90–107. Pune: Film & Television Institute of India.
Bailey, F. G. 1977. *Morality and Expediency: The Folklore of Academic Politics*. Chicago: Aldine Publishing Co.
  1988 *Humbuggery and Manipulation*. Ithaca, NY: Cornell University Press.
Barnett, Marguerite Ross. 1976. *The Politics of Cultural Nationalism in South India*. Princeton: Princeton University Press.
Barnouw, Erik and S. Krishnaswamy. 1980. *Indian Film*, 2nd ed. New York: Oxford University Press.
Baskaran, S. Theodore. 1981. *The Message Bearers: The Nationalist Politics and the Entertainment Media in South India, 1880–1945*. Madras: Cre-A:.

Beck, Brenda E. F. 1972. *Peasant Society in Konku: A Study of Right and Left Subcastes in South India*. Vancouver: University of British Columbia Press.
Beeman, William O. 1981. "The Use of Music in Popular Film: East and West," *India International Centre Quarterly* 8, 1: 77–87.
Bennett, Lynn. 1983. *Dangerous Wives and Sacred Sisters*. New York: Columbia University Press.
Beteille, Andre. 1965. *Caste, Class and Power: Changing Patterns of Stratification in a Tanjore Village*. Berkeley: University of California Press.
   1974. *Studies in Agrarian Social Structure*. Delhi: Oxford University Press.
Bharati, Swami Agehananda. 1977. "Anthropology of Hindi Films," *Folklore* 18, 8: 288–300.
Bobo, Jacqueline. 1988. "*The Color Purple*: Black Women as Cultural Readers." In E. Deidre Pribram, ed., *Female Spectators: Looking at Film and Television*, pp. 90–109. London: Verso.
Bourdieu, Pierre. 1984. *Distinction*, trans. by Richard Nice. Cambridge, MA: Harvard University Press.
Burra, Rani, ed. 1981. *Film India: Looking Back, 1896–1960*. New Delhi: The Directorate of Film Festivals.
Caplan, Lionel. 1984. "Bridegroom Price in Urban India: Class, Caste and 'Dowry Evil' among Christians in Madras," *Man* (N.S.) 19: 216–33.
   1987. *Class and Culture in Urban India: Fundamentalism in a Christian Community*. Oxford: Clarendon Press.
Caplan, Patricia. 1985. *Class & Gender in India: Women and their Organizations in a South Indian City*. London: Tavistock Publications.
Chandavarkar, Bhaskar. 1985. "Indian Film Song." In T. M. Ramachandran and S. Rukmini, eds., *70 Years of Indian Cinema (1913–1983)*, pp. 244–51. Bombay: CINEMA India-International.
Daniel, E. Valentine. 1984. *Fluid Signs: Being a Person the Tamil Way*. Berkeley: University of California Press.
Daniel, Sheryl B. 1980. "Marriage in Tamil Culture: The Problem of Conflicting 'Models'." In S. S. Wadley, ed., *The Powers of Tamil Women*, pp. 61–91. Syracuse: Maxwell School of Citizenship and Public Affairs, Syracuse University.
Das Gupta, Chidananda. 1981. *Talking About Films*. New Delhi: Orient Longman.
   1991. *The Painted Face*. New Delhi: Roli Books.
David, C. R. W. 1983. *Cinema as Medium of Communication in Tamil Nadu*. Madras: Christian Literature Society.
David, Kenneth. 1980. "Hidden Powers: Cultural and Socio-Economic Accounts of Jaffna Women." In S. S. Wadley, ed., *The Powers of Tamil Women*, pp. 93–136. Syracuse: Maxwell School of Citizenship and Public Affairs, Syracuse University.
Debord, Guy. 1983. *The Society of the Spectacle*. Detroit: Red and Black.
Derné, Steve. n.d. "Market Forces at Work: Religious Themes in Commercial Hindi Films." Unpublished ms.
Dharap, B. V. 1983. "The Mythological or Taking Fatalism for Granted." In A. Vasudev and P. Lenglet, eds., *Indian Cinema Superbazaar*. New Delhi: Vikas.

1985. "Facts and Figures about the Industry." In T. M. Ramachandran and S. Rukmini, eds., *70 Years of Indian Cinema (1913–1983)*, p. 626. Bombay: CINEMA India-International.
Dhondy, Farrukh. 1985. "Keeping Faith: Indian Film and its World," *Daedalus* 114, 4: 125–40.
Dickey, Sara. 1993. "The Politics of Adulation: Cinema and the Production of Politicians in South India." *The Journal of Asian Studies*, 52, 2 (May 1993).
Driver, Edwin D. and Aloo E. Driver. 1987. *Social Class in Urban India: Essays on Cognitions and Structures*. Leiden: E. J. Brill.
D'Souza, Victor. 1986. "Social Inequality and Stratification in India." In S. C. Malik, ed., *Determinants of Social Status in India*. Delhi: Motilal Banarsidass.
Dumont, Louis. 1970. *Homo Hierarchicus: The Caste System and its Implications*, trans. by Mark Sainsbury. Chicago: University of Chicago Press.
1989. *A South Indian Subcaste: Social Organization and Religion of the Pramalai Kallar*, trans. by M. Moffatt, L. and A. Morton; rev. by L. Dumont and A. Stern; ed. with an introduction by M. Moffatt. Delhi: Oxford University Press.
Dushkin, Lelah. 1972. "Scheduled Caste Politics." In J. M. Mahar, ed., *The Untouchables in Contemporary India*, pp. 165–226. Tucson: University of Arizona Press.
Dyer, Richard. 1985. "Entertainment and Utopia." In B. Nichols, ed., *Movies and Methods*, vol. II, pp. 220–32. Berkeley: University of California Press.
Elsaesser, Thomas. 1985. "Tales of Sound and Fury: Observations on the Family Melodrama." In B. Nichols, ed., *Movies and Methods,* vol. II, pp. 165–89. Berkeley: University of California Press.
Enzensberger, Hans Magnus. 1982. "Constituents of a Theory of the Media," trans. by Stuart Hood. In R. Grimm and B. Armstrong, eds., *Hans Magnus Enzensberger: Critical Essays*, pp. 46–76. New York: Continuum.
Epstein, Arnold Leonard. 1978. *Ethos and Identity*. London: Tavistock.
Ganguli, B. N. 1977. "Conceptualising the Indian Middle Class." In K. S. Krishnaswamy *et al.*, eds., *Society and Change: Essays in Honour of Sachin Chaudhuri*. Bombay: Oxford University Press.
Geertz, Clifford. 1963. "The Integrative Revolution: Primordial Sentiments and Civil Politics in the New States." In C. Geertz, ed., *Old Societies and New States*, pp. 105–57. New York: The Free Press.
1973. "Deep Play: Notes on the Balinese Cockfight." In C. Geertz, *The Interpretation of Cultures*, pp. 412–53. New York: Basic Books.
Gledhill, Christine. 1987. "The Melodramatic Field: An Investigation." In Gledhill, ed., *Home is Where the Heart Is: Studies in Melodrama and the Woman's Film*. London: BFI Publishing.
1988. "Pleasurable Negotiations." In E. Deidre Pribram, ed., *Female Spectators: Looking at Film and Television*, pp. 64–89. London: Verso.
Gluckman, Max. 1959. *Custom and Conflict in Africa*. Glencoe, IL: The Free Press.
Gough, Kathleen. 1981. *Rural Society in Southeast India*. Cambridge: Cambridge University Press.
Government of India. 1969. *Report of the Enquiry Committee on Film Censorship*. New Delhi: Ministry of Information and Broadcasting.

Grossberg, Lawrence. 1984. "I'd Rather Feel Bad Than Not Feel Anything at All: Rock and Roll, Pleasure and Power," *Enclitic* 8, 1–2: 94–110 (Spring/Fall).
Guy, Randor. 1985. "Tamil Cinema." In T. M. Ramachandran and S. Rukmini, eds., *70 Years of Indian Cinema*, pp. 462–75. Bombay: CINEMA India-International.
———. 1990. "Communists in Showbiz," *Aside* 14, 13: 38–39 (15 July 1990).
Hall, Stuart and Tony Jefferson, eds. 1976. *Resistance through Rituals*. London: Hutchinson, in association with the Centre for Contemporary Cultural Studies, University of Birmingham.
Hardgrave, Robert L., Jr. 1965a. "The DMK and the Politics of Tamil Nationalism." *Pacific Affairs* 37: 396–411.
———. 1965b. *The Dravidian Movement*. Bombay: Popular Prakashan.
———. 1969. *The Nadars of Tamilnad*. Berkeley: University of California Press.
———. 1975. "When Stars Displace the Gods: The Folk Culture of Cinema in Tamil Nadu." Occasional Paper Series, No. 3. Center for Asian Studies, The University of Texas, Arlington.
Hardgrave, Robert L., Jr., and Anthony C. Neidhart. 1975. "Films and Political Consciousness in Tamil Nadu," *Economic and Political Weekly* 10, 1/2: 27–35.
Hariharan, N. 1987. "Confusion All Around," *Cinema in India* 1, 1: 50–51.
Hartmann, Paul, B. R. Patil, and Anita Dighe. 1989. *The Mass Media and Village Life: An Indian Study*. New Delhi: Sage.
Hebdige, Dick. 1979. *Subculture*. London: Methuen.
Heider, Karl. 1991. *Indonesian Cinema: National Culture on Screen*. Honolulu: University of Hawaii Press.
Heston, Alan. 1990. "Poverty in India: Some Recent Policies." In Marshall M. Bouton and Philip Oldenburg, eds., *India Briefing, 1990*, pp. 101–28. Boulder, CO: Westview Press. (Published in cooperation with The Asia Society.)
Holmström, Mark. 1984. *Industry and Inequality: The Social Anthropology of Indian Labour*. Cambridge: Cambridge University Press.
Horkheimer, Max. 1941. "Art and Mass Culture," *Studies in Philosophy and Social Science* 9, 2: 290–304.
Irschick, Eugene. 1969. *Politics and Social Conflict in South India: The Non-Brahman Movement and Tamil Separatism, 1916–1929*. Berkeley: University of California Press.
Jagathrakshakan, S. 1984. *Dr. M. G. R.: A Phenomenon*. Madras: Apollo Veliyeetagam.
Jameson, Fredric. 1979. "Reification and Utopia in Mass Culture," *Social Text* 1: 130–48.
Jeyakanthan. 1972. *Cinimaavukku Poona Cittaaḷ*. Madurai: Meenakshi Puthaka Nilayam.
Kakar, Sudhir. 1981. "The Ties that Bind: Family Relationships in the Mythology of Hindi Cinema," *India International Centre Quarterly* 8, 1: 11–21.
———. 1989. *Intimate Relations: Exploring Indian Sexuality*. New Delhi: Viking.
Kohli, Atul. 1987. *The State and Poverty in India: The Politics of Reform*. Cambridge: Cambridge University Press.

Kolenda, Pauline. 1984. "Woman as Tribute, Woman as Flower: Images of 'Woman' in Weddings in North and South India." *American Ethnologist* 11: 98–117.

Konvitz, Milton Ridvas, ed. 1963. *First Amendment Freedoms*. Ithaca, NY: Cornell University Press.

Krishen, Pradip. 1981. "Introduction." *India International Centre Quarterly* 8, 1: 3–9.

Kulkarni, V. B. 1965. *Heroes Who Made History*. Bombay: Bharatiya Vidya Bhavan.

Kumar, Nita. 1988. *The Artisans of Banaras: Popular Culture and Identity, 1880–1986*. Princeton: Princeton University Press.

Lele, Jayant. 1981. *Elite Pluralism and Class Rule*. Toronto: University of Toronto Press, 1981.

Lever, Janet. 1983. *Soccer Madness*. Chicago: University of Chicago Press.

Limón, José. 1982. "History, Chicano Joking, and the Varieties of Higher Education: Tradition and Performance as Critical Symbolic Action," *Journal of the Folklore Institute* 19, 2/3: 141–66.

1989. "*Carne, Carnales*, and the Carnivalesque: Bakhtinian *Batos*, Disorder, and Narrative Discourses," *American Ethnologist* 16, 3: 471–86.

Lloyd, Peter Cutt. 1982. *A Third World Proletariat?* London: G. Allen & Unwin.

Lombardi-Satriani, Luigi. 1974. "Folklore as Culture of Contestation," *Journal of the Folklore Institute* 11, 1/2: 99–121.

MacAloon, John J. 1984a. "Cultural Performances, Culture Theory." In J. J. MacAloon, ed., *Rite, Drama, Festival, Spectacle*, pp. 1–15. Philadelphia: Institute for the Study of Human Issues.

1984b. "Olympic Games and the Theory of Spectacle in Modern Societies." In J. J. MacAloon, ed., *Rite, Drama, Festival, Spectacle*, pp. 241–80. Philadelphia: Institute for the Study of Human Issues.

Marchetti, Gina. n.d. "Excess and Understatement: War, Romance, and the Melodrama in Contemporary Vietnamese Cinema." Unpublished ms.

Marglin, Frederique. 1985. *Wives of the God-King: The Rituals of the Devadasis of Puri*. Delhi: Oxford University Press.

Marriott, McKim. 1968. "Caste Ranking and Food Transactions: A Matrix Analysis." In Milton Singer and Bernard S. Cohn, eds., *Structure and Change in Indian Society*. Chicago: University of Chicago Press.

Marriott, McKim and Ronald Inden. 1977. "Toward an Ethnosociology of South Asian Caste Systems." In Kenneth David, ed., *The New Wind: Changing Identities in South Asia*, pp. 227–38. The Hague: Mouton.

Marx, Karl. 1978. "Preface" to *A Contribution to the Critique of Political Economy*. In R. C. Tucker, ed., *The Marx-Engels Reader*, 2nd ed., pp. 3–6. New York: W. W. Norton.

Marx, Karl and Friedrich Engels. 1978. "Part I," *The German Ideology*. In R. C. Tucker, ed., *The Marx-Engels Reader*, 2nd ed., pp. 147–200. New York: W. W. Norton.

Modleski, Tania, ed. 1986. *Studies in Entertainment*. Bloomington, IN: Indiana University Press.

Morley, David. 1986. *Family Television: Cultural Power and Domestic Leisure*. London: Comedia.
Mulvey, Laura. 1989a. "Afterthoughts on 'Visual Pleasure and Narrative Cinema' Inspired by King Vidor's *Duel in the Sun* (1946)." (Originally published 1981.) In L. Mulvey, *Visual and Other Pleasures*, Bloomington, IN: Indiana University Press.
  1989b "Visual Pleasure and Narrative Cinema." (Originally published 1975.) In Mulvey, *Visual and Other Pleasures*, Bloomington, IN: Indiana University Press.
Nowell-Smith, Geoffrey. 1985. "Minnelli and Melodrama." In B. Nichols, ed., *Movies and Methods*, vol. II, pp. 190–94. Berkeley: University of California Press.
Omvedt, Gail. 1989. "Class, Caste and Land in India." In Hamza Alavi and John Harriss, eds., *South Asia*, pp. 134–48. New York: Monthly Review Press.
Pandian, M. S. S. 1992. *The Image Trap: MG Ramachandran in Film and Politics*. New Delhi: Sage Publications.
Peacock, James L. 1968. *Rites of Modernization: Symbolic and Social Aspects of Indonesian Proletarian Drama*. Chicago: University of Chicago Press.
Pfleiderer, Beatrix. 1985. "An Empirical Study of Urban and Semi-Urban Audience Reactions to Hindi Films." In B. Pfleiderer and L. Lutze, eds., *The Hindi Film*, pp. 81–130.
Pfleiderer, Beatrix and Lothar Lutze, eds. 1985. *The Hindi Film: Agent and Re-Agent of Cultural Change*. New Delhi: Manohar Publications.
Radway, Janice A. 1984. *Reading the Romance: Women, Patriarchy, and Popular Literature*. Chapel Hill: The University of North Carolina Press.
Ramachandran, R. K. n.d. "The Eternal Cinema." Unpublished ms.
Ramachandran, T. M. and S. Rukmini, eds. 1985. *70 Years of Indian Cinema (1913–1983)*. Bombay: CINEMA India-International.
Ramachandran, T. M. and Jyoti Venkatesh. 1985. "Film Censorship in India." In T. M. Ramachandran and S. Rukmini, eds., *70 Years of Indian Cinema*, pp. 537–43.
Rao, Sridevi. 1986. "Leave Me Alone, Please," *Aside* 10, 5: 10–15.
Reynolds, Holly Baker. 1980. "The Auspicious Married Woman." In S. S. Wadley, ed., *The Powers of Tamil Women*, pp. 35–60. Syracuse: Maxwell School of Citizenship and Public Affairs, Syracuse University.
Roberge, Gaston. 1985. *Another Cinema for Another Society*. Calcutta: Seagull Books.
Roy, Manisha. 1975. *Bengali Women*. Chicago: University of Chicago Press.
Sarkar, Kobita. 1975. *Indian Cinema Today – An Analysis*. New Delhi: Sterling Publishers.
  1982. *You Can't Please Everyone! Film Censorship: The Inside Story*. Bombay: I.B.H. Publishing Co.
Sastri, K. A. Nilakanta. 1966. *A History of South India*. Oxford: Oxford University Press.
Schrøder, Kim. 1988. "The Pleasure of *Dynasty*: The Weekly Reconstruction of Self-Confidence." In Phillip Drummond and Richard Paterson, eds.,

Television and its Audience: International Research Perspectives. London: BFI Publishing.
Segal, Mohan. 1985. "Dance In Indian Cinema." In T. M. Ramachandran and S. Rukmini, eds., *70 Years of Indian Cinema*, pp. 252–57. Bombay: CINEMA India-International.
Sharma, Miriam. 1978. *The Politics of Inequality: Competition and Control in an Indian Village.* Honolulu: University of Hawaii Press.
Silverman, Kaja. 1988. *The Acoustic Mirror: The Female Voice in Psychoanalysis and Cinema.* Bloomington, IN: Indiana University Press.
Singer, Milton. 1959. "The Great Tradition in a Metropolitan Center: Madras." In M. Singer, ed., *Traditional India: Structure and Change*, pp. 141–82. Philadelphia: American Folklore Society.
  1972. *When a Great Tradition Modernizes.* New York: Praeger.
Sivathamby, Karthigesu. 1981. *The Tamil Film as a Medium of Political Communication.* Madras: New Century Book House.
Slingo, Carol. 1990. "The Malayalam Commercial Cinema and the Films of Mammootty," *Asian Cinema* 5, 1: 2–7.
South Indian Film Chamber of Commerce. 1985. *Annual Report for the Year 1984–85.* Madras.
Srinivasan, C. M. 1964. *The Heroes of Hind.* Madras: Aiyar and Company.
Stam, Richard. 1988. "Mikhail Bakhtin and Left Cultural Critique." In E. Ann Kaplan, ed., *Postmodernism and its Discontents.* New York: Verso.
Sunil, K. P. 1986. "The Colossus" (interview with Shivaji Ganesan), *Filmfare* 35, 2: 60–63.
Thomas, Rosie. 1985. "Indian Cinema: Pleasures and Popularity," *Screen* 26, 3/4: 116–31.
Thompson, E. P. 1963. *The Making of the English Working Class.* London: Victor Gollancz.
Thorner, Daniel. 1956. *The Agrarian Prospect in India.* Delhi: Oxford University Press.
Trawick, Margaret. 1990. *Notes on Love in a Tamil Family.* Berkeley: University of California Press.
Turner, Victor. 1957. *Schism and Continuity in an African Society.* Manchester: Manchester University Press.
  1967. *The Forest of Symbols: Aspects of Ndembu Ritual.* Ithaca, NY: Cornell University Press.
  1984. "Liminality and the Performative Genres." In J. J. MacAloon, ed., *Rite, Drama, Festival, Spectacle*, pp. 19–41. Philadelphia: Institute for the Study of Human Issues.
  1986. *The Anthropology of Performance.* New York: PAJ Publications.
Varadachar, Beba D. 1979. "The Bottom View Up: Some Cognitive Categories – Slums in Madras." In M. N. Srinivas, A. M. Shah and E. A. Ramaswamy, eds., *The Fieldworker and the Field: Problems and Challenges in Sociological Investigation*, pp. 127–40. Delhi: Oxford University Press.
Wadley, Susan S. 1980. "The Paradoxical Powers of Tamil Women." In S. S. Wadley, ed., *The Powers of Tamil Women*, pp. 153–70. Syracuse: Maxwell School of Citizenship and Public Affairs, Syracuse University.

Walsh, Andrea. 1989. "'Life Isn't Yet Over': Older Heroines in American Popular Cinema of the 1930s and 1970s/80s." *Qualitative Sociology* 12, 1: 72–95.

Washbrook, D. A. 1989. "Caste, Class and Dominance in Modern Tamil Nadu: Non-Brahmanism, Dravidianism and Tamil Nationalism." In Francine R. Frankel and M. S. A. Rao, eds., *Dominance and State Power in Modern India*, vol. I, pp. 204–64. Delhi: Oxford University Press.

Weinstein, Jay A. 1974. *Madras: An Analysis of Urban Ecological Structure in India*. Beverly Hills: Sage.

Wiebe, Paul. 1981. *Tenants and Trustees: A Study of the Poor in Madras*. Delhi: MacMillan India.

Williams, Raymond. 1977. *Marxism and Literature*. Oxford: Oxford University Press.

1982. *The Sociology of Culture*. New York: Schocken Books.

Wood, Robin. 1985. "An Introduction to the American Horror Film." In B. Nichols, ed., *Movies and Methods*, pp. 195–220. Berkeley: University of California Press.

Index

AIDS, 163
Aariliruntu Arupatu Varai, 137
acting style, 64, 152
actors, 6, 29, 31, 33, 36, 42, 50, 51, 52, 56, 59, 60, 61, 63–64, 120, 121, 127, 128, 134, 147, 153, 155, 165, 172, 188n (*see also* actresses; film stars; heroes; heroines; performers)
   acting ability of, 152–54
   dancing skills of, 152, 153–54
   fighting skills of, 152
   identification with film roles, 169, 172
   identification with the poor, 63, 153, 154, 156–57, 168–70, 172 (*see also* Ramachandran, M. G., as defender of poor)
   images of, *see* film stars, images of
   importance of, 55
   relationship with fans, 153, 154
actresses, 6, 29, 31, 36, 50, 52, 56, 59, 60, 61–64, 120, 121, 147, 153, 188n (*see also* actresses; film stars; heroines; performers)
   as fighters, 59, 184n
   stigma attached to, 50, 56, 61, 146–47
adolescents, 28, 29, 31, 36, 39, 149
adoptive families, kindness of in films, 95–96
adultery, 90, 96–97, 98, 138, 140, 185n
advertisements (projected before films), 39–40
advertising of films, 3, 121–22 (*see also* film songs, role in film promotion)
Alam Ara, 52
alcohol and drugs, 53, 91, 110, 111, 140, 169, 187n (*see also* film themes, imposed, evils of alcohol and drugs)
   glorification of in films, 103–104, 177
All India Radio (AIR), 58
Althusser, L., 144
Ambika, 63, 84
ambivalence
   regarding cinema, 6, 42–43, 146, 176 (*see also* cinema, public and private opinions on)
   regarding class identity, 172, 173, 176 (*see also* fan club members, ambivalent relationship to urban poor; urban poor, views on class)
Amman Koovil Kizhakkaalee, 71, 78–83, 91, 92–94, 95, 96, 98–99, 101, 102, 111, 112, 113, 115, 135, 184n, 186n, 187n
Andhra Pradesh, 127, 179n, 193n
Andhra Pradesh Film Development Corporation, 128
Anglo–Indians, 34, 50
Annadurai, C. N., 22, 54–55, 155, 162, 166, 179n, 190n
Annadurai-Dravida Munnetra Kazhagam (ADMK), 22, 162, 170, 171, 191n, 193n
anti-Brahman sentiments, 21, 22, 54
anti-North sentiments, 21, 22, 23, 54, 187n
anxieties of viewers, 17, 65, 66, 69–70, 89, 91, 92, 93, 97, 99, 110–114, 115, 138, 173, 174, 175, 185n, 186n, 187n, 194n
appeal of cinema, 3, 14, 32, 68, 69, 145, 147, 184n, 189n
"art," "parallel" or "new wave" cinema, 5, 123, 129

203

Index

audience participation, 40, 92, 158
audiences, 3–5, 6, 11, 13, 25, 39, 49, 51, 58, 60, 63, 66, 67, 68, 71, 90, 92, 100, 101, 104, 105, 107, 109, 110, 115, 119, 127, 130–31, 134–47 *passim*, 165, 173, 184n, 188n, 194n
   ambivalence regarding cinema, 6, 146, 176
   and popular culture, 11–14
   as active viewers, 12, 174–75, 176
   as childlike, 130–32
   entertainment needs and desires of, 57–58, 65, 109, 115, 126, 133, 143, 146, 174, 175, 189n
   influence on cinema, 6, 32, 119, 126, 130, 140–41, 143–44, 147, 175
   personalizing of situations, 137–38, 173
   reactions to middle and upper class values, 144, 145
   representation of selves, 133, 140–41, 142, 143, 175
   view of others on, 5, 64, 125, 126, 189n
Avantaan Manitan, 104

Bachchan, Amitabh, 193n
backward castes and classes, 19, 181n
Balachandar, K., 90, 98
Balaje, K., 61, 127, 128–29, 146–47, 189n
Bangalore, 123, 191n
Bengal, 48, 53
Beteille, A., 9, 10
Bhagyaraj, 184n
Bhanumathi Ramakrishna, 183n, 189n
bharatanatyam, 59
Bharatiar, C. S., 73, 185n
Bharatiraja, 69, 98, 105, 109, 125, 126, 128, 189n
Bombay, 49, 51–52, 119, 123, 130, 183n, 188n
Brahmans, 8, 19, 21, 22, 34, 52, 55, 105, 108, 109, 180n, 181n, 187n
Britain, 12, 43
British, as colonial rulers, 48, 53, 123, 124, 180n, 183n

cakti, 27, 28, 29, 181–82n (*see also* female sexuality; women, power of)
   binding of, 27, 28, 29 (*see also* female sexuality, binding of; women, power of, binding of)
Calankai Oli, 59
Calcutta, 123, 130

Camsaaram Atu Minsaaram, 95, 114, 140
Caplan, L., 7, 9, 10, 11, 27, 180n
Carnatic music, 59, 71, 72, 115
caste, 7, 10, 15, 17–19, 24, 25, 26, 27, 29, 33, 34, 48, 98, 100, 103, 107–108, 109, 135, 138, 139, 180n, 181n, 182n, 186n, 187n, 189n
   and education, 24–25
   and politics, 18, 19
   definition of, 17
   in films, 104, 105, 177
   significance and expression of, 18–19, 108, 109, 190n
caste identity, 17–19, 108, 109 (*see also* film themes, avoided, caste)
caste relations, 19, 108, 110 (*see also* film themes, avoided, caste relations)
caste reservations, 19, 180–81n
censor boards, 53–54, 109, 123–25, 132, 177
censor code, 103, 177–78, 188n
censor rating, process of appeal of, 124
censors, 14, 33, 109, 110, 120, 123–25, 131, 132–33
   as teachers and protectors of audience, 130–32, 133, 143–44
   views on audience, 130–32, 143
   views on filmmakers, 132, 143
censorship, 54, 55, 59, 121, 122, 130–33, 177
   circumvention of, 124, 132
   "double standard" in, 130–31
   process, 123–24
Central Board of Film Censors, 123
Central Board of Film Certification, 121, 123, 177
certificates (censor), 40, 120, 121, 123, 124
   "A," 123
   "S," 123
   "U," 120, 123
   "UA," 123
certification, 124, 177
Chakkiliyars, 140, 180n
Chandralekha, 54, 55
Chaplin, Charlie, 55
charity, relationship to leadership, 161–62, 170, 171, 191n, 192n
Chettiars, 34, 140
children, 3, 16, 17, 20, 24–25, 26, 27, 28–29, 36, 39, 43, 69, 70, 90, 94, 95, 97, 99, 130, 131–32, 138, 139, 154, 155, 156, 157, 159, 161, 169, 170, 182n

as audience, 25
 rebellion of against parental authority, 99–100, 112
Christianity, 20
Christians, 17, 20, 93, 98, 104, 135, 149, 187n
Church of South India, 20
Cilappatikaaram, 90
cinema, 13, 25, 30, 35, 48
 and class, 6–7, 9, 11, 16, 17, 142, 143–46, 168, 174, 179n, 194n
 and crime, 43, 139, 140, 177, 189n
 and politics, 3, 6, 14, 22, 42, 43, 52–56, 64, 129, 148, 152, 155, 165–72, 176, 184n, 193n
 and social commentary, 54, 65–66, 127, 185n
 and stigma, 6–7, 42–43, 52, 149, 176
 artificiality of, 173, 174, 193–94n
 definition of, 14
 effects and influence of, 5, 14, 32, 37, 43, 126, 128–29, 130–32, 134, 139–42, 172, 173, 175, 182n, 189n, 193n
 history, *see* history of Tamil cinema
 influence on of other dramatic forms, 47–49
 popularity of, 3, 6, 31, 32, 42, 69, 182n
 "proper" attitudes toward, 142
 public and private opinions on, 6, 36, 41, 42, 43, 141–42, 147, 149
 relation to and connections with viewers' lives, 5, 14, 60, 71, 91, 115, 134, 136–38, 141, 142, 173, 175
 roots in reality, 65, 66–67, 68, 69, 110, 141, 173, 174, 175
 social censure of, 6, 43, 142
 usefulness as political tool, 42, 165
"cinema madness," 142
Cinematograph Act of 1918, 53
Cinna Viitu, 90
Cippikkul Muttu, 154, 186n, 190n
Civil Disobedience movement, 53
class, 6–7, 8–11, 15–17, 18, 48, 61, 68, 70, 98, 114, 119, 136, 137, 138, 141, 165, 174, 180n (*see also* cinema and class; film themes, class identity and class relations; dominant class; subordinate class)
 difficulties in applying categories in India, 9–11
 difficulties in defining in India, 9–11
 in fan clubs, 149–50

local categories of, 8, 9
 relation to power, 15–17
class conflict, seen in *Nadodi Mannan,* 168
class consciousness, 9, 10
class differences, 8–9, 24, 58, 70, 102
class identity, 11, 15, 142 (*see also* film themes, class identity and class relations)
 ambivalence regarding, 172, 173, 176 (*see also* fan club members, ambivalent relationship to urban poor; urban poor, views on class)
class ideology(ies), 10, 143, 144, 145, 164, 185n (*see also* dominant ideology; subordinate ideology)
 purpose in films, 145–47
class relations, 16
comedy, 54, 55, 58, 60, 126
communication
 between audiences and filmmakers, 143–44, 145, 175
 through media, 12–13, 68, 174–75
Communists, 184n
Congress party, 55, 105, 152, 168
consumer items, 6, 27, 34, 62, 186n
contradictions
 between images of utopia, *see* utopian images, contradictions and conflicts in
 within films, 66–67
conventions of Tamil and other Indian cinema, 14, 47, 48–49, 58–61, 64, 71, 90, 185n
 aesthetic, 47
 narrative, 47, 95
 of verisimilitude, 47, 52, 183n
criticism of Tamil and other Indian cinema, 5–6, 13, 47–48, 58, 173, 193–94n
cultural performance studies, 12–13, 175
cumankali, 28, 97

Dallas, 13
dance, 3, 33, 48, 50, 52, 150, 156, 183n, 191n
dance, classical, 59
dances, 54, 56, 58, 59, 60, 61, 71, 154 (*see also* song and dance scenes)
Das Gupta, C., 5, 110
Debord, G., 13, 68, 174–75
deities, 20, 36, 40, 50, 90, 91, 92, 103, 157, 184n, 185n, 187n, 191n
Delhi, 124

*devadasi*s, 48, 94, 105, 183n
devotion, 20, 157–58, 170, 184n, 191n
dialogue(s), 3, 54, 55, 108, 168, 192n
directors, 29, 33, 40, 41, 50, 53, 56, 58, 61, 104, 119–30 *passim*, 132, 145, 146, 152, 154, 156, 188n (*see also* filmmakers)
disdain for cinema, 5, 42, 43, 54, 58, 59, 63, 146, 176 (*see also* criticism of Tamil and other Indian cinema)
distribution, 51, 120, 121
division of labor, 24, 28, 29
documentary films, 49, 122–23, 125
dominant class, 9–10, 12, 65, 185n
dominant ideology, 10, 11, 68, 145
dowry, 26, 27, 137, 182n
drama, 52, 53, 56, 166, 194n
  classical, 47, 48, 52
  European, 48
  folk, 47, 48, 52
  exodus of personnel to cinema, 52, 183n
Dramatic Performances Act of 1876, 53
Dravida Kazhagam (DK), 22, 54
Dravida Munnetra Kazhagam (DMK), 22, 54, 151, 152, 166, 168, 170, 184n, 185n, 190n, 191n, 193n
Dravidian movement, 21, 155 (*see also* non-Brahman movement)
drugs, *see* alcohol and drugs
dubbing, of films, 120, 188n
dubbing, of voice parts, 121, 188n
Dyer, R., 57–58, 65, 66–67, 110, 115

education and schooling, 9, 17, 19, 23, 24, 26, 27, 29, 43, 64, 95, 97, 99, 100, 101, 102, 115, 130, 135, 137, 150, 155, 157, 161, 165, 169, 180n, 181n, 182n
education, cinema and, 128–29, 139, 142, 143
"educational" films (censor category), 123
Elsaesser, T., 64–65, 66, 67, 68
Emergency, 124
En Uyir Thoozhan, 69
endings, happy, 61, 65, 66, 97, 114–15
endings, tragic, 67, 98, 114–15
England, nineteenth-century, 164
English (language), 8, 23, 24, 33, 51, 73, 77, 78, 82, 84, 122, 158, 182n
Enok, Joseph, 189n
Enzensberger, H. M., 12, 13, 111
escape, 13–14, 67–68, 69, 115, 128, 129, 138, 139, 141, 142, 145, 148, 173, 174–76, 194n

and conflict between class roots and individual desires, 174
escapism, 13, 54, 66, 174
ethnicity, 21–23, 54, 98, 181n, 187n, 193n
European cinema, 5, 51
Europeans in India, 21, 49, 50 (*see also* British, as colonial rulers)

family(ies), 8, 16–17, 24–27, 28–29, 36, 37, 41, 43, 61, 66, 70, 93, 96, 99, 112, 114, 138, 140, 141, 142, 147, 149, 169, 180n, 184n, 186n
  extended or joint, 94–95, 136
  members' transgressions of responsibilities, 17, 95, 136, 137, 138, 186n, 187n
fan club activities, 42, 53, 149, 150, 151, 158–64, 173, 190n, 192n
  compared with filmwatching, 175
  recreation vs. service, 163–64, 176
  recreational, 158–60, 191n
  social service, 63, 148, 157, 158, 159–65, 176, 192n; as support for star's reputation, 159–60, 161, 170, 171, 172; ethos of, 159, 161, 163–64; presentation ceremonies, 161–63
fan club finances, 158, 161, 162–63
fan club members, 33, 148, 149, 158, 159, 170, 171–72, 190n
  ambivalent relationship to urban poor, 164–65, 173, 176
  as helpers of poor, 161, 164–65, 172, 176
  attributes of, 149–50
  depictions of heroes, 148
  feelings for film stars, 151, 153
  image of selves, 156, 172, 175
  qualities praised in film stars, 153–57, 176; compassion, 154, 155, 157, 171; generosity, 153, 154, 155, 156, 157, 159, 171, 176; good-naturedness, 153; hospitality, 153, 154, 156; humility, 153, 157, 191n; ingenuousness, 154, 157; physical prowess and virility, 153, 154, 155–56, 157, 171, 172; political power, 155, 157, 171, 172
  respect for film stars, 155, 157
fan club membership, 152
fan club officers, 33, 136, 148, 150, 151, 154, 155, 158, 159, 160–61, 162–63, 168, 171, 189–90n, 191n
fan clubs, 3, 14, 23, 25, 29, 32, 33, 40, 42, 53, 63–64, 122, 148–65, 170–72, 173

and caste, 148, 150, 190n
and politics, 42, 53, 159, 160, 161–62, 163, 165, 170–71, 190n, 192n
and violence, 158, 191n, 193n
as mutual aid societies, 164–65, 173
assistance to poor, 160, 161, 163, 164–65, 193n
branch clubs, 148, 150–51, 154, 159–60, 161, 190n
compared with upper class welfare organizations, 163–64
complaints regarding, 159, 192n
head clubs (city, district and state), 148, 150–51, 154, 155, 158, 160–61, 162–63, 171, 190n
Kamalhasan, 148, 150, 151, 160, 163, 189n, 190n, 191n
MGR, 148, 149–51, 158, 161–63, 165, 189–90n, 191n, 192n
neighborhood base of, 150
number of, 148, 189–90n
organizational structure of, 148, 150–51, 170
Rajinikanth, 136, 148, 150, 151, 159–60, 161, 189n, 190n, 191n
relationship with neighborhood residents, 158–59, 161, 162–63, 164, 192n
Shivaji, 149–50, 190n
unofficial, 189n
Vijaykanth, 161
fantasy, 5, 57, 67, 68, 69, 110, 115, 120, 126, 127, 128, 146, 174, 175, 176, 194n
female sexuality, 28, 91, 92–94, 111–12 (*see also cakti*)
binding of, 91, 92, 93–94, 111–12 (*see also cakti*, binding of)
festivals, 3, 20, 48, 51, 58, 170, 191n
fieldwork, 14, 15, 29–35, 125–26, 134, 148, 151, 188n, 190n
fights and fight scenes, 47, 54, 58, 59–60, 61, 79, 82, 85, 120, 155–56, 157, 168
Film Advisory Board, 123
Film Certification Appellate Tribunal, 124
Film Federation of India, 122
Film Finance Corporation, 123
film critics, 5, 11, 14, 33, 58, 104, 121–22, 130, 141, 173, 174, 179n, 188n, 189n, 193n
film industry, 50, 119–25, 146, 187–88n
Madras, 119–20
size of, 3

film magazines, 122, 150, 161
film paraphernalia, 41
film personnel, 120
film production, 47, 49, 50
film reviews, 36, 122
film sets, 49, 69, 110
film songs, 3, 27, 36, 40, 47, 52, 53, 54, 58–59, 60, 61, 71, 87, 120, 126, 165, 168, 183n, 192n, 193n (*see also* song and dance scenes)
role in film promotion, 58
role in narrative, 59
film stars, 3, 6, 40, 42, 49, 52–53, 58, 63, 64, 121, 127, 148–59 *passim*, 169, 184n, 191n, 194n (*see also* actors; actresses)
control over films of, 50, 53
images of, 62, 63, 148, 152–53, 154, 156, 157, 169, 170, 171, 172 (*see also* fan club members, qualities praised in film stars)
importance to film's success, 52
significance of rise from poverty for fans, 156–57, 172, 173, 176
film stories, 41, 58, 60–61, 120, 184n
recounted by viewers, 134, 135, 136, 137–38, 141
film studios, 3, 49, 120, 121, 183n
film themes, 69, 70–71, 99, 103, 110, 142, 148, 172, 174, 185n
avoided, 58, 71, 103, 105, 115, 143; caste, 103, 105; caste relations, 103, 105, 115
class identity and class relations, 69, 78, 84, 89, 100–103, 113–14, 141, 144; interaction of rich and poor, 78, 100, 101–102, 135; nature of rich and poor, 78, 84, 100–101, 113, 135, 144, 157; value of different educations, 100, 102, 113
directors', *see* film themes, imposed
family relations, 69, 72, 78, 84, 89, 94–100, 112, 114, 135, 138, 141, 185n, 186n; adultery, 72, 96–97, 112; loyalty to natal vs. marital families, 78, 96, 112; love marriages, 96, 97–100, 112, 114; transgression of responsibilities, 95–96, 112
imposed, 58, 71, 103–105, 142; evils of alcohol and drugs, 103–104, 115, 142; goodness of religious minorities, 103, 104–105, 115

relationships between men and women, 69, 72, 78, 89–94, 112, 138, 141, 185n; transformed woman, 78, 89, 91–94, 111–12, 135; woman disrupting male family, 89, 94–95, 112, 114, 185n, 186n; woman sacrificing for a man, 78, 89, 90–91, 111, 135
viewers', *see* film themes, avoided
filmgoing, 25, 31, 32, 36–39, 42. 60, 139–41, 183n
filmmakers, 5, 6–7, 11, 14, 50, 52, 58, 65, 66, 67, 71, 104–105, 110, 114–15, 119–30, 132, 141, 142–47, 175, 185n, 187n, 188n, 194n (*see also* directors; producers)
 ambivalence regarding cinema, 145–47
 and creativity, 119, 126, 127, 143, 177
 and North Indian market, 54
 as teachers of audience, 104–105, 115, 129–30, 133, 143, 144, 164, 175
 definition of, 119
 desires of, 57
 determining legitimacy of audience needs and desires, 104, 109, 115
 reactions to lower class values, 145, 146
 relation to middle and upper classes, 143, 145–47, 175
 views on and attitudes toward audiences, 6, 14, 104–105, 119, 126–30, 142, 143, 144, 164, 175
filmmaking, 14, 50, 120, 126–27
 financial constraints on, 57, 120, 146, 183n, 184n
 process, 120–22
Films Division, Ministry of Information and Broadcasting, 40, 122–23
films, 30, 41
 family (*kuṭumpa paṭankaḷ*), 55, 60, 99, 136, 139, 143
 historical, 50, 60
 mythological, 49, 53, 54, 56, 60, 183n
 number produced, 3, 119–20
 number unreleased, 121
 older, compared with contemporary films, 40
 "progressive," 65, 114
 "reactionary," 65
 religious (*caami paṭankaḷ*), 36, 40, 60
 romance, 56, 136
 silent, 48, 49–51, 53
 social, 50, 53, 55, 60, 99
 stunt, 50, 53, 131

filmwatching, 14, 36, 39–40, 42, 138, 139–41, 184n, 194n
 reasons for, 14, 128–29, 134, 139, 142, 173
financing, 119, 120, 123, 145, 188n
"folk culture of cinema," 41
food exchange, 19, 181n
foreign cinema, 47–48, 55
 in India, 50–51, 130–31
foreign influence on Tamil and other Indian cinema, 47, 49, 50, 58, 59
foreign views on and criticisms of Indian and Tamil cinema, 5, 47–48, 179n
formula, 58, 71, 126, 143, 188–89n
forward castes, 19, 181n
Frankfurt School, 11, 12, 13, 144

Gandhi, Mahatma, 18, 53, 105, 110, 180n
Gandhi, Rajiv, 40
Gemini Studio, 54
gender, 15, 18, 28, 29, 119
gender relations, 28, 91–92
Gledhill, C., 12, 13, 14, 65–66
"good" films
 as defined by audiences, 90, 136, 141, 143
 as defined by filmmakers, 126–27, 129, 143
government, 18, 24, 35, 53, 129, 131, 155, 156, 162, 163, 169, 181n, 192n, 193n
 Indian, 19, 21, 123, 184n
 involvement of in film industry, 121, 122–25
Gujarat, 122

Hardgrave, R. L., 21, 22, 41, 61, 63, 64, 149–50, 156, 158, 168, 190n, 191n
Harijans, 19, 53, 107, 135, 136, 138, 180n (*see also* scheduled castes; and specific caste names)
"heart of a child," quality praised in film stars, 153, 154, 157
heroes, 40, 42, 52, 60, 61, 105, 127, 148, 152, 156–58, 165, 169, 172
heroines, 52, 60, 61, 152, 158, 168
Himalayas, 120
Hindi, 21, 22, 23, 51, 52, 54, 181n
Hindi cinema, 66, 119–20, 124, 127, 153, 183n (*see also* North Indian films)
Hindu Munnani, 21
Hinduism, 20, 22, 30–31

Index 209

Hindus, 17, 18, 19–20, 26, 96, 98, 104, 135, 149, 185n, 186n, 187n
history of Tamil cinema, 47–56
Hollywood, domination of international film market, 51–52
Hollywood films, *see* US cinema
horoscopes, 26
housework, 24, 29, 43, 149
Hyderabad, 20

identification of fans with film stars, 131, 171, 172, 193n, 194n
identity, 7, 8, 9, 11, 14, 15, 17–18, 35, 137, 165, 176 (*see also* class identity; caste identity)
ideology, *see* class ideology; dominant ideology; subordinate ideology
illusion, role of, 68, 174–75, 176
image in film, *see* illusion, role of
India, national security and sovereignty of, 130, 177
Indian Congress government, 53
Indian nationalism, 52, 53–54, 185n
individualizing in film, 68, 108, 145, 173–74 (*see also* melodrama, individualizing tendencies of)
individualizing in fan clubs, 173
inter-caste love relationships, 107–108, 109–110
Iruvar Uḷḷam, 135

Jains, 17
Janaki Ramachandran, 170, 179n
Janata Dal, 152, 184n, 193n
jati, *see* caste
jatra, 48
Jayalalitha Jayaram, 104, 155, 165, 166–67, 179n, 191n, 193n
Justice Party, 21–22

Kakar, S., 42, 57, 66, 179n
Kamalhasan, 59, 63, 127–28, 150, 151, 152–53, 156, 157, 160, 163, 188–89n, 190n
Kannada films, 119–20
Kannagi, 90
Karakaaṭṭakkaaran, 61, 141
Karnataka, 123, 152, 179n
Karunanidhi, Mu., 22, 54–55, 155, 179n, 191n
Kaṭaloora Kavitaikaḷ, 98, 135
kathakali, 48

Kavithalaiya Productions, 72
Kerala, 20, 48, 120, 123, 124, 179n, 188n, 193n
Kodaikanal, 120
Kohli, A., 9, 10
*kolam*s, 31, 81, 185n
Kommineni, 147, 189n
Konars, 34
Krishnan, N. S., 55, 59

"lack" in cinema, 193–94n
language and politics, 21–23
language chauvinism, 21, 22–23, 54, 187n
leisure, 25, 184n
love (*see also* romance), 27, 99, 105–106, 107–108, 135, 141, 153, 155, 157, 158, 187n
love marriage (*see* marriage, love)
lower class values, 144
lower class(es), 6, 8, 10, 24, 34, 35, 42, 49, 101, 102, 128, 129–30, 142, 147, 152, 156, 157, 169
 attitudes to higher classes, 16, 100, 102
 views of higher classes on, 126, 127, 130
 Raja in *Paṭikkaatavan* as epitome of, 113
 resistance to middle and upper class values, 16, 144, 164
Lumière brothers, 47, 49

MGR, *see* Ramachandran, M. G.
MGR Women's Association, 190n
MacAloon, J. J., 12–13, 174
Madhuram, T. A., 55
Madras, 3, 10, 29, 33, 34, 50, 51–52, 54, 96–97, 100, 119, 120, 123, 125, 132, 151, 153, 156, 166, 177n, 180n, 183n, 185n, 187n
Madurai, 3, 6, 8, 15–16, 19–20, 21, 30, 33–35, 37, 38, 40, 42, 61, 69, 71, 90, 100, 108, 148, 150, 151, 154, 155, 160, 161, 168, 169, 183n, 184n, 189–90n, 191n, 192n, 193n
 research neighborhoods in, 14, 15, 34–35, 151
Mahabalipuram, 120
Mahabharata, 90, 184n
Malayalam films, 119–20, 124, 188n
male bonds, 94–95
manipulation through popular culture, 13, 144, 145, 174–75
Marathavars, 135, 140, 189n

Index

marriage, 17, 24, 25–29, 91, 98, 141, 149, 161, 186n
  arranged, 25–27, 98, 99, 135, 137
  binding symbolism in, 28, 182n
  ideal spouses in, 26, 27, 90, 99, 182n, 184–86n
  love, 26, 98, 99, 185n
Marxist class analysis, 9, 145
  difficulties of applying in India, 9–11
mass culture, 11, 12, 13 (*see also* popular culture)
mass media and culture, 11
Masud, I., 179n
meaning in cinema, 5, 7, 14, 42, 143, 179n
meaning in popular culture, 13
meaning-making, 5, 7
melodrama, 13, 47, 49, 55, 60, 64–68, 95, 108, 114, 115, 173, 175
  individualizing tendencies of, 65–66, 108, 145, 173
  social functions of, 64–66
men, 20, 21, 23, 24, 25, 26, 27, 28, 29, 32, 36, 37, 39, 42, 43, 61, 91, 92, 94, 96, 107, 111–12, 114, 138, 141, 142, 150, 171, 182n, 183n, 186n, 190n
  as audiences, 25
  as fan club members, 148, 149, 171
  as fans, 152
  in films, 89, 177
middle and upper class values, 9, 130, 132, 143–47 *passim*
  imparted by filmmakers and censors, 143–44
  resistance to by lower class, 16, 144, 164
middle and upper classes, 6, 8–9, 24, 26, 34, 39, 42, 49, 65, 70, 100, 105, 126, 130, 146, 164, 176, 180n, 182n, 185n, 188n, 189n
  and filmwatching, 6, 42, 152, 189n
  as combined category, 8–9
  attitudes to lower class, 16, 43, 100, 164
  represented in films, 144–45
Ministry of Information and Broadcasting, 40, 122–23
Modleski, T., 12
moocam, 61–63, 184–85n
morality, 5, 6, 9, 43, 96, 100, 101, 103, 129, 132, 133, 136, 141, 142, 143, 144–45, 146, 157, 164, 172, 175, 184n, 185n
morals and messages of films, 90, 127, 130, 134, 135–36, 140, 142, 173, 175
Muktha Srinivasan, 128, 189n

Mulvey, L., 13, 194n
music directors, 52, 120
music, 48, 50, 52, 56, 58, 102, 183n
Muslims, 17, 20–21, 34, 48, 95, 104, 105, 137, 149, 187n
Mutal Mariyaatai, 105–108, 109, 135
Mutaliyars, 34

Nadars, 34
Nadodi Mannan, 168, 193n
Naidus, 34
Narayanan, A. V., 128, 129, 189n
narrative, 47 (*see also* conventions of Tamil and other Indian cinema, narrative)
National Awards, 105, 109
National Film Development Corporation (NFDC), 129
negotiation
  through cinema, 5, 14
  through popular culture, 12, 174–75
newspapers, 25, 37, 161, 165, 191n, 192n, 193n
newsreels, 39, 40
non-Brahman movement, 21–22, 181n
non-Brahmans, 8, 21, 22, 181n
Non-cooperation movement, 53
North Indian films, 57, 183–84n, 187–88n
  (*see also* Hindi cinema)

Ooty, 120

Palaniappan, S. P., 78
Pandian, M. S. S., 150, 170, 190n
Pantam, 137
Parasakthi, 54, 55
Parsis, 17
"particulate" actors, 52, 121
Paṭikkaatavan, 71, 84–88, 94, 95–96, 98, 100–102, 103, 104, 112, 113, 115, 135–36, 152, 186n
patrilineage, 94, 96
performers, 41, 42, 43, 63
  stigma attached to, 50, 56, 61
Phalke, D. G., 49, 50
Pillais, 135, 189n
playback singers, 52, 120
pleasure, 13–14, 138, 175–76, 194n
political leaders, 23, 56, 165, 171, 172, 187n, 191n
political parties, 6, 21, 23, 56, 155, 170, 171, 181n, 193n (*see also* specific parties)

popular culture
  and audiences 11–14
  manipulation through, 11, 12, 13, 144, 145, 174–75
  meaning in, 13
  negotiation through, 12, 174–75
  subaltern uses of, 11–12, 13, 144, 194n
pornography, 124
poverty, 8, 10, 101, 111, 139, 153, 156, 172, 173, 179–80n
  in films, 69, 187n
Prasad, L. V., 127, 129, 189n
Prasad Studios, 127, 129
producers, 29, 33, 40, 51, 58, 104, 119–30 *passim*, 132, 146, 152, 156, 188n (*see also* filmmakers)
production rates, 3, 119–20
profits, 120, 136, 188n
prostitutes, 43, 50, 94
puberty (of girls), 29
Punnakai Mannan, 97–98, 114
Putu Vacantam, 141
Puu Onru Puyalaanatu, 56, 184n
Puukkalai Parikkaatiirkal, 98

*racikai manram*s, 149
*racikar manram*s, *see* fan clubs
Radha, 78
Radio Ceylon, 58–59
radio, 58–59, 165, 193n
Rajashekar, 84
Rajnikanth, 59, 84, 136, 137, 150, 152–53, 154, 156, 157, 159–60
Raju, D. V. S., 128, 129, 189n
Rakaciya Pooliis, 55
Rama Rao, N. T. (NTR), 165, 193n
Ramachandran, M. G. (MGR), 22, 23, 40, 42, 43, 52, 56, 59, 63, 99, 101, 122, 150, 151, 152, 154–56, 157, 162, 163, 165–72, 176, 179n, 184n, 191n, 193n
  as defender of poor, 63, 152, 165, 169, 170, 171–72, 176
  rise of, 55
Ramachandran, R. K., 54, 123, 132–33
Ramasamy, E. V. (EVR), 22
Ramayana, 90, 184n
Rambo, 127
Ramesh, A., 129, 189n
Ravichandran, V., 84
realism in performance (*see also* cinema, roots of in reality), 69, 110, 115, 127–28, 141, 174, 176, 185n, 187n, 194n

Reevati, 94
regional cinema, 47, 51
religion, 7, 11, 43, 55, 91, 98, 104, 187n
  in cinema, 49, 50, 54, 55, 60, 90, 184n, 191n
  similarities to cinema, 184n
religious chauvinism, 21
religious conflict, 21, 181n
religious groups, in films, 104, 177
religious practice, 20
religious tolerance, 110
Report of the Enquiry Committee on Film Censorship, 131
Report of the Working Group on National Film Policy, 188n
research assistants, 32–33
resolution in cinema, 65, 66–67, 68, 71, 88, 89, 104, 111–15, 141, 148, 174, 175
Revathi, 63
Roman Catholic church, 20
romance, 27, 28, 43, 55, 58, 60, 99–100, 112, 141, 152, 165 (*see also* love)
rural vs. urban poor, 179n, 180n

Sanskrit, 72, 187n
Sanskrit drama, *see* drama, classical
Saurashtrian, 21
Saurashtrians, 34
scheduled castes, 18, 19, 34, 35, 107, 180n, 181n (*see also* Harijans; and specific caste names)
Selvakumar, 78
sex, 26, 27, 29, 55, 59, 74, 124–25, 127–28, 130, 141, 143, 144, 146
shakti, *see* cakti
Shivaji Ganesan, 40, 52, 55, 63, 64, 84, 104, 127, 137–38, 150, 152, 155, 156, 165, 184n, 193n
shrines, 3, 19–20, 34
Sikhs, 17
Sindhu Bairavi, 59, 71, 72–78, 90–91, 94, 96, 97, 98, 102–103, 105, 111, 112, 113, 115, 187n
Singer, M., 12
Sivakumar, 72
social life, 14, 15–29
social services, *see* fan club activities, social service
song and dance scenes, 59, 71, 120, 184n (*see also* dances; film songs)
  role of in film narrative, 59
sound in film, 48, 51, 183n

South Indian Film Chamber of Commerce, 128, 129
South Indian Liberal Federation, 21–22
spectacle, 13, 54, 55, 68, 110–11, 174–75, 176, 183n
spectators, 174, 175, 194n
split between image and reality in Tamil cinema, 173, 175–76
Sri Lanka, 165
Sri Lankan Tamils, 64
Subbulakshmi, M. S., 52
subordinate class, 9, 11, 12, 145, 194n
subordinate ideology, 145
success of a film, 58, 122, 126, 127, 188–89n
Suhasini, 72
Sulakshana, 72
Sundarambal, K. B., 52
Sundarrajan, R., 78

Tamil, 20, 21, 22, 23, 32, 33, 54, 72, 127, 181n, 187n, 193n
tax revenues, 122, 129, 188n
taxes, 37, 122
technical personnel, 49, 119, 120
television, 13, 34, 39, 193n
Telugu, 21, 59, 72, 181n, 187n
Telugu cinema, 29, 59, 119–20, 127
temples, 3, 19, 20, 25, 30, 33, 48, 183n, 184n
terukkuuttu, 48
thali, 28, 92, 93, 96, 111–12, 135, 154, 182n, 186n
theaters, 3, 22, 37–38, 39, 41, 51, 107, 121, 122, 123, 158, 169, 179n, 183n, 191n, 192n
  "temporary," 38
  touring, 37, 51, 179n
Thevar Association, 109
Thevars, 34, 108, 109, 140, 187n, 189n
Thomas, R., 5, 47, 179n
Thompson, E. P., 164
ticket prices, 37, 158
Trivandrum, 123

US, 43, 49, 163, 188–89n
US cinema, 50–51, 58, 59, 123, 186n, 188–89n
unions, 8, 193n
urban poor, 6, 7, 9, 23, 24, 71, 95, 99, 105, 110, 126, 140, 146, 179n, 182n, 183n
  as category, 8, 10–11

definition of, 7
incomes, 34, 35, 179–80n
insecurity(ies) of, 7, 8, 10, 16–17, 34, 35, 68, 69–70, 110, 171–72, 173, 174, 176, 180n, 187n, 194n
lack of power of, 10, 17
MGR and, 155
neighborhoods in Madurai, 34–35
occupations of, 8, 24
perceptions of selves, 135–36, 144, 156, 157, 164, 172
political power of, 17
represented in films, 54, 69, 113, 144, 152, 175, 187n
values of, 144
views of others on, 9, 43, 100, 130–31
views on class, 136, 173
views on the wealthy, 14, 102, 136, 144, 157, 164
Urdu, 20
utopia, 110–11, 113–14, 141, 145, 148, 175, 176
utopian images, contradictions and conflicts in, 14, 114, 172

VCRs, 6, 107, 184n
VNS Productions, 78
Vaazhkai, 138
Vasan, S. S., 54
Veerappan, Arun, 189n
Veeraswamy, N., 84
Veetam Putitu, 105, 108–109, 110, 187n
verisimilitude, 47 (*see also* conventions of Tamil and other Indian cinema, verisimilitude)
videos, 124
Vijaykanth, 78
Vikram, 154
villains, 40, 60, 104, 168, 187n
violence, 21, 43, 55, 56, 124–25, 127–28, 130, 143, 144, 146, 177
voluntary associations, 25, 192–93n
voting, 17, 23, 172
Vyjayanthimala, 193n

Weberian class categories, 9
Williams, R., 11
widows, 28, 139, 154, 186n
women, 20–21, 23, 24, 25, 26, 27, 28, 29, 32, 37, 39, 43, 50, 53, 60, 61, 63, 69, 70, 90, 91, 92, 94, 96, 97, 107, 111–12, 114, 125, 127, 136, 138, 141, 142,

146–47, 148, 171, 185–86n, 187n, 189n, 190n (*see also* film themes, relationships between men and women)
and MGR, 168, 169, 193n
as audience, 25, 49, 126, 127, 146
as fan club members, 149, 190n
as fans, 152
chastity of, 28, 90, 101, 181–82n, 183n
duties to husband, 135 (*see also* marriage, ideal spouses in)
in films, 53, 89, 177 (*see also* film themes, relationships between men and women)
power of, 91, 111–12 (*see also cakti*); binding of, 91, 111–12 (*see also cakti*, binding of)
Wood, R., 65
work and employment, 7–8, 9, 10–11, 16, 17–18, 19, 23–24, 25, 26, 27, 29, 34, 39, 43, 97, 99, 101, 137, 138, 150, 153, 156, 180n, 181n, 182n, 187n, 193n
worship, 20, 184n, 192n

Cambridge Studies in Social and Cultural Anthroplogy

Editors: ERNEST GELLNER, JACK GOODY, STEPHEN GUDEMAN, MICHAEL HERZFELD, JONATHAN PARRY

11 Rethinking Symbolism*
    DAN SPERBER. Translated by Alice L. Morton
15 World Conqueror and World Renouncer: A Study of Buddhism and Polity in Thailand against a Historical Background*
    S. J. TAMBIAH
16 Outline of a Theory of Practice*
    PIERRE BOURDIEU. Translated by Richard Nice
17 Production and Reproduction: A Comparative Study of the Domestic Domain*
    JACK GOODY
27 Day of Shining Red: An Essay on Understanding Ritual*
    GILBERT LEWIS
28 Hunters, Pastoralists and Ranchers: Reindeer Economies and their Transformations*
    TIM INGOLD
32 Muslim Society*
    ERNEST GELLNER
36 Dravidian Kinship
    THOMAS R. TRAUTMANN
39 The Fish-People: Linguistic Exogamy and Tukanoan Identity in Northwest Amazonia
    JEAN E. JACKSON
41 Ecology and Exchange in the Andes
    Edited by DAVID LEHMANN
42 Traders without Trade: Responses to Trade in Two Dyula Communities
    ROBERT LAUNAY
45 Actions, Norms and Representations: Foundations of Anthropological Inquiry*
    LADISLAV HOLY and MILAN STUCKLIK

46 Structural Models in Anthropology*
   PER HAGE and FRANK HARARY
47 Servants of the Goddess: The Priests of a South Indian Temple
   C. J. FULLER
49 The Buddhist Saints of the Forest and the Cult of Amulets: A Study in Charisma, Hagiography, Sectarianism, and Millennial Buddhism*
   S. J. TAMBIAH
51 Individual and Society in Guiana: A Comparative Study of Amerindian Social Organizations*
   PETER RIVIERE
53 Inequality among Brothers: Class and Kinship in South China
   RUBIE S. WATSON
54 On Anthropological Knowledge
   DAN SPERBER
55 Tales of the Yanomami: Daily Life in the Venezuelan Forest*
   JACQUES LIZOT. Translated by Ernest Simon
56 The Making of Great Men: Male Domination and Power among the New Guinea Baruya*
   MAURICE GODELIER. Translated by Ruper Swyer
57 Age Class Systems: Social Institutions and Politics Based on Age*
   BERNARDO BERNARDI. Translated by David I. Kertzer
58 Strategies and Norms in a Changing Matrilineal Society: Descent, Succession and Inheritance among the Toka of Zambia
   LADISLAV HOLY
59 Native Lords of Quito in the Age of the Incas: The Political Economy of North-Andean Chiefdoms
   FRANK SALOMON
60 Culture and Class in Anthropology and History: A Newfoundland Illustration*
   GERALD SIDER
61 From Blessing to Violence: History and Ideology in the Circumcision Ritual of the Merina of Madagascar*
   MAURICE BLOCH
62 The Huli Response to Illness
   STEPHEN FRANKEL
63 Social Inequality in a Northern Portugese Hamlet: Land, Late Marriage, and Bastardy, 1870–1978
   BRIAN JUAN O'NEILL
64 Cosmologies in the Making: A Generative Approach to Cultural Variation in Inner New Guinea*
   FREDRIK BARTH
65 Kinship and Class in the West Indies: A Genealogical Study of Jamaica and Guyana*
   RAYMOND T. SMITH
66 The Making of the Basque Nation
   MARIANNE HEIBERG
67 Out of Time: History and Evolution in Anthropological Discourse
   NICHOLAS THOMAS

68 Tradition as Truth and Communication
   PASCAL BOYER
69 The Abandoned Narcotic: Kava and Cultural Instability in Melanesia
   RON BRUNTON
70 The Anthropology of Numbers*
   THOMAS CRUMP
71 Stealing People's Names: History and Politics in a Sepik River Cosmology
   SIMON J. HARRISON
72 The Bedouin of Cyrenaica: Studies in Personal and Corporate Power
   EMRYS L. PETERS. Edited by Jack Goody and Emanuel Marx
73 Bartered Brides: Politics, Gender and Marriage in an Afghan Tribal Society
   NANCY TAPPER
74 Property, Production and Family in Neckerhausen*
   DAVID WARREN SABEAN
75 Fifteen Generations of Bretons: Kinship and Society in Lower Brittany, 1720–1980
   MARTINE SEGALEN. Translated by J. A. Underwood
76 Honor and Grace in Anthropology
   Edited by J. G. PERISTIANY and JULIAN PITT-RIVERS
77 The Making of the Modern Greek Family: Marriage and Exchange in Nineteenth-Century Athens
   PAUL SANT CASSIA and CONSTANTINA BADA
78 Religion and Custom in a Muslim Society: The Berti of Sudan
   LADISLAV HOLY
79 Quiet Days in Burgundy: A Study of Local Politics
   MARC ABÉLÈS. Translated by Annella McDermott
80 Sacred Void: Spatial Images of Work and Ritual among the Giriama of Kenya
   DAVID PARKIN
81 A Place of their Own: Family Farming in Eastern Finland
   RAY ABRAHAMS
82 Power, Prayer and Production: The Jola of Casamance, Senegal
   OLGA F. LINARES
83 Identity through History: Living Stories in a Solomon Island Society
   GEOFFREY M. WHITE
84 Monk, Householder and Tantric Priest: Newar Buddhism and its Hierarchy of Ritual
   DAVID GELLNER
85 Hunters and Herders of Southern Africa: A Comparative Ethnography of the Khoisan Peoples*
   ALAN BARNARD
86 Belonging in the Two Berlins: Kin, State, Nation*
   JOHN BORNEMAN
87 Power and Religiosity in a Post-Colonial Setting: Sinhala Catholics in Contemporary Sri Lanka
   R. L. STIRRAT

88 Dialogues with the Dead: The Discussion of Mortality among the Sora of Eastern India
    PIERS VITEBSKY
89 South Coast New Guinea Cultures: A Regional Comparison*
    BRUCE M. KNAUFT
90 Pathology and Identity: The Work of Mother Earth in Trinidad
    ROLAND LITTLEWOOD
91 The Cultural Relations of Classification: An Analysis of Nuaulu Animal Categories in Central Seram
    ROY ELLEN

* available in paperback